flexText

MACROECONOMICS

Avi J. Cohen and Harvey B. King

PEARSON

Toronto

D1208617

Editorial Director: Claudine O'Donnell
Acquisitions Editor: Megan Farrell
Marketing Manager: Claire Varley
Program Manager: Emily Dill
Project Manager: Pippa Kennard
Developmental Editor: Heather Sangster/Strong Finish Editorial Design
Composition: Cenveo® Publishing Services

Vice-President, Cross Media and Publishing Services: Gary Bennett

3 16

ISBN: 978-0-13-454431-1

PEARSON

Contents

Introduction

Before You Begin …

Our experience has taught us that what first-year economics students want most from a *flexText* is help in mastering course material to do well on examinations. We have developed this *flexText* to respond specifically to that demand. Using this *flexText* alone, however, is not enough to guarantee that you will do well in your course. In order to help you overcome the problems and difficulties that most first-year students encounter, we have some general advice on how to study, as well as some specific advice on how to best use this *flexText*.

Don't rely solely on your high school economics. If you took high school economics, you will have seen the material on demand and supply, which your instructor will lecture on in the first few weeks. Don't be lulled into feeling that the course will be easy. Your high school knowledge of economic concepts will be useful, but it will not be enough to guarantee high marks on exams. Your college or university instructors will demand much more detailed knowledge of concepts and ask you to apply them in new circumstances.

Keep a good set of lecture notes. Good lecture notes are vital for focusing your studying. Your instructor will only lecture on a subset of topics from the textbook. The topics your instructor covers in a lecture should usually be given priority when studying. Also give priority to studying the figures and graphs covered in the lecture.

Instructors do differ in their emphasis on lecture notes or the textbook, so early on in the course ask which is more important in reviewing for exams—lecture notes or the textbook. If your instructor answers that both are important, then ask the following, typically economic question: at the margin, which will be more beneficial—spending an extra hour rereading your lecture notes or an extra hour rereading the textbook? This question assumes that you have read each textbook chapter twice (once before lecture for a general understanding and then later for a thorough understanding); that you have prepared a good set of lecture notes; and that you have worked through all of the problems in the appropriate *flexText* chapters. By applying this style of analysis to the problem of efficiently allocating your study time, you are already beginning to think like an economist!

Some Friendly Advice

The study of economics requires a different style of thinking from what you may encounter in other courses. Economists make extensive use of assumptions to break down complex problems into simple, analytically manageable parts. This analytical style, while not ultimately more demanding than the styles of thinking in other disciplines, feels unfamiliar to most students and requires practice. As a result, it is not as easy to do well in economics simply on the basis of your raw intelligence and high school knowledge as it is in many other first-year courses. Many students who come to our offices are frustrated and puzzled by the fact that they are getting A's and B's in their other courses but only a C or worse in economics. They have not recognized that the study of economics is different and requires practice. In order to avoid a frustrating visit to your instructor after your first test, we suggest you do the following:

Use your instructor and/or teaching assistants for help. When you have questions or problems with course material, come to the office to ask questions. Remember, you are paying for your education and instructors are there to help you learn. We are often amazed at how few students come to see us during office hours. Don't be shy. The personal contact that comes from one-on-one tutoring is professionally gratifying for us as well as (hopefully) beneficial to you.

Form a study group. A useful way to motivate your studying and to learn economics is to discuss the course material and problems with other students. Explaining the answer to a question out loud is an effective way of discovering how well you understand the question. When you answer a question only in your head, you often skip steps in the chain of reasoning without realizing it. When you are forced to explain your reasoning out loud, gaps and mistakes quickly appear, and you (with your fellow group members) can quickly correct your reasoning. The true/false and explain questions in the *flexText* and the questions at the end of each textbook chapter are good study-group material. You might also get together after having worked the *flexText* problems, but before looking at the answers, and help each other solve unsolved problems.

Work old exams. One of the most effective ways of studying is to work through exams your instructor has given in previous years. Old exams give you a feel for the style of questions your instructor may ask and give you the opportunity to get used to time pressure if you force yourself to do the exam in the allotted time. Studying from old exams is not cheating, as long as you have obtained a copy of the exam legally. Some institutions post old exams online; others keep them in the library, the department, or at the student union. Upper-year students who have previously taken the course are usually a good source as well. Remember, though, that old exams are a useful study aid only if you use them to understand the reasoning behind each question. If you simply memorize answers in the hopes that your instructor will repeat the identical question, you are likely to fail. From year to year, instructors routinely change the questions or change the numerical values for similar questions.

Using the *flexText*

Each *flexText* chapter contains the following sections:

Key Concepts This first section is a one- to two-page summary, in point form, of all key definitions, concepts, and material from the textbook chapter. The summary is organized using the same major section headings from the textbook chapter. Key terms from the textbook appear in bold. This section is designed to focus you quickly and precisely on the core material that you must master. It is an excellent study aid for the night before an exam. Think of it as crib notes that will serve as a final check of the key concepts you have studied.

Helpful Hints   When you encounter difficulty in mastering concepts or techniques, you will not be alone. Many students find certain concepts difficult and often make the same kinds of mistakes. We have seen these common mistakes often enough to have learned how to help students avoid them. The hints point out these mistakes and offer tips to avoid them. The hints focus on the most important concepts, equations, and techniques for problem solving. They also review crucial graphs that appear on every instructor's exams. We hope that this section will be useful, since instructors always ask exam questions designed to test these possible mistakes in your understanding.

Self-Test   This should be one of the most useful sections of this *flexText*. The questions are designed to give you practice and to test skills and techniques you must master to do well on exams. You are encouraged to write directly in the *flexText*. There are plenty of the multiple-choice questions (25 for each chapter) you are most likely to encounter on course tests and exams. There are also other types of questions, described below, each with a specific pedagogical purpose.

Before we describe the three parts of the Self-Test section, here are some tips that apply to all parts:

Use a pencil. This will allow you to erase your mistakes and have neat, completed pages from which to study. Draw graphs wherever applicable. Some questions will ask explicitly for graphs; many others will not, but will require a chain of reasoning that involves shifts of curves on a graph. *Always draw the graph.* Don't try to work through the reasoning in your head—you are much more likely to make mistakes that way. Whenever you draw a graph, even in the margins of this *flexText*, label the axes. You may think that you can keep the labels in your head, but you will be confronting many different graphs with many different variables on the axes. Avoid confusion: label! As an added incentive, remember that on exams where graphs are required, instructors will deduct marks for unlabelled axes.

Do the Self-Test questions as if they were real exam questions, which means do them without looking at the answers. This is the single most important tip we can give you. Struggling for the answers to questions that you find difficult is one of the most effective ways to learn. The athletic adage "No pain, no gain" applies equally to studying. You will learn the most from right answers you had to struggle for and from your wrong answers and mistakes. Only after you have attempted all the questions should you look at the answers. When you finally do check the answers, be sure to understand where you went wrong and why the right answer is right.

If you want to impose time pressure on yourself to simulate the conditions of a real exam, allow two minutes for each true/false and multiple-choice question. The short answer problems vary considerably in their time requirements, so it is difficult to give time estimates for them. However, we believe that such time pressure is probably not a good idea for *flexText* questions. A state of relaxed concentration is best.

There are many questions in each chapter, and it will take you somewhere between two and four hours to answer all of them. If you get tired (or bored), don't burn yourself out by trying to work through all of the questions in one sitting. Consider breaking up your Self-Test over two (or more) study sessions.

One other tip about the Self-Test: *Before* you jump in and do the questions, be sure to read through the Key Concepts and Helpful Hints. This will save you the frustration of getting wrong answers to questions. When you do get wrong answers, you will often find an explanation of the right answers in the Key Concepts or Helpful Hints. The three parts of the Self-Test section are as follows:

True/False and Explain These questions test basic knowledge of chapter concepts and your ability to apply the concepts. Some challenge your understanding, to see whether you can identify mistakes in statements using basic concepts. These questions will quickly identify gaps in your knowledge and are useful to answer out loud in a study group. There are 15 of these questions, organized using the same major section headings from the textbook. The Test Bank that your instructor will likely use to make up tests and exams also contains true/false questions like those in the Self-Test.

When answering, identify each statement as *true* or *false*. Explain your answer in one sentence. The space underneath each question should be sufficient in every case for writing your answer.

Multiple-Choice These more difficult questions test your analytical abilities by asking you to apply concepts to new situations, manipulate information, and solve numerical and graphical problems.

This is the most frequently used type of test and exam question, and the Self-Test contains 25 of them for each chapter organized using the same major section headings from the textbook. Your instructor's Test Bank contains all of the *flexText* multiple-choice questions, numerous questions that closely parallel the *flexText* questions, plus many similar questions.

Before you answer, read each question and all five choices carefully. Many of the choices will be plausible and will differ only slightly. You must choose the one *best* answer. A useful strategy is to first eliminate any obviously wrong choices and then focus on the remaining alternatives. Be aware that sometimes the correct answer will be "none of the above." Don't get frustrated or think that you are dim if you can't immediately see the correct answer. These questions are designed to make you work to find the correct choice.

Short Answer Problems The best way to learn to do economics is to do problems. Problems are also a popular type of test and exam question—practise them as much as possible! Each Self-Test concludes with eight short answer, numerical, or graphical problems, often based on economic policy issues. In many chapters, this is the most challenging part of the Self-Test. It is also likely to be the most helpful for deepening your understanding of the chapter material. We have, however, designed the questions to teach as much as to test. We have purposely arranged the parts of each multipart question to lead you through the problem-solving analysis in a gradual and sequential fashion, from easier to more difficult parts.

Problems that require critical thinking are marked with the symbol ⓒ, to alert you to the need for extra time and effort. This symbol gives you the same indication you would have on a test or exam from the number of marks or minutes allocated to a problem.

Answers The Self-Test is followed by a section that gives answers to all the questions. But do not look at any answer until you have attempted the question.

When you finally do look, use the answer to understand where you went wrong, and think about why the answer is right. Every true/false and multiple-choice answer includes a brief, point-form explanation to suggest where you might have gone wrong and the economic reasoning behind the answer. At the end of each answer are page references to the textbook, so you can read a more complete explanation.

Answers to critical thinking questions are marked with ⓒ to indicate why you might have struggled with that question! (We purposely did not mark which true/false and multiple-choice questions were critical thinking, to stay as close as possible to a real test or exam format. In an exam, all multiple-choice questions, for example, are worth the same number of marks, and you would have no idea which questions are the more difficult ones requiring critical thinking.)

The detailed answers to the short answer problems should be especially useful in clarifying and illustrating typical chains of reasoning involved in economic analysis. Answers to critical thinking problems are marked with ⓒ.

If the answers alone do not clear up your confusion, go back to the appropriate sections of the textbook and to the Key Concepts and Helpful Hints in this *flexText*. If that still does not suffice, go to your instructor's or teaching assistants' office or to your study-group members for help and clarification.

Pearson *flexText*…setting you up for success in school and at work

Regardless of the course you're taking — whether you are in a Business, Practical Nursing, ECE, or Police Foundations program — you want to leave with skills that can help you get the job you want. Some of these skills will be specific to your course of study or major. These are basic skills your employers will want you to have. An accountant, for example, will be expected to know how to read a balance sheet and use Microsoft Excel. But there are other skills essential to your success in the workplace that might not seem so obvious but are important enough that the many governments call them "Essential" Employability Skills. The Conference Board of Canada goes even further, calling them "the skills you need to enter, stay in, and progress in the world of work — whether you work on your own or as a part of a team." (http://www.conferenceboard. ca/topics/education/learning-tools/employability-skills. aspx)

This Pearson *flexText* was designed to help you develop these skills.

What are Essential Employability Skills? They can be grouped into six broad categories: Communication, Numeracy, Critical Thinking & Problem Solving, Information Management, Interpersonal, and Personal. The Government of Ontario thinks that these skills are so important that they expect that everyone who graduates with a certificate or diploma should have them. Other provincial governments place an equal emphasis on them. Many of these skills could also be called "soft skills," or "21st century skills," and represent areas such as writing that are not specific to the core content of any one course but are important to your success in *all* courses, and in the working world. Being able to show prospective employers that you have these skills can make a huge difference in your ability to get the job that you want.

Pearson *flexText* is designed with the needs of college students in mind, including the need to develop and demonstrate Essential Employability Skills. Here's how:

Communication Skills   *Defining skill areas: reading, writing, speaking, listening, presenting, and visual literacy*

One of the reasons why students don't develop their reading skills is simply because they have not bought their textbook. *flexTexts* are affordable, and available at a price that will encourage as many students as possible to buy — and read — their course materials. *flexTexts* often include chapter summaries and outlines to help support reading comprehension and many will include short answer questions or writing activities that provide opportunities for students to practise their writing and develop their written communication skills.

Numeracy Skills   *Defining skill areas: understanding and applying mathematical concepts and reasoning, analyzing and using mathematical data, and conceptualizing*

flexTexts in disciplines such as Accounting, Economics and Finance, which require students to understand and apply mathematical concepts to the course content, will include practice questions. The spiral-bound *flexText* format encourages their use as in-class activity workbooks, where faculty can provide instructional support to students as they work through these problems.

Critical Thinking & Problem Solving Skills   *Defining skill areas: analyzing, synthesizing, evaluating, decision making, and creativity and innovative thinking*

The exercises and activities found in Pearson's *flexTexts* are not simply factual, recall, or "skill and drill" type activities. They are created to engage students at many different levels of Bloom's Taxonomy to help them develop their critical thinking and problem solving skills. And because the *flexText* is affordable, a greater number of students will have the opportunity to develop these skills through practice because they have purchased their course materials.

Information Management Skills   *Defining skill areas: gathering and managing information, selecting and using appropriate tools and technology for a task or project, computer literacy, and internet skills*

Not all of the exercises in a *flexText* are pen and paper activities. Many also require students to engage with online multimedia assets, with applications such as Microsoft

Excel, or to explain how they would bring these tools to bear to the solution of a problem.

Interpersonal Skills   *Defining skill areas: teamwork, relationship management, conflict resolution, leadership, and networking*

Because *flexTexts* are designed to be brought to class, they facilitate group work and collaborative problem solving. Activities that, in the past, would have been assigned as homework and be done individually can now be implemented in ways that help students develop their interpersonal skills.

Personal Skills   *Defining skill areas: managing self, managing change and being flexible and adaptable, engaging in reflexive practice, and demonstrating personal responsibility*

Making the decision to purchase course materials and actively engage with course content is one of the first steps toward demonstrating a degree of personal responsibility for your own success in school. The page layout of a *flexText* also encourages note taking and supports the development of good study skills.

1 What Is Economics?

Key Concepts
Definition of Economics

All economic questions arise from **scarcity**.

- Because wants exceed the resources available to satisfy them, we cannot have everything we want and must make choices.

  - Choices depend on **incentives**—rewards that encourage actions and penalties that discourage action.

- **Economics** is the social science that studies the choices people make to cope with scarcity.

  - **Microeconomics** studies choices of individuals and businesses.
  - **Macroeconomics** studies national and global economies.

Two Big Economic Questions

Two questions summarize the scope of economics:

- How do choices determine *what*, *how*, and *for whom* **goods and services** are produced, and in what quantities?

- How can choices made in the pursuit of self-interest also promote the social interest?

Notes:

The **factors of production** used to produce goods and services are

- **land** (shorthand for all natural resources), which earns **rent.**
- **labour** (includes **human capital**—knowledge and skills from education, training, experience), which earns **wages.**
- **capital** (machinery), which earns **interest.**
- **entrepreneurship,** which earns **profit.**

Choices made in **self-interest** are best for the person making them. Choices that are in the **social interest** are best for society as a whole. Society achieves **efficiency** when available resources are used to produce goods and services at the lowest cost.

- Markets often provide incentives so that the pursuit of our self-interest also promotes the social interest; but self-interest and social interest sometimes conflict.

- Economic principles allow us to understand when self-interest promotes the social interest, when they conflict, and policies to reduce those conflicts.

The Economic Way of Thinking

A choice is a **tradeoff**—we give up one thing to get something else—and the **opportunity cost** of any action is the highest-valued alternative forgone. Opportunity cost is the single most important concept for making choices.

- A **rational choice** compares costs and benefits and achieves the greatest benefit over cost.
- **Benefit**—gain or pleasure of a choice, is determined by a person's **preferences**—likes and dislikes and their intensity.
- The **big tradeoff** is between equality and efficiency. Government redistribution using taxes and transfers weaken incentives, so a more equally shared pie results in a smaller pie.

We make choices in small steps, or at the **margin**, and choices are influenced by incentives.

- Economic choices are made by comparing the *additional* benefit—**marginal benefit**—and *additional* opportunity cost—**marginal cost**—of a small increase in an activity. If marginal benefit exceeds marginal cost, we choose to increase the activity.

- By choosing only activities that bring greater benefits than costs, we use our scarce resources in the way that makes us as well off as possible.

Economics as Social Science and Policy Tool

Economics, as a social science, distinguishes between

- *positive* statements—statements about what *is*; they can be tested by checking them against the facts.
- *normative* statements—statements about what *ought* to be; they depend on values and cannot be tested.

Economics attempts to understand the economic world and is concerned with positive statements. Economists try to discover positive statements that are consistent with observed facts by

- unscrambling cause and effect.
- creating **economic models**—a simplified description of the economic world that includes only features needed for purpose of explanation.
- testing economic models, comparing predictions with the facts, using
  - natural experiments—where one factor is different in real world; other things are equal.
  - statistical investigations—correlations between variables.
  - economic experiments—putting people in decision-making situations and changing one variable to see the response.

Economics is a useful toolkit for

- personal decisions
- advising businesses on economic policy
- advising government on economic policy

For any *normative* policy objective, economics provides a method of evaluating alternative solutions—evaluate marginal benefits and marginal costs to find solutions that make the best use of resources.

Helpful Hints

1. The definition of economics (explaining the choices we make using limited resources to try to satisfy unlimited wants) leads us directly to two important economic concepts: choice and opportunity cost. If wants exceed resources, we cannot have everything we want and therefore must make *choices* among alternatives. In making a choice, we forgo other alternatives, and the *opportunity cost* of any choice is the highest-valued alternative forgone.

2. Marginal analysis is a fundamental tool economists use to predict people's choices. The key to understanding marginal analysis is to focus on *additional*, rather than total, benefits and costs. For example, to predict whether or not Taejong will eat a fourth Big Mac, the economist compares Taejong's *additional* benefit or satisfaction from the fourth Big Mac with its *additional* cost. The total benefits and costs of all four Big Macs are not relevant. Only if the marginal benefit exceeds the marginal cost will Taejong eat a fourth Big Mac.

3. In attempting to understand how and why something works (e.g., an airplane, a falling object, an economy), we can try to use description or theory. A description is a list of facts about something. But it does not tell us which facts are essential for understanding how an airplane works (the shape of the wings) and which facts are less important (the colour of the paint).

    Scientists use theory to abstract from the complex descriptive facts of the real world and focus only on those elements essential for understanding. Those essential elements are fashioned into models—highly simplified representations of the real world.

    In physics and some other natural sciences, if we want to understand the essential force (gravity) that causes objects to fall, we use theory to construct a simple model and then test it by performing a controlled experiment. We create a vacuum to eliminate less important forces like air resistance.

    Economic models are also attempts to focus on the essential forces (competition, self-interest) operating in the economy, while abstracting from less important forces (whims, advertising, altruism). Unlike physicists, economists cannot easily perform

Notes: _____

controlled experiments to test their models. As a result, it is difficult to conclusively prove or disprove a theory and its models. Economists rely on naturally occurring experiments, statistical investigations of correlations between variables, and artificial laboratory economic experiments about choices.

4. Models are like maps, which are useful precisely because they abstract from real-world detail. A map that reproduced all of the details of the real world (street lamps, fireplugs, electric wires) would be useless. A useful map offers a simplified view that is carefully selected according to the purpose of the map. Remember that economic models are not claims that the real world is as simple as the model. Models claim to capture the simplified effect of some real force operating in the economy. Before drawing conclusions about the real economy from a model, we must be careful to consider whether, when we reinsert all of the real-world complexities the model abstracted from, the conclusions will be the same as in the model.

5. The most important purpose of studying economics is not to learn what to think about economics but rather *how* to think about economics. The "what"—the facts and descriptions of the economy—can always be found in books. The value of an economics education is the ability to think critically about economic problems and *to understand how* an economy works. This understanding of the essential forces governing how an economy works comes through the mastery of economic theory and model-building.

Self-Test
True/False and Explain

Definition of Economics

1. Economics explains how we use unlimited resources to satisfy limited wants.

2. Economics studies the choices people make to cope with scarcity and the institutions that influence and reconcile choices.

Two Big Economic Questions

3. In economics, the definition of "land" includes nonrenewable resources but excludes renewable resources.

4. In economics, the definition of "capital" includes financial assets like stocks and bonds.

5. Entrepreneurs bear the risks arising from the business decisions they make.

6. "How do choices determine *what*, *how*, and *for whom* goods and services are produced?" is one of the big economic questions.

7. "When do choices made in the pursuit of the social interest also promote self-interest?" is one of the big economic questions.

8. Choices made in the pursuit of self-interest always promote the social interest.

The Economic Way of Thinking

9. When the opportunity cost of an activity increases, the incentive to choose that activity increases.

10. Tradeoffs and opportunity costs are the key concepts for understanding the economic way of thinking.

11. Economists assume that it is human nature for all people to act selfishly.

Economics as Social Science and Policy Tool

12. A positive statement is about what is, while a normative statement is about what will be.

13. Economists test positive statements about how the world works to weed out those that are wrong.

14. The main economics policy tool is to compare total costs and total benefits to find the solution with the greatest gain.

15. Economics is a useful policy tool for governments and businesses, but not for individuals.

Multiple-Choice

Definition of Economics

1. The fact that human wants cannot be fully satisfied with available resources is called the problem of
   a. opportunity cost.
   b. scarcity.
   c. normative economics.
   d. what to produce.
   e. who will consume.

2. The problem of scarcity exists
   a. only in economies with government.
   b. only in economies without government.
   c. in all economies.
   d. only when people have not optimized.
   e. now, but will be eliminated with economic growth.

3. Scarcity differs from poverty because
   a. resources exceed wants for the rich.
   b. wants exceed resources even for the rich.
   c. the rich do not have to make choices.
   d. the poor do not have any choices.
   e. the poor do not have any wants.

4. The branch of economics that studies the choices of individual households and firms is called
   a. macroeconomics.
   b. microeconomics.
   c. positive economics.
   d. normative economics.
   e. home economics.

7. The first big economic question about goods and services includes all of the following *except*

a. *what* to produce.

b. *why* produce.

c. *how* to produce.

d. *what* quantities to produce.

e. *who* gets what is produced.

8. The trends over the past 60 years in what we produce show that _____ has expanded and _____ has shrunk.

a. manufacturing; services

b. manufacturing; agriculture

c. agriculture; services

d. agriculture; manufacturing

e. services; agriculture

---

5. Microeconomics studies all of the following *except* the

a. decisions of individual firms.

b. effects of government safety regulations on the price of cars.

c. global economy as a whole.

d. prices of individual goods and services.

e. effects of taxes on the price of beer.

Two Big Economic Questions

6. The two big economic questions

a. arise from scarcity.

b. summarize the scope of economics.

c. describe choices we make.

d. examine incentives that influence choices.

e. are all of the above.

9. All of the following are resources *except*
   a. natural resources.
   b. tools.
   c. entrepreneurship.
   d. government.
   e. land.

10. The knowledge and skill obtained from education and training is
    a. labour.
    b. human capital.
    c. physical capital.
    d. entrepreneurship.
    e. technological know-how.

11. Which statement about incomes earned by factors of production is *false?*
    a. Land earns rent.
    b. Natural resources earn rent.
    c. Labour earns wages.
    d. Capital earns profit.
    e. Entrepreneurship earns profit.

12. When boats fish in international waters, that is certainly a(n)
    a. self-interested choice.
    b. altruistic choice.
    c. globalization choice.
    d. factor of production choice.
    e. choice in the social interest.

The Economic Way of Thinking

13. When the government chooses to use resources to build a dam, those resources are no longer available to build a highway. This illustrates the concept of

 a. a market.
 b. macroeconomics.
 c. opportunity cost.
 d. a "how" tradeoff.
 e. the big tradeoff.

14. The opportunity cost of attending university

 a. depends on what you expect to earn with your degree.
 b. must be greater than the money cost of attending university.
 c. must be less than the money cost of attending university.
 d. depends on your major.
 e. depends on what you could earn now.

15. Renata has the chance to either attend an economics lecture or play tennis. If she chooses to attend the lecture, the value of playing tennis is

 a. greater than the value of the lecture.
 b. not comparable to the value of the lecture.
 c. equal to the value of the lecture.
 d. the opportunity cost of attending the lecture.
 e. zero.

16. Which of the following sayings best describes opportunity cost?

 a. "Make hay while the sun shines."
 b. "Money is the root of all evil."
 c. "Boldly go where no one has gone before."
 d. "There's no such thing as a free lunch."
 e. "Baseball has been very good to me."

17. Marginal benefit is the

  a. total benefit of an activity.

  b. additional benefit of a decrease in an activity.

  c. additional benefit of an increase in an activity.

  d. opportunity cost of a decrease in an activity.

  e. opportunity cost of an increase in an activity.

18. Monika will choose to eat a seventh pizza slice if

  a. the marginal benefit of the seventh slice is greater than its marginal cost.

  b. the marginal benefit of the seventh slice is less than its marginal cost

  c. the total benefit of all seven slices is greater than their total cost.

  d. the total benefit of all seven slices is less than their total cost.

  e. she is training to be a Sumo wrestler.

19. Economists assume that

  a. self-interested actions are all selfish actions.

  b. consumers and producers pursue their self-interest while politicians and public servants pursue the social interest.

  c. incentives are key in reconciling self-interest and the social interest.

  d. all people pursue the social interest.

  e. human nature changes as incentives change.

Economics as Social Science and Policy Tool

20. A positive statement is

  a. about what ought to be.

  b. about what is.

  c. always true.

  d. capable of evaluation as true or false by observation and measurement.

  e. **b** and **d**.

21. Which of the following is a positive statement?

a. Low rents will restrict the supply of housing.

b. High interest rates are bad for the economy.

c. Housing costs too much.

d. Owners of apartment buildings ought to be free to charge whatever rent they want.

e. Government should control the rents that apartment owners charge.

22. A normative statement is a statement regarding

a. what is usually the case.

b. the assumptions of an economic model.

c. what ought to be.

d. the predictions of an economic model.

e. what is.

23. Which of the following statements is normative?

a. Scientists should not make normative statements.

b. Warts are caused by handling toads.

c. As compact disc prices fall, people will buy more of them.

d. If income increases, sales of luxury goods will fall.

e. None of the above.

24. Which of the following statements is *false?* An economic model

a. is tested by comparing predictions with the facts.

b. is difficult to test because of the simultaneous operation of many factors.

c. tests only positive economic statements.

d. can be tested using natural and economic experiments

e. includes all aspects of the economic world.

25. The common element to making personal, business, and government policy decisions is to evaluate
    a. total benefits and total costs to find greatest gain.
    b. marginal benefits and marginal costs to find greatest gain.
    c. marginal benefits and marginal costs to find highest marginal benefit.
    d. marginal benefits and marginal costs to find lowest marginal costs.
    e. average benefits and average costs to find greatest gain.

Short Answer Problems

1. "If all people would only economize, the problem of scarcity would be solved." Agree or disagree, and explain why.

2. Ashley, Doug, and Mei-Lin are planning to travel from Halifax to Sydney. The trip takes one hour by airplane and five hours by train. The air fare is $100 and train fare is $60. They all have to take time off from work while travelling. Ashley earns $5 per hour in her job, Doug $10 per hour, and Mei-Lin $12 per hour.

Calculate the opportunity cost of air and train travel for each person. Assuming they are all economizers, how should each of them travel to Sydney?

3. Suppose the government builds and staffs a hospital to provide "free" medical care.

a. What is the opportunity cost of the free medical care?

b. Is it free from the perspective of society as a whole?

@ **4.** Branko loves riding the bumper cars at the amusement park, but he loves the experience a little less with each successive ride. In estimating the benefit he receives from the rides, Branko would be willing to pay $10 for his first ride, $7 for his second ride, and $4 for his third ride. Rides actually cost $5 apiece for as many rides as Branko wants to take. This information is summarized in Table 1.

TABLE 1			
Ride	1st	2nd	3rd
Marginal benefit	10	7	4
Marginal cost	5	5	5

a. If Branko chooses by comparing total benefit and total cost, how many rides will he take?

b. If Branko chooses by comparing marginal benefit and marginal cost, how many rides will he take?

c. Is Branko better off by choosing according to total or marginal benefit and cost? Explain why.

⊕ **5.** Assume Branko's benefits are the same as in Short Answer Problem **4**. Starting fresh, if the price of a bumper car ride rises to $8, how many rides will Branko now take? Explain why.

6. Indicate whether each of the following statements is positive or normative. If it is normative (positive), rewrite it so that it becomes positive (normative).

a. The government ought to reduce the size of the deficit to lower interest rates.

b. Government imposition of a tax on tobacco products will reduce their consumption.

7. Perhaps the biggest economic question is "How can we organize our lives so that when each of us makes choices in our self-interest, these choices also promote the social interest?" When Nike builds a factory in Malaysia and pays workers far less than North American wages, it is acting in its own corporate self-interest. What questions do you need to ask to decide if this is also in the social interest?

℗ **8.** Suppose your friend, who is a history major, claims that economic models are useless because they are so unrealistic. He claims that since the models leave out so many descriptive details about the real world, they can't possibly be useful for understanding how the economy works. How would you defend your decision to study economics?

Answers

True/False and Explain

1. **F** Limited resources and unlimited wants. (1–2)

2. **T** This is the full definition of economics—the institutional aspect is often omitted for brevity. (1–2)

3. **F** "Land" includes all natural resources, whether non-renewable (oil) or renewable (forests). (3–7)

4. **F** "Capital" only consists of physical equipment like tools and buildings used in production. (3–7)

5. **T** Entrepreneurs earn profits in return for bearing the risks of organizing labour, land, and capital. (3–7)

6. **T** See text discussion. (3–7)

7. **F** When do choices made in the pursuit of self-interest also promote the social interest? (3–7)

8. **F** Markets often provide incentives so that pursuit of self-interest also promotes social interest, but self-interest and social interest sometimes conflict. (3–7).

9. **F** Incentive decreases because activity is now more expensive. (8–9)

10. **T** Scarcity requires choice, choice involves tradeoffs, and tradeoffs involve opportunity cost. (8–9)

11. **F** Economists assume people act in their self-interest, but self-interested actions are not necessarily selfish actions, if what makes you happy is to help others. (10)

12. **F** Normative statements are about what *ought* to be. (10)

13. **T** Test *positive* statements. (10)

14. **F** Compare *marginal* benefits and *marginal* costs. (10)

15. **F** Useful for personal, business, government policy. (10)

Multiple-Choice

1. **b** Definition. (1–2)

2. **c** With infinite wants and finite resources, scarcity will never be eliminated. (1–2)

3. **b** Poverty is a low level of resources. But wants exceed resources for everyone, necessitating choice. (1–2)

4. **b** Definition. (1–2)

5. **c** Macroeconomic topic. (1–2)

6. **e** Economics explains choices created by scarcity and incentives that help reconcile self-interest and social interest. (3–7)

7. **b** *Why* is not part of first big question. (3–7)

8. **e** Services have expanded; agriculture and manufacturing have shrunk. (3–7)

9. **d** Government is a social institution. (3–7)

10. **b** Definition. (3–7)

11. **d** Capital earns interest. (3–7)

12. **a** Certainly in the fishing company's self-interest; not altruistic or in social interest depending on benefits and costs. (3–7)

13. **c** Highway is forgone alternative. (8–9)

14. **e** What you must give up, *not* what you will earn. May be more or less than money cost. (8–9)

15. **d** Choosing lecture means its value > tennis. Tennis = (highest-valued) forgone alternative to lecture. (8–9)

16. **d** Every choice involves a cost. (8–9)

17. **c** Definition; **e** is marginal cost, **b** and **d** are nonsense. (8–9)

18. **a** Choices are made at the margin, when marginal benefit exceeds marginal cost. (8–9)

19. **c** Assume human nature is given and all people pursue self-interest. When self-interested choices are not in the social interest, there are wrong incentives. (8–9)

20. **e** Definition. (10)

21. **a** While **a** may be evaluated as true or false, other statements are matters of opinion. (10)

22. **c** Key word for normative statements is *ought*. (10)

23. **a** Key word is *should*. Even statement **b** is positive. (10)

24. **e** Includes only relevant aspects and ignores others. (10)

25. **b** See text discussion. (10)

Short Answer Problems

1. Disagree. If everyone economized, then we would be making the best possible use of our resources and would be achieving the greatest benefits or satisfaction possible, given the limited quantity of resources. But this does not mean that we would be satisfying all of our limitless needs. The problem of scarcity can never be "solved" as long as people have infinite needs and finite resources for satisfying those needs.

2. The main point is that the total opportunity cost of travel includes the best alternative value of travel time as well as the train or air fare. The total costs of train and air travel for Ashley, Doug, and Mei-Lin are calculated in Table 2.

   On the basis of the cost calculation in Table 2, Ashley should take the train, Mei-Lin should take the plane, and Doug could take either.

TABLE 2		
Traveller	**Train**	**Plane**
Ashley		
(a) Fare	$ 60	$ 100
(b) Opportunity cost of travel time at $5/hr	$ 25	$ 5
Total cost	**$ 85**	**$ 105**
Doug		
(a) Fare	$ 60	$ 100
(b) Opportunity cost of travel time at $10/hr	$ 50	$ 10
Total cost	**$ 110**	**$ 110**
Mei-Lin		
(a) Fare	$ 60	$ 100
(b) Opportunity cost of travel time at $12/hr	$ 60	$ 12
Total cost	**$ 120**	**$ 112**

3. a. Even though medical care may be offered without charge ("free"), there are still opportunity costs. The opportunity cost of providing such health care is the highest-valued alternative use of the resources used in the construction of the hospital, and the highest-valued alternative use of the resources (including human resources) used in the operation of the hospital.

b. These resources are no longer available for other activities and therefore represent a cost to society.

4. a. If Branko rides as long as total benefit is greater than total cost, he will take 3 rides.

Total benefit (cost) can be calculated by adding up the marginal benefit (cost) of all rides taken. Before taking any rides, his total benefit is zero and his total cost is zero. The first ride's marginal benefit of is $10, which when added to 0 yields a total benefit of $10. The first ride's marginal cost is $5, which when added to zero yields a total cost of $5. Total cost is less than total benefit, so Branko takes the first ride. For the first and second rides together, total benefit is $17, which is greater than total cost of $10. For all 3 rides together, total benefit is $21, which is greater than total cost of $15.

b. If Branko compares the marginal benefit of each ride with its marginal cost, he will only take 2 rides. He will take the first ride because its marginal benefit ($10) is greater than its marginal cost ($5). After the first ride, he will still choose to take the second ride because its marginal benefit ($7) is greater than its marginal cost ($5). But he will quit after the second ride. The third ride would add a benefit of $4, but it costs $5, so Branko would be worse off by taking the third ride.

c. The marginal rule for choosing will make Branko better off. It would be a mistake to pay $5 for the third ride when it is only worth $4 to Branko. He would be better off taking that final $5 and spending it on something (the roller coaster?) that gives him a benefit worth at least $5.

You will learn much more about applying marginal analysis to choices like Branko's in Chapters 2 and 5.

5. a. If the price of a bumper car rises to $8, Branko now takes only 1 ride. He will take the first ride because its marginal benefit ($10) is greater than its marginal cost ($8). After the first ride, he will quit. The marginal benefit of the second ride ($7) is now less than its marginal cost ($8).

6. a. The given statement is normative. The following is positive: If the government reduces the size of the deficit, interest rates will fall.

b. The given statement is positive. The following is normative: The government ought to impose a tax on tobacco products.

7. Questions must identify benefits and costs that need to be compared. Some of the many possible questions are: Even though the Malaysian workers earn less than North Americans, are they better off or worse off with these jobs? As consumers in North America, are we better off or worse off with shoes being produced more cheaply in Malaysia? Are workers in North America better off or worse off with the Malaysian

Nike plant? How do we define the social interest when people from many countries are involved?

You don't yet have enough information to answer these questions, but economics provides a way of thinking about them that makes it easier to come to a well-reasoned conclusion.

8. A brief answer to your friend's challenge appears in Helpful Hint **3**. Models are like maps, which are useful precisely because they abstract from real-world detail. A useful map offers a simplified view, which is carefully selected according to the purpose of the map. No mapmaker would claim that the world is as simple as her map, and economists do not claim that the real economy is as simple as their models. What economists claim is that their models isolate the simplified effect of some real forces (like optimizing behaviour) operating in the economy, and yield predictions that can be tested against real-world data.

Another way to answer your friend would be to challenge him to identify what a more realistic

model or theory would look like. You would do well to quote Milton Friedman (a Nobel Prize winner in economics) on this topic: "A theory or its 'assumptions' cannot possibly be thoroughly 'realistic' in the immediate descriptive sense.... A completely 'realistic' theory of the wheat market would have to include not only the conditions directly underlying the supply and demand for wheat but also the kind of coins or credit instruments used to make exchanges; the personal characteristics of wheat-traders such as the color of each trader's hair and eyes, … the number of members of his family, their characteristics,… the kind of soil on which the wheat was grown,… the weather prevailing during the growing season;… and so on indefinitely. Any attempt to move very far in achieving this kind of 'realism' is certain to render a theory utterly useless." From Milton Friedman, "The Methodology of Positive Economics," in *Essays in Positive Economics* (Chicago: University of Chicago Press, 1953), p. 32.

1 Appendix: Graphs in Economics

Key Concepts
Graphing Data

Graphs represent quantity as a distance. On a two-dimensional graph,

- horizontal line is *x-axis*.
- vertical line is *y-axis*.
- intersection (0) is the *origin*.

A **scatter diagram** shows the relationship between two variables, one measured on the *x*-axis, the other measured on the *y*-axis. Correlation between variables does not necessarily imply causation.

  Misleading graphs often break the axes or stretch/compress measurement scales to exaggerate or understate variation. Always look closely at the values and labels on axes before interpreting a graph.

Graphs Used in Economic Models

Graphs showing relationships between variables fall into four categories:

- **Positive (direct) relationship**—variables move together in same direction: upward-sloping.
- **Negative (inverse) relationship**—variables move in opposite directions: downward-sloping.

- Relationships with a maximum/minimum:

  - Relationship slopes upward, reaches a maximum (zero slope), and then slopes downward.

  - Relationship slopes downward, reaches a minimum (zero slope), and then slopes upward.

- Unrelated (independent) variables—one variable changes while the other remains constant; graph is a vertical or horizontal straight line.

The Slope of a Relationship

Slope of a relationship is change in value of a variable on y-axis divided by change in value of a variable on x-axis.

- Δ means "change in."
- Formula for slope is $\Delta y / \Delta x = $ rise/run.
- Straight line (**linear relationship**) has a constant slope.

  - A positive, upward-sloping relationship has a positive slope.
  - A negative, downward-sloping relationship has a negative slope.

- A curved line has a varying slope, calculated

  - *at a point*—draw straight line tangent to curve at that point and calculate slope of the line.

  - *across an arc*—draw straight line across two points on curve and calculate slope of the line.

Graphing Relationships Among More Than Two Variables

Relationships among more than two variables can be graphed by holding constant the values of all variables except two. This is done by making a *ceteris paribus* assumption—"other things remain the same."

Notes: _____

Notes: <u>   </u>

Helpful Hints

1. Throughout the text, relationships among economic variables will almost invariably be represented and analyzed graphically. An early, complete understanding of graphs will greatly facilitate your mastery of the economic analysis in later chapters. Avoid the common mistake of assuming that a superficial understanding of graphs will be sufficient.

2. If you have limited experience with graphical analysis, this appendix is crucial to your ability to understand later economic analysis. You will likely find significant rewards in occasionally returning to this appendix for review. If you are experienced in constructing and using graphs, this appendix may be "old hat." Even so, you should skim it and work through the Self-Test in this *FlexText Workbook*.

3. Slope is a *linear* concept since it is a property of a straight line. For this reason, the slope is constant along a straight line but is different at different points on a curved (nonlinear) line. For the slope of a curved line, we actually calculate the slope of a straight line. The text presents two alternatives for calculating the slope of a curved line: (1) slope at a point and (2) slope across an arc. The first of these calculates the slope of the *straight line* that just touches (is tangent to) the curve at a point. The second calculates the slope of the *straight line* formed by the arc between two points on the curved line.

4. A straight line on a graph can also be described by a simple equation. The general form for the equation of a straight line is

$$y = a + bx$$

If you are given such an equation, you can graph the line by finding the y-intercept (where the line intersects the vertical y-axis), finding the x-intercept (where the line intersects the horizontal x-axis), and then connecting those two points with a straight line:

To find the y-intercept, set $x = 0$.

$$y = a + b(0)$$
$$y = a$$

To find the *x*-intercept, set *y* = 0.

$$0 = a + bx$$
$$x = -a/b$$

Connecting these two points (($x = 0$, $y = a$) and ($x = -a/b$, $y = 0$)) or (0, a) and ($-a/b$, 0)) allows you to graph the straight line. For any straight line with the equation of the form $y = a + bx$, the slope of the line is *b*. Fig. A1 illustrates a line where *b* is a *negative* number, so there is a *negative* relationship between the variables *x* and *y*.

To see how to apply this general equation, consider this example:

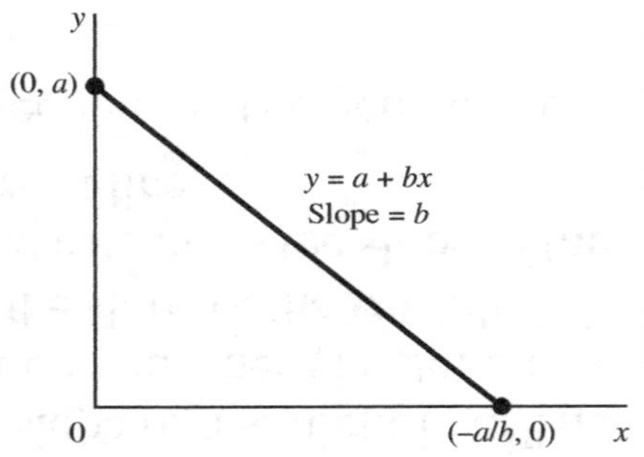

$$y = 6 - 2x$$

To find the *y*-intercept, set *x* = 0.

$$y = 6 - 2(0)$$
$$y = 6$$

To find the *x*-intercept, set *y* = 0.

$$0 = 6 - 2x$$
$$x = 3$$

Connecting these two points, (0, 6) and (3, 0), yields the line in Fig. A2.

The slope of this line is −2. Since the slope is negative, there is a negative relationship between the variables *x* and *y*.

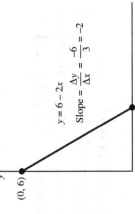

$y = a + bx$
Slope = b

(0, a)

(−a/b, 0)

▲ **FIGURE A1**

$y = 6 - 2x$
Slope = $\dfrac{\Delta y}{\Delta x} = \dfrac{-6}{3} = -2$

(0, 6)

(3, 0)

▲ **FIGURE A2**

Self-Test

True/False and Explain

Graphing Data

1. Stretching or compressing the scale on an axis can be misleading.

2. A graph with a break in the axes must be misleading.

3. If a scatter diagram shows a clear relationship between variables x and y, then x must cause y.

Graphs Used in Economic Models

4. If the graph of the relationship between two variables slopes upward (to the right), the graph has a positive slope.

5. The graph of the relationship between two variables that are in fact unrelated is always vertical.

6. In Fig. A3, the relationship between y and x is first negative, reaches a minimum, and then becomes positive as x increases.

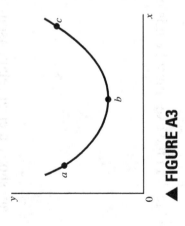

▲ **FIGURE A3**

7. In Fig. A3, the value of x is a minimum at point b.

The Slope of a Relationship

8. In Fig. A3, the slope of the curve is increasing as we move from point b to point c.

9. In Fig. A3, the slope of the curve is approaching zero as we move from point a to point b.

10. The slope of a straight line is calculated by dividing the change in the value of the variable measured on the horizontal axis by the change in the value of the variable measured on the vertical axis.

11. For a straight line, if a small change in y is associated with a large change in x, the slope is large.

12. For a straight line, if a large change in y is associated with a small change in x, the line is steep.

13. The slope of a curved line is not constant.

Graphing Relationships Among More Than Two Variables

14. *Ceteris paribus* means "other things change."

15. Relationships between three variables can be displayed on a two-dimensional graph.

Multiple-Choice

Graphing Data

1. A point with a negative *x-coordinate* must be
   a. below the horizontal axis.
   b. above the horizontal axis.
   c. to the left of the vertical axis.
   d. to the right of the vertical axis.
   e. below the vertical axis.

2. A point's position on a graph is best described by its
   a. slope.
   b. coordinates.
   c. origin.
   d. causation.
   e. correlation.

3. Which of the following statements is *false?*
   a. The intersection of the *x-axis* and *y-axis* is the origin.
   b. Breaks in a graph's axes can be misleading.
   c. Breaks in a graph's axes can highlight a relationship.
   d. A causal relationship must imply a correlation.
   e. A correlation must imply a causal relationship

Graphs Used in Economic Models

4. From the data in Table A1, it appears that
   a. *x* and *y* have a negative relationship.
   b. *x* and *y* have a positive relationship.
   c. there is no relationship between *x* and *y*.
   d. there is first a negative and then a positive relationship between *x* and *y*.
   e. there is first a positive and then a negative relationship between *x* and *y*.

TABLE A1

Year	x	y
2004	6.2	143
2005	5.7	156
2006	5.3	162

5. If variables x and y move up and down together, they are said to be

  a. positively related.
  b. negatively related.
  c. conversely related.
  d. unrelated.
  e. trendy.

6. The relationship between two variables that move in opposite directions is shown graphically by a line that is

  a. positively sloped.
  b. relatively steep.
  c. relatively flat.
  d. negatively sloped.
  e. curved.

The Slope of a Relationship

7. In Fig. A4 the relationship between x and y as x increases is

  a. positive with slope decreasing.
  b. negative with slope decreasing.
  c. negative with slope increasing.
  d. positive with slope increasing.
  e. positive with slope first increasing then decreasing.

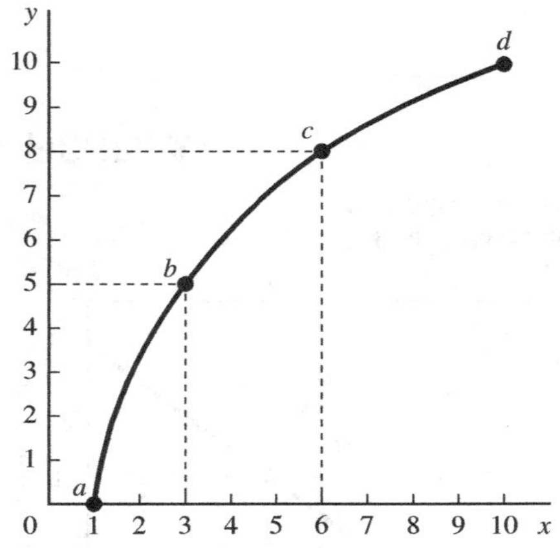

▲ **FIGURE A4**

8. What is the slope across the arc between b and c in Fig. A4?

  a. 1/2
  b. 2/3
  c. 1
  d. 2
  e. 3

9. In Fig. A4, consider the slopes of arc *ab* and arc *bc*. The slope at point *b* is difficult to determine exactly, but it must be

a. greater than 5/2.

b. about 5/2.

c. between 5/2 and 1.

d. about 1.

e. less than 1.

10. In Table A2, suppose that *w* is the independent variable measured along the horizontal axis. The slope of the line relating *w* and *u* is

a. positive with a decreasing slope.

b. negative with a decreasing slope.

c. positive with an increasing slope.

d. negative with a constant slope.

e. positive with a constant slope.

TABLE A2

w	2	4	6	8	10
u	15	12	9	6	3

11. Refer to Table A2. Suppose that *w* is the independent variable measured along the horizontal axis. The slope of the line relating *w* and *u* is

a. +3.

b. −3.

c. −2/3.

d. +3/2.

e. −3/2.

12. In Fig. A5, if household income increases by $1,000, household expenditure will

a. increase by $1,333.

b. decrease by $1,333.

c. remain unchanged.

d. increase by $1,000.

e. increase by $750.

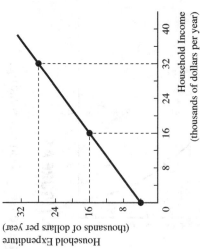

▲ **FIGURE A5**

13. In Fig. A5, if household income is zero, household expenditure is

a. 0.

b. − $4,000.

c. $4,000.

d. $8,000.

e. impossible to determine from the graph.

14. In Fig. A5, if household expenditure is $28,000, household income is

a. $36,000.

b. $32,000.

c. $28,000.

d. $25,000.

e. none of the above.

15. At all points along a straight line, slope is

a. positive.

b. negative.

c. constant.

d. zero.

e. none of the above.

16. What is the slope of the line in Fig. A6?

a. 2

b. 1/2

c. 3

d. 1/3

e. − 3

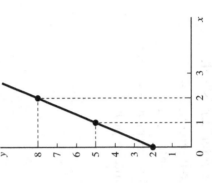

▲ **FIGURE A6**

17. If the line in Fig. A6 were to continue down to the x-axis, what would the value of x be when y is zero?

a. 0
b. 2
c. 2/3
d. −2/3
e. −3/2

18. If the equation of a straight line is $y = 6 + 3x$, the slope is

a. −3 and the y-intercept is 6.
b. −3 and the y-intercept is −2.
c. 3 and the y-intercept is 6.
d. 3 and the y-intercept is −2.
e. 3 and the y-intercept is −6.

19. If the equation of a straight line is $y = 8 − 2x$, then the slope is

a. −2 and the x-intercept is −4.
b. −2 and the x-intercept is 4.
c. −2 and the x-intercept is 8.
d. 2 and the x-intercept is −4.
e. 2 and the x-intercept is 4.

Graphing Relationships Among More Than Two Variables

20. To graph a relationship among more than two variables, what kind of assumption is necessary?

a. normative
b. positive
c. linear
d. independence of variables
e. *ceteris paribus*

21. Given the data in Table A3, holding income constant, the graph relating the price of strawberries (vertical axis) to the purchases of strawberries (horizontal axis)

   a. is a vertical line.

   b. is a horizontal line.

   c. is a positively sloped line.

   d. is a negatively sloped line.

   e. reaches a minimum.

TABLE A3

Weekly Family Income ($)	Price per Box of Strawberries ($)	Number of Boxes Purchased per Week
300	$1.00	5
300	$1.25	3
300	$1.50	2
400	$1.00	7
400	$1.25	5
400	$1.50	4

22. Given the data in Table A3, suppose family income decreases from $400 to $300 per week. Then the graph relating the price of strawberries (vertical axis) to the purchases of strawberries (horizontal axis) will

   a. become negatively sloped.

   b. become positively sloped.

   c. shift rightward.

   d. shift leftward.

   e. no longer exist.

23. Given the data in Table A3, holding price constant, the graph relating family income (vertical axis) to the purchases of strawberries (horizontal axis) is a

   a. vertical line.

   b. horizontal line.

   c. positively sloped line.

   d. negatively sloped line.

   e. positively or negatively sloped line, depending on the price that is held constant.

24. In Fig. A7, x is

  a. positively related to y and negatively related to z.

  b. positively related to both y and z.

  c. negatively related to y and positively related to z.

  d. negatively related to both y and z.

  e. greater than z.

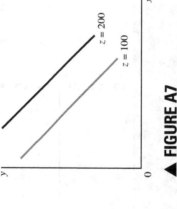

▲ **FIGURE A7**

25. In Fig. A7, a decrease in the value of z will cause, *ceteris paribus*,

  a. a decrease in the value of x.

  b. an increase in the value of x.

  c. an increase in the value of y.

  d. no change in the value of y.

  e. no change in the value of x.

Short Answer Problems

1. On the grid on the next page, draw a graph of variables x and y that illustrates each of the following relationships:

  a. x and y move up and down together.

  b. x and y move in opposite directions.

  c. as x increases y reaches a maximum.

  d. as x increases y reaches a minimum.

  e. x and y move in opposite directions, but as x increases y decreases by larger and larger increments for each unit increase in x.

  f. y is unrelated to the value of x.

  g. x is unrelated to the value of y.

2. What does it mean to say that the slope of a line is $-2/3$?

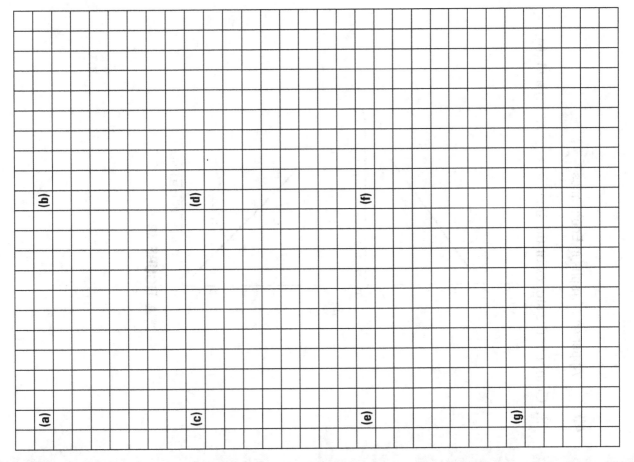

3. Compute the slopes of the lines in Fig. A8(a) and (b).

(a)

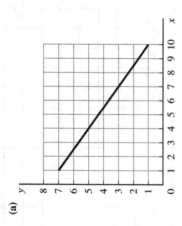

(b)

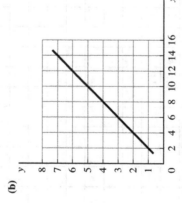

▲ **FIGURE A8**

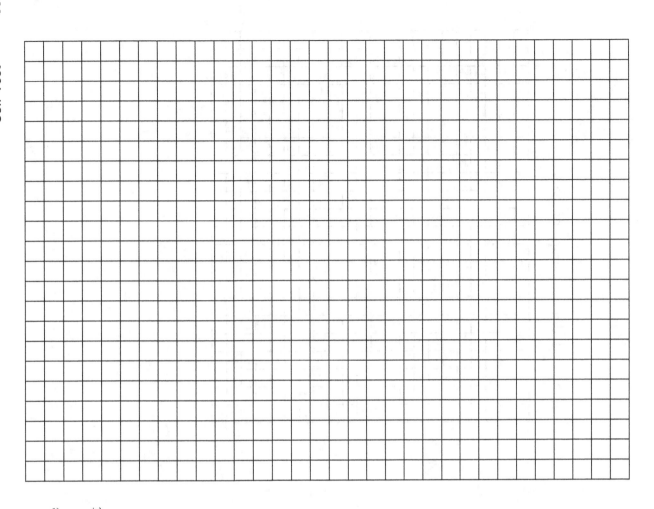

4. On the grid, draw each of the following:

a. a straight line with slope −10 and passing through the point (2, 80).

b. a straight line with slope 2 and passing through the point (6, 10).

5. The equation for a straight line is $y = 4 - 2x$.

a. Calculate the y-intercept, the x-intercept, and the slope.

b. On the grid, draw the graph of the line.

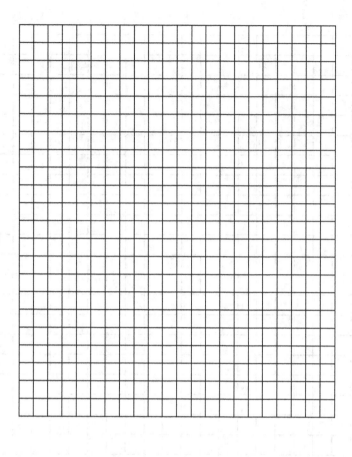

6. Explain two ways to measure the slope of a curved line.

7. Use the graph in Fig. A9 to compute the slope

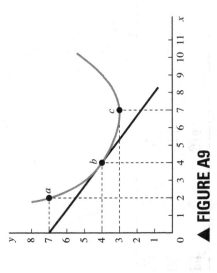

▲ **FIGURE A9**

a. across the arc between points *a* and *b*.

b. at point *b*.

c. at point *c*, and explain your answer.

8. In Table A4, *x* represents the number of umbrellas sold per month, *y* represents the price of an umbrella, and *z* represents the average number of rainy days per month.

TABLE A4

Umbrellas Sold per Month (x)	Price per Umbrella (y)	Average Number of Rainy Days per Month (z)
120	$10	4
140	$10	5
160	$10	6
100	$12	4
120	$12	5
140	$12	6
80	$14	4
100	$14	5
120	$14	6

a. Using the grid below, on the same diagram, graph the relationship between x (horizontal axis) and y (vertical axis) when $z = 4$, when $z = 5$, and when $z = 6$.

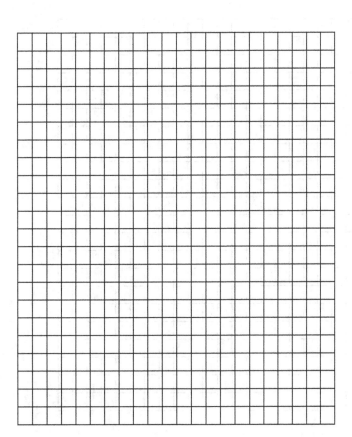

b. On average, it rains six days per month. This implies a certain average relationship between monthly umbrella sales and umbrella price. Suppose that the "greenhouse effect" reduces the average monthly rainfall to four days per month. What happens to the graph of the relationship between umbrella sales and umbrella prices?

c. Using the grid below, graph the relationship between x (horizontal axis) and z (vertical axis) when $y = \$10$ and when $y = \$12$. Is the relationship between x and z positive or negative?

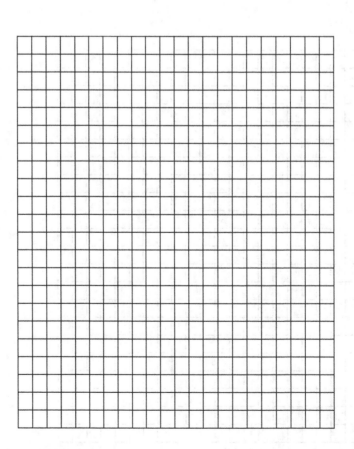

d. Using the grid below, graph the relationship between y (horizontal axis) and z (vertical axis) when $x = 120$ and when $x = 140$. Is the relationship between y and z positive or negative?

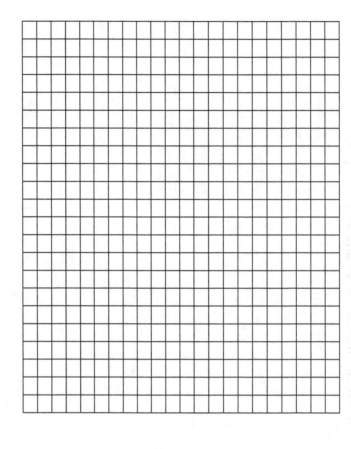

Answers

True/False and Explain

1. **T** Can exaggerate or hide relationships. (13–16)

2. **F** Breaks in the axes may be misleading, or may bring information into clearer view. (13–16)

3. **F** x and y are correlated, but correlation does not guarantee causation. (13–16)

4. **T** Upward-sloping curves/lines have positive slopes. (16–19)

5. **F** A graph of unrelated variables may be vertical or horizontal. (16–19)

6. **T** Arc ab would have negative slope, arc bc positive slope. (16–19)

7. **F** Value of y is minimum at point b. (16–19)

8. **T** Curve becomes steeper, meaning Δy is increasing faster than Δx, so slope is increasing. (20–22)

9. **T** At b, tangent has slope = 0, since $\Delta y = 0$ along the horizontal line through b. (20–22)

10. **F** Slope = (Δ variable on vertical (y) axis)/(Δ variable on horizontal (x) axis). (20–22)

11. **F** Large slope means large Δy associated with small Δx. (20–22)

12. **T** The steep line has a large slope, meaning large Δy is associated with small Δx. (20–22)

13. **T** Slope of a straight line is constant. (20–22)

14. **F** "Other things remain the same." Only variables being studied are allowed to change. (22–23)

15. **T** A *ceteris paribus* assumption holds one variable constant, allowing the other two variables to be plotted in two dimensions. (22–23)

Multiple-Choice

1. **c** Where x values are less than 0. Depending on y-coordinate, may be above or below the horizontal axis. (13–16)

2. **b** Combination of *x-coordinate* and *y-coordinate*. (13–16)

3. **e** A high correlation may be a coincidence. (13–16)

4. **a** Higher values x (6.2) associated with lower values y (143). (16–19)

5. **a** Definition. (16–19)

6. **d** Graph may be steep, flat, or curved, but must have a negative slope. (16–19)

7. **a** Slope of arc $ab = +2.5$. Slope of arc $bc = +1$. (20–22)

8. **c** $\Delta y = 3(8 - 5)$; $\Delta x = 3(6 - 3)$. (20–22)

9. **c** $5/2$ is slope of ab, while 1 is slope of bc. (20–22)

10. **d** As w increases, u decreases. $\Delta u / \Delta w$ is constant. (20–22)

11. **e** Between any two points, $\Delta u = 3$, $\Delta w = -2$. (20–22)

12. **e** Slope ($\Delta y / \Delta x$) = $3/4$. If Δx (Δ household income) = $1,000, then Δy (Δ household expenditure) = $750 = ¾ of $1,000. (20–22)

13. c Where the line intersects the household expenditure (*y*) axis. (20–22)

14. b From $28,000 on vertical (expenditure) axis, move across to line, then down to $32,000 on horizontal (income) axis. (20–22)

15. c Along straight line, the slope may or may not be **a**, **b**, or **d**. (20–22)

16. c Between any two points, $\Delta y = 3$ and $\Delta x = 1$. (20–22)

17. d Equation of line is $y = 2 + 3x$. Solve for *x*-intercept (set $y = 0$). (20–22, 24–25)

18. c Use formula $y = a + bx$. Slope $= b$, *y*-intercept $= a$. (20–22, 24–25)

19. b Use formula $y = a + bx$. Slope $= b$, *x*-intercept $= -a/b$. (20–22, 24–25)

20. e Must hold constant other variables to isolate relationship between two variables. (22–23)

21. d Look either at data in the top 3 rows (income $= 300$) or data in bottom 3 rows (income $= 400$). Higher price is associated with lower purchases. (22–23)

22. d At each price, fewer boxes will be purchased. (22–23)

23. c For $P = 1$, two points on line are (5 boxes, $300) and (7 boxes, $400). Same relationship for other prices. (22–23)

24. c Increased *y* causes decreased *x* holding *z* constant. Increased *z* causes increased *x* holding *y* constant. (22–23)

25. a Decreased *z* causes decreased *x* holding *y* constant. Decreased *z* causes decreased *y* holding *x* constant. (22–23)

Short Answer Problems

1. Figures A10(a) through (g) illustrate the desired graphs.

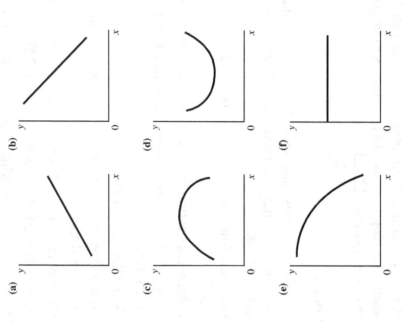

▲ **FIGURE A10**

2. The negative sign in the slope of $-2/3$ means that there is a negative relationship between the two variables. The value of $2/3$ means that when the variable measured on the vertical axis decreases by 2 units (the rise or Δy), the variable measured on the horizontal axis increases by 3 units (the run or Δx).

3. To find the slope, pick any two points on a line and compute $\Delta y/\Delta x$. The slope of the line in Fig. A8(a) is $-2/3$, and the slope of the line in Fig. A8(b) is $1/2$.

4. a. The requested straight line is graphed in Fig. A11(a). First plot the point (2, 80). Then pick a second point whose y-coordinate decreases by 10 for every 1 unit increase in the x-coordinate, for example, (5, 50). The slope between the two points is $-30/3 = -10$.

b. The requested straight line is graphed in Fig. A11(b). First plot the point (6, 10). Then pick a second point whose y-coordinate decreases by 2 for every 1 unit decrease in the x-coordinate, for example, (5, 8). The slope between the two points is $-2/-1 = 2$.

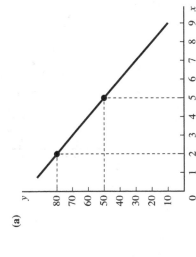

(a)

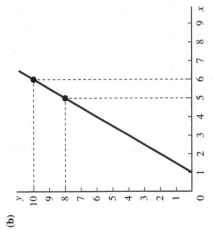

(b)

▲ **FIGURE A11**

5. a. To find the y-intercept, set $x = 0$.
$$y = 4 - 2(0)$$
$$y = 4$$

To find the x-intercept, set $y = 0$.
$$0 = 4 - 2x$$
$$x = 2$$

The slope of the line is -2, the value of the "b" coefficient on x.

d. The relationships between y and z when $x = 120$ and when $x = 140$ are graphed in Fig. A13(c). The relationship between y and z is positive.

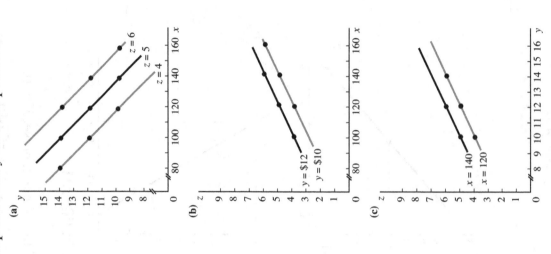

▲ **FIGURE A13**

b. The graph of the line is shown in Fig. A12.

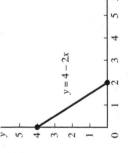

▲ **FIGURE A12**

6. The slope of a curved line can be measured at a point or across an arc. The slope at a point is measured by calculating the slope of the straight line that is tangent to (just touches) the curved line at the point. The slope across an arc is measured by calculating the slope of the straight line that forms the arc.

7. a. The slope across the arc between points a and b is $-3/2$.

b. The slope at point b is $-3/4$.

c. The slope at point c is zero because it is a minimum point. Nearby a minimum point the slope changes from negative to positive and must pass through zero, or no slope, to do so.

8. a. The relationships between x and y for $z = 4$, 5, and 6 are graphed in Fig. A13(a).

b. If the average monthly rainfall drops from 6 days to 4 days, the curve representing the relationship between umbrella sales and umbrella prices will shift from the curve labelled $z = 6$ to $z = 4$.

c. The relationships between x and z when y is $10 and when y is $12 are graphed in Fig. A13(b). The relationship between x and z is positive.

2 The Economic Problem

Key Concepts
Production Possibilities and Opportunity Cost

The production possibility frontier (*PPF*)

- is the boundary between unattainable and attainable production possibilities.

- shows maximum combinations of outputs (goods and services) that can be produced with given resources and technology.

PPF characteristics:

- points on *PPF* represent **production efficiency**—outputs produced at the lowest possible cost.

- points inside *PPF* are inefficient—attainable, but not maximum combinations of outputs; they represent unused or misallocated resources.

- points on *PPF* are preferred to points inside *PPF*.

- points outside *PPF* are unattainable.

- choosing among efficient points on *PPF* involves an **opportunity cost** (highest-valued opportunity foregone) and a *tradeoff*.

*PPF*s are generally bowed outward (concave), reflecting increasing opportunity costs as more of a good is produced.

- *PPF* is bowed outward because resources are not equally productive in all activities (non-homogeneous). Resources most suitable for a given activity are the first to be used.

- Outward-bowed shape of *PPF* represents increasing opportunity cost—opportunity cost of good increases as its quantity produced increases.

- In moving between two points on *PPF* more of good *X* can be obtained only by producing less of good *Y*. Opportunity cost on *PPF* of additional *X* is amount of *Y* forgone.

- There is no opportunity cost in moving from point inside *PPF* to point on *PPF*.

Using Resources Efficiently

To choose among points on *PPF*, compare

- **marginal cost**—the opportunity cost of producing one more unit of a good.
  - marginal cost curve slopes upwards because of *increasing opportunity cost*.

- **marginal benefit**—the benefit (measured in willingness to forgo other goods) from consuming one more unit of a good. Depends on **preferences**—likes, dislikes, and intensity of feelings.
  - **marginal benefit curve** slopes downwards because of *decreasing marginal benefit*.

We choose a point on *PPF* of **allocative efficiency** where

- outputs are produced at lowest possible cost, and in quantities providing greatest possible benefit
  - marginal benefit = marginal cost.

Economic Growth

Economic growth is the expansion of production possibilities—an outward shift of *PPF*.

- *PPF* shifts from changes in resources or technology.
- **Capital accumulation** and **technological change** shift *PPF* outward—economic growth.

- Opportunity cost of increased goods and services in future (economic growth through capital accumulation and technological progress) is decreased consumption today.

Gains from Trade

Production increases if people *specialize* in the activity in which they have a comparative advantage.

- Person has **comparative advantage** in producing a good if she can produce at a lower opportunity cost than anyone else.
- When each person specializes in producing a good at which she has comparative advantage and exchanges for other goods, there are gains from trade.
- Specialization and exchange allow consumption (not production) at points outside *PPF*.
- Person has **absolute advantage** in producing a good if, using the same quantity of resources, she can produce more than anyone else.
    - Absolute advantage is irrelevant for specialization and gains from trade.
    - Even a person with an absolute advantage in producing all goods gains by specializing in an activity in which she has a comparative advantage and trading.

Economic Coordination

Gains from trade and specialization require coordination. Decentralized coordination through markets depends on the social institutions of

- **firms**—hire and organize factors of production to produce and sell goods and services. Firms coordinate much economic activity, but the efficient size of a firm is limited.
- **markets**—coordinating buying and selling decisions through price adjustments.
- **property rights**—governing ownership, use, and disposal of resources, goods, and services.
- **money**—any generally acceptable means of payment; makes trading more efficient.

Helpful Hints

1. This chapter reviews the absolutely critical concept of opportunity cost—the best alternative forgone—that was introduced in Chapter 1. Opportunity cost is a *ratio*. A helpful formula for opportunity cost, which works well in solving problems, especially problems that involve moving up or down a production possibility frontier (*PPF*), is:

$$\text{Opportunity Cost} = \frac{\text{Give Up}}{\text{Get}}$$

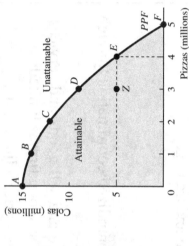

▲ **FIGURE 1 Production Possibilities Frontier**

Opportunity cost equals the quantity of goods you must give up divided by the quantity of goods you will get. This formula applies to all *PPF*s, whether they are linear or bowed out. To illustrate, look again at the bowed-out *PPF* as illustrated in Fig. 1:

First, consider an example of moving down the *PPF*. In moving from *C* to *D*, what is the opportunity cost of an additional pizza? This economy must give up 3 colas (12 − 9) to get 1 pizza (3 − 2). Substituting into the formula, the opportunity cost is:

$$\frac{3 \text{ colas}}{1 \text{ pizza}} = 3 \text{ colas per pizza}$$

Next, consider an example of moving up the *PPF*. In moving from *D* to *C*, what is the opportunity cost of an additional cola? We must give up 1 pizza (3 − 2) to get 3 colas (12 − 9). Substituting into the formula, the opportunity cost is:

$$\frac{1 \text{ pizza}}{3 \text{ colas}} = \frac{1}{3} \text{ pizza per colas}$$

Opportunity cost is always measured in the units of the forgone good.

2. Opportunity cost can also be related to the slope of the *PPF*. As we move down between any two points on the *PPF*, the opportunity cost of an additional unit of the good on the horizontal axis is:

$$|\text{slope of } PPF|$$

The slope of the *PPF* is negative, but economists like to describe opportunity cost in terms of a positive quantity of forgone goods. Therefore, we must use the absolute value of the slope to calculate the desired positive number.

As we move up between any two points on the *PPF*, the opportunity cost of an additional unit of the good on the vertical axis is:

$$\frac{1}{|\text{slope of } PPF|}$$

This is the *inverse* relation we saw between possibilities *C* and *D*. The opportunity cost of an additional pizza (on the horizontal axis) between *C* and *D* is 3 colas. The opportunity cost of an additional cola (on the vertical axis) between *D* and *C* is 1/3 pizza.

3. All points on a *PPF* achieve production efficiency in that they fully employ all resources. But how do we pick a point on the *PPF* and decide *what* combination of goods we want? The *PPF* provides information about resources and *costs*. But choosing what goods we want also requires information about *benefits*.

This choice, like all economic choices, is made at the margin. To decide what goods we want, compare the marginal cost (*MC*) and marginal benefit (*MB*) of different combinations. Marginal cost is the opportunity cost of producing one more unit. The marginal cost of producing more of any good increases as we move along the *PPF*. Marginal benefit is the benefit received from consuming one more unit. Marginal benefit decreases as we consume more of any good.

If the marginal cost of a good exceeds the marginal benefit, we decrease production of the good. If the marginal benefit exceeds the marginal cost, we increase production. When marginal cost equals marginal benefit for every good, we have chosen the goods that we value most highly. The decision rule of *MB* = *MC* yields an *efficient* allocation of resources.

4. The colas and pizza production possibility frontier assumes that resources are *not* equally productive in all activities. Resources with such differences are also called nonhomogeneous resources. As a result of this assumption, opportunity cost increases as we increase the production of either good. In moving from possibility C to D, the opportunity cost per unit of pizza is 3 colas. But in increasing pizza production from D to E, the opportunity cost per unit of pizza increases to 4 colas. In producing the first 1 (million) pizzas, we use the resources best suited to pizza production. As we increase pizza production, however, we must use resources that are less well suited to pizza production—hence increasing opportunity cost. A parallel argument accounts for the increasing opportunity cost of increasing cola production.

It is also possible to construct an even simpler model of a *PPF* that assumes resources are equally productive in all activities, or homogeneous resources. As a result of this assumption, opportunity cost is constant as we increase production of either good. Constant opportunity cost means that the *PPF* will be a straight line (rather than bowed out). As you will see in some of the following exercises, such a simple model is useful for illustrating the principle of comparative advantage, without having to deal with the complications of increasing opportunity cost.

5. This chapter gives us our first chance to develop and use economic models. It is useful to think about the nature of these models in the context of the general discussion of models in Chapter 1. For example, one model in this chapter is a representation of the production possibilities in the two-person and two-good world of Liz and Joe. The model abstracts greatly from the complexity of the real world in which there are billions of people and numerous different kinds of goods and services. The model allows us to explain a number of phenomena that we observe in the world such as specialization and exchange.

The production possibilities model also has some implications or predictions. For example, countries that devote a larger proportion of their resources to capital accumulation will have more rapidly expanding production possibilities. The model can be subjected to "test" by comparing these predictions to the facts we observe in the real world.

Notes:

Self-Test

True/False and Explain

Production Possibilities and Opportunity Cost

Refer to the production possibility frontier (*PPF*) in Fig. 2 for Questions 1 to 4.

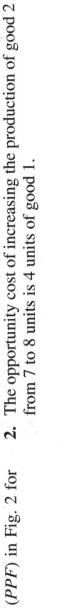

▲ **FIGURE 2**

2. The opportunity cost of increasing the production of good 2 from 7 to 8 units is 4 units of good 1.

1. Point *a* is not attainable.

3. Point *c* is not attainable.

4. In moving from point *b* to point *d*, the opportunity cost of increasing the production of good 2 equals the absolute value of the slope of the *PPF* between *b* and *d*.

7. The principle of decreasing marginal benefit states that the more we have of a good, the *less* we are willing to pay for an additional unit of it.

Using Resources Efficiently

5. The marginal cost of the 4th pizza is the cost of producing all 4 pizzas.

8. All points on a *PPF* represent both production efficiency and allocative efficiency.

Economic Growth

6. The marginal benefit of good *X* is the amount of good *Y* a person is willing to forgo to obtain one more unit of *X*.

9. Economic growth, by shifting out the *PPF*, eliminates the problem of scarcity.

10. In a model where capital resources can grow, points on the *PPF* that have more consumption goods yield faster growth.

11. With specialization and trade, a country can produce at a point outside its *PPF*.

12. Canada has no incentive to trade with a cheap-labour country like Mexico.

13. Nadim definitely has a comparative advantage in producing skateboards if he can produce more than Elle.

Economic Coordination

14. The incentives for specialization and exchange do not depend on property rights but only on differing opportunity costs.

15. Price adjustments coordinate decisions in goods markets but not in factor markets.

Gains from Trade

Multiple-Choice

Production Possibilities and Opportunity Cost

1. If Harold can increase production of good X without decreasing the production of any other good, he
   a. is producing on his *PPF*.
   b. is producing outside his *PPF*.
   c. is producing inside his *PPF*.
   d. must have a linear *PPF*.
   e. must prefer good X to any other good.

2. The bowed-out (concave) shape of a *PPF*
   a. is due to the equal usefulness of resources in all activities.
   b. is due to capital accumulation.
   c. is due to technological change.
   d. reflects the existence of increasing opportunity cost.
   e. reflects the existence of decreasing opportunity cost.

3. The economy is at point b on the *PPF* in Fig. 3. The opportunity cost of producing one more unit of X is
   a. 1 unit of Y.
   b. 20 units of Y.
   c. 1 unit of X.
   d. 8 units of X.
   e. 20 units of X.

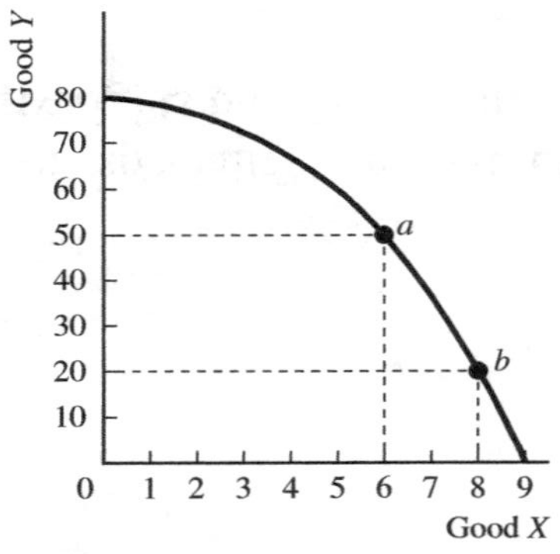

▲ **FIGURE 3**

4. Refer to the *PPF* in Fig. 3. Which of the following statements is *false*?

a. Resources are not equally productive in all activities.

b. Points inside the frontier represent unemployed resources.

c. Starting at point *a*, an increase in the production of good *Y* will shift the frontier out.

d. The opportunity cost of producing good *Y* increases as production of *Y* increases.

e. Shifts in preferences for good *X* or good *Y* will not shift the frontier.

5. Refer to Fig. 4, which shows the *PPF* for an economy without discrimination operating at maximum efficiency. If discrimination against women workers is currently occurring in this economy, the elimination of discrimination would result in a(n)

a. movement from *a* to *b*.

b. movement from *b* to *c*.

c. movement from *a* to *c*.

d. outward shift of the *PPF*.

e. inward shift of the *PPF*.

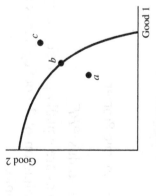

▲ **FIGURE 4**

Suppose a society produces only two goods—hockey sticks and maple leaves. Three alternative combinations on its *PPF* are given in Table 1. Use the information in Table 1 to answer Questions **6** and **7**.

TABLE 1 Production Possibilities

Possibility	Units of Hockey Sticks	Units of Maple Leaves
a	3	0
b	2	3
c	0	9

6. In moving from combination *c* to combination *b*, the opportunity cost of producing one additional hockey stick is

a. 2 maple leaves.

b. 1/2 a maple leaf.

c. 6 maple leaves.

d. 1/6 a maple leaf.

e. 3 maple leaves.

7. According to this *PPF*

a. resources are equally productive in all activities.

b. a combination of 3 hockey sticks and 9 maple leaves is attainable.

c. a combination of 3 hockey sticks and 9 maple leaves would not employ all resources.

d. the opportunity cost of producing hockey sticks increases as more hockey sticks are produced.

e. the opportunity cost of producing hockey sticks decreases as more hockey sticks are produced.

Using Resources Efficiently

8. The marginal benefit curve for a good

a. shows the benefit a firm receives from producing one more unit.

b. shows the amount a consumer is willing to pay for one more unit.

c. is upward sloping.

d. is bowed out.

e. is none of the above.

9. With increasing production of food, its marginal benefit

a. increases and marginal cost increases.

b. increases and marginal cost decreases.

c. decreases and marginal cost increases.

d. decreases and marginal cost decreases.

e. decreases and marginal cost is constant.

10. Suppose the *PPF* for skirts and pants is a straight line. As the production of skirts increases, the marginal benefit of skirts

a. increases and marginal cost is constant.

b. is constant and marginal cost increases.

c. decreases and marginal cost decreases.

d. decreases and marginal cost increases.

e. decreases and marginal cost is constant.

11. With allocative efficiency, for each good produced, marginal

   a. benefit equals marginal cost.

   b. benefit is at its maximum.

   c. benefit exceeds marginal cost by as much as possible.

   d. cost exceeds marginal benefit by as much as possible.

   e. cost is at its minimum.

Economic Growth

12. The *PPF* for wine and wool will shift if there is a change in

   a. the price of resources.

   b. the unemployment rate.

   c. the quantity of resources.

   d. preferences for wine and wool.

   e. all of the above.

13. A movement *along* a given *PPF* will result from

   a. technological change.

   b. change in the stock of capital.

   c. change in the labour force.

   d. all of the above.

   e. none of the above.

14. The opportunity cost of pushing the *PPF* outward is

   a. capital accumulation.

   b. technological change.

   c. reduced current consumption.

   d. the gain in future consumption.

   e. all of the above.

15. In general, the higher the proportion of resources devoted to technological research in an economy, the

a. greater will be current consumption.

b. faster the *PPF* will shift outward.

c. faster the *PPF* will shift inward.

d. closer it will come to having a comparative advantage in the production of all goods.

e. more bowed out the shape of the *PPF* will be.

16. Refer to the *PPF* in Fig. 5. A politician who argues that "if our children are to be better off, we must invest now for the future" is recommending a current point like

a. *a.*

b. *b.*

c. *c.*

d. *d.*

e. *e.*

17. Refer to the *PPF* in Fig. 5. The statement that "unemployment is a terrible waste of human resources" refers to a point like

a. *a.*

b. *b.*

c. *c.*

d. *d.*

e. *e.*

Gains from Trade

In an 8-hour day, Andy can produce either 24 loaves of bread or 8 kilograms of butter. In an 8-hour day, Rolfe can produce either 8 loaves of bread or 8 kilograms of butter. Use this information to answer Questions **18** and **19**.

18. Which of the following statements is *true?*

a. Andy has an absolute advantage in butter production.

b. Rolfe has an absolute advantage in butter production.

c. Andy has an absolute advantage in bread production.

d. Andy has a comparative advantage in butter production.

e. Rolfe has a comparative advantage in bread production.

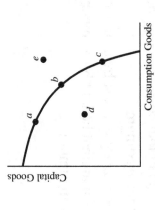

▲ **FIGURE 5**

19. Andy and Rolfe

- **a.** can gain from exchange if Andy specializes in butter production and Rolfe specializes in bread production.
- **b.** can gain from exchange if Andy specializes in bread production and Rolfe specializes in butter production.
- **c.** cannot gain from exchange.
- **d.** can exchange, but only Rolfe will gain.
- **e.** can exchange, but only Andy will gain.

20. Mexico and Canada produce both oil and apples using labour only. A barrel of oil is produced with 4 hours of labour in Mexico and 8 hours of labour in Canada. A bushel of apples is produced with 8 hours of labour in Mexico and 12 hours of labour in Canada. Canada has

- **a.** an absolute advantage in oil production.
- **b.** an absolute advantage in apple production.
- **c.** a comparative advantage in oil production.
- **d.** a comparative advantage in apple production.
- **e.** none of the above.

21. In Portugal, the opportunity cost of a bale of wool is 3 bottles of wine. In England, the opportunity cost of 1 bottle of wine is 3 bales of wool. Given this information,

- **a.** England has an absolute advantage in wine production.
- **b.** England has an absolute advantage in wool production.
- **c.** Portugal has a comparative advantage in wine production.
- **d.** Portugal has a comparative advantage in wool production.
- **e.** no trade will occur.

22. To gain from comparative advantage, countries must not only trade, they must also

- **a.** save.
- **b.** invest.
- **c.** engage in research and development.
- **d.** engage in capital accumulation.
- **e.** specialize.

23. It takes Mom 30 minutes to cook dinner. In the same time she can iron 6 of your shirts. Dad takes 1 hour to cook dinner and 30 minutes to iron a single shirt. In this situation

  a. Dad has an absolute advantage in cooking dinner.
  b. Dad has an absolute advantage in ironing shirts.
  c. Mom should not cook dinner, as her opportunity cost is 6 shirts.
  d. there are no gains from trade.
  e. Mom should cook dinner, even though the opportunity cost is 12 shirts.

Economic Coordination

24. Trade is organized using the social institutions of

  a. firms.
  b. property rights.
  c. money.
  d. markets.
  e. all of the above.

25. Markets

  1. enable buyers and sellers to get information.
  2. are defined by economists as geographical locations where trade occurs.
  3. coordinate buying and selling decisions through price adjustments.

  a. 1 only
  b. 3 only
  c. 1 and 3 only
  d. 2 and 3 only
  e. 1, 2, and 3

Short Answer Problems

1. Why is a *PPF* negatively sloped? Why is it bowed out?

2. Suppose that an economy has the *PPF* shown in Table 2.

| **TABLE 2 Production Possibilities** | | |
Possibility	Maximum Units of Butter per Week	Maximum Units of Guns per Week
a	200	0
b	180	60
c	160	100
d	100	160
e	40	200
f	0	220

   a. On the grid, plot these possibilities, label the points, and draw the *PPF*. (Put guns on the *x*-axis.)

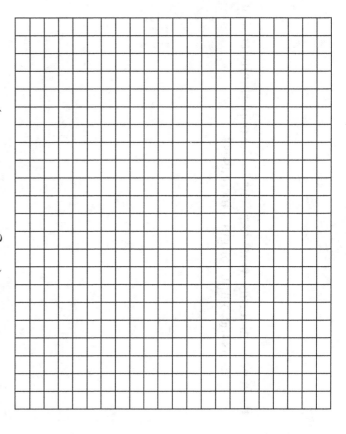

b. If the economy moves from possibility *c* to possibility *d*, the opportunity cost *per unit of guns* will be how many units of butter?

c. If the economy moves from possibility *d* to possibility *e*, the opportunity cost *per unit of guns* will be how many units of butter?

d. In general terms, what happens to the opportunity cost of guns as the output of guns increases?

e. In general terms, what happens to the opportunity cost of butter as the output of butter increases? What do the results in parts **d** and **e** imply about resources?

f. If (instead of the possibilities given) the *PPF* were a straight line joining points *a* and *f*, what would that imply about opportunity costs and resources?

g. Given the original *PPF* you have plotted, is a combination of 140 units of butter and 130 units of guns per week attainable? Would you regard this combination as an efficient one? Explain.

h. Given the original *PPF*, is a combination of 70 units of butter and 170 units of guns per week attainable? Does this combination achieve productive efficiency? Explain.

3. If the following events occurred (each is a separate event, unaccompanied by any other event), what would happen to the *PPF* in Short Answer Problem **2**?

a. A new, easily exploited energy source is discovered.

b. A large number of skilled workers immigrate into the country.

c. The output of butter increases.

d. A new invention increases output per person in the butter industry but not in the guns industry.

e. A new law is passed compelling workers, who could previously work as long as they wanted, to retire at age 60.

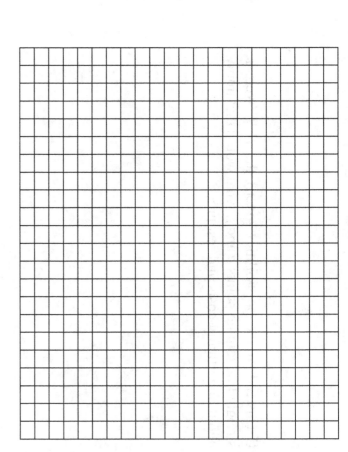

4. The Borg produce only two goods—cubes and transwarp coils—and want to decide where on their *PPF* to operate. Table 3 shows the marginal benefit and marginal cost of cubes, measured in the number of transwarp coils per cube.

TABLE 3

Borg Cubes	Marginal Benefit	Marginal Cost
1	12	3
2	10	4
3	8	5
4	6	6
5	4	7
6	2	8

a. If the Borg are efficient (and they are!), what quantity of cubes will they produce?

b. If the Borg were to produce one more cube than your answer in **a**, why would that choice be inefficient?

5. Suppose the country of Quark has historically devoted 10 percent of its resources to the production of new capital goods. On the grid on the next page, use *PPF* diagrams to compare the consequences (costs and benefits) of each of the following:

a. Quark continues to devote 10 percent of its resources to the production of capital goods.

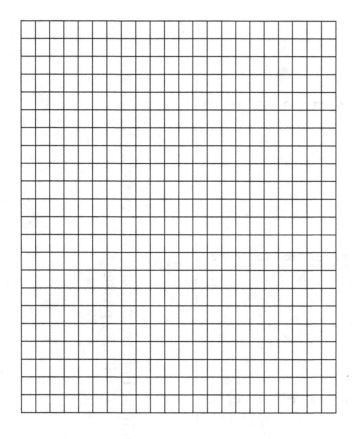

b. Quark begins now to permanently devote 20 percent of its resources to the production of capital goods.

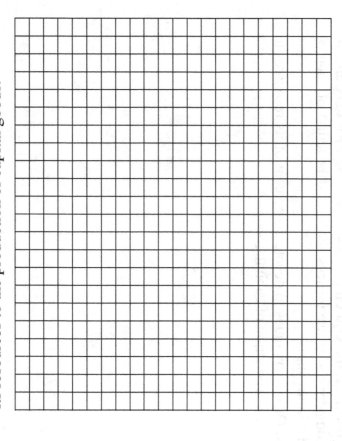

6. Lawyers earn $200 per hour while secretaries earn $15 per hour. Use the concepts of absolute and comparative advantage to explain why a lawyer who is a better typist than her secretary will still specialize in doing only legal work and will trade with the secretary for typing services.

7. France and Germany each produce both wine and beer, using a single, homogeneous input—labour. Their production possibilities are:

- France has 100 units of labour and can produce a maximum of 200 bottles of wine or 400 bottles of beer.
- Germany has 50 units of labour and can produce a maximum of 250 bottles of wine or 200 bottles of beer.

a. Complete Table 4.

TABLE 4	Bottles Produced by I Unit of Labour		Opportunity Cost of I Additional Bottle	
	Wine	Beer	Wine	Beer
France				
Germany				

Use the information in part **a** to answer the following questions.

b. Which country has an absolute advantage in wine production?

c. Which country has an absolute advantage in beer production?

d. Which country has a comparative advantage in wine production?

e. Which country has a comparative advantage in beer production?

f. If trade is allowed, describe what specialization, if any, will occur.

ⓒ **8.** Tova and Ron are the only two remaining inhabitants of the planet Melmac. They spend their 30-hour days producing widgets and woggles, the only two goods needed for happiness on Melmac. It takes Tova 1 hour to produce a widget and 2 hours to produce a woggle, while Ron takes 3 hours to produce a widget and 3 hours to produce a woggle.

a. For a 30-hour day, draw on the grid an individual *PPF* for Tova, then for Ron.

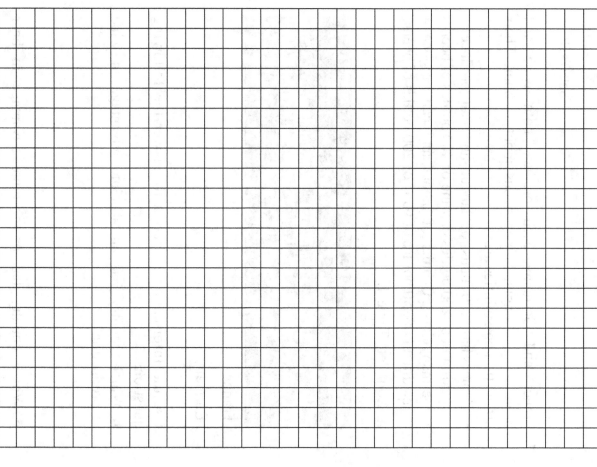

b. What does the shape of the *PPF*s tell us about opportunity costs? about resources?

c. Assume initially that Tova and Ron are each self-sufficient. Define self-sufficiency. Explain what the individual consumption possibilities are for Tova, then for Ron.

d. Who has an absolute advantage in the production of widgets? of woggles?

e. Who has a comparative advantage in the production of widgets? of woggles?

f. Suppose Tova and Ron each specialize in producing only the good in which she or he has a comparative advantage (one spends 30 hours producing widgets, the other spends 30 hours producing woggles). What will be the total production of widgets and woggles?

g. Suppose Tova and Ron exchange 7 widgets for 5 woggles. On your *PPF* diagrams, plot the new point of Tova's consumption, then of Ron's consumption. Explain how these points illustrate the gains from trade.

Answers

True/False and Explain

1. **F** Attainable but not an efficient point. (30–32)

2. **T** Moving from *b* to *d*, production good 1 decreases by 4 units. (30–32)

3. **T** Outside *PPF*. (30–32)

4. **T** See Helpful Hint **2**. (30–32)

5. **F** Marginal cost is the *additional* cost of producing the 4th pizza alone. (33–35)

6. **T** Marginal benefit is also the amount a person is willing to pay for one more unit, but payment in money ultimately represents an opportunity cost in goods forgone. (33–35)

7. **T** The more we have of a good, the smaller is the marginal benefit and hence the willingness to pay for it. (33–35)

8. **F** All points represent productive efficiency (efficient use of resources). But allocative efficiency only occurs at the single point (combination of goods) that we prefer above all others (where *MB* = *MC*). (33–35)

9. **F** Cost of growth is forgone current consumption. (36–37)

10. **F** Points with more capital goods yield faster growth. (36–37)

11. **F** Can *consume* at a point outside the *PPF*. (38–40)

12. **F** Mutually beneficial trade depends on comparative advantage, not absolute advantage. (38–40)

13. **F** Nadim has absolute advantage in skateboard production, but without information about opportunity costs, we don't know if he has comparative advantage. (38–40)

14. **F** Property rights are a prerequisite for specialization and exchange. (41–43)

15. **F** Price adjustments coordinate buying and selling decisions in all markets. (41–43)

Multiple-Choice

1. **c** For 0 opportunity cost, there must be unemployed resources. (30–32)

2. **d** **a** would be true if *unequal* resources; **b** and **c** shift the *PPF*. (30–32)

3. **b** To increase quantity *X* to 9, must decrease quantity *Y* from 20 to 0. (30–32)

4. **c** Increased production of *Y* moves up *along* the *PPF*. (30–32)

5. **a** Discrimination causes underemployment of resources. Women are not allowed to produce up to their full abilities. (30–32)

6. **e** Give up 6 maple leaves to get 2 hockey sticks: 6/2 = 3 maple leaves per hockey stick. (30–32)

7. **a** Constant opportunity cost means resources are equally productive for producing all goods—see Helpful Hint **4**. (30–32)

8. **b** Benefits apply to consumers; the curve is downward sloping. (33–35)

9. **c** Principles of diminishing marginal benefit and increasing marginal cost. (33–35)

10. e Diminishing marginal benefit, but a linear *PPF* means constant opportunity and marginal costs. (33–35)

11. a Whenever *MB* ≠ *MC*, efficiency improves by reallocating resources to produce more goods with high marginal benefits, causing a decrease in their marginal benefit and increase in marginal cost. (33–35)

12. c Only changes in resources or technology shift the *PPF*. (36–37)

13. e a, b, and **c** all shift the *PPF*. (36–37)

14. c a and **b** cause an outward shift of the *PPF*, not opportunity cost; **d** is an effect of an outward shift in the *PPF*. (36–37)

15. b Technological change shifts *PPF* outward at the cost of current consumption. (36–37)

16. a Producing more capital goods now, shifts the *PPF* outward in the future. (36–37)

17. d Points inside the *PPF* represent unemployed resources, whether labour, capital, or land. (36–37)

18. c Andy produces 3 loaves bread per hour; Rolfe produces 1 loaf per hour—see Helpful Hint **5**. (38–40)

19. b Andy has comparative advantage (lower opportunity cost) in bread, Rolfe has comparative advantage in butter production. (38–40)

20. d Opportunity cost of oil in bushels of apples—Canada 2/3, Mexico 1/2. Opportunity cost of apples in barrels of oil—Canada 3/2, Mexico 2. (38–40)

21. c Opportunity cost of wine in bales of wool—Portugal 1/3, England 3. Opportunity cost of wool in bottles of wine—Portugal 3, England 1/3. (38–40)

22. e Gains from trade require specialization based on comparative advantage. **a–d** may increase productivity and absolute advantage, but not necessarily comparative advantage. (38–40)

23. c Dad has a comparative advantage cooking. (38–40)

24. e All 4 institutions are required for gains from trade and specialization through decentralized coordination. (41–43)

25. c 2 is the ordinary meaning of markets, not the economist's definition. (41–43)

Short Answer Problems

1. The negative slope of the *PPF* reflects opportunity cost: in order to have more of one good, some of the other must be forgone. It is bowed out because the existence of resources not equally productive in all activities creates increasing opportunity cost as we increase the production of either good.

2. a. The graph of the *PPF* is given in Fig. 6.

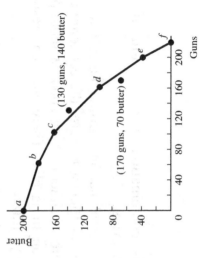

▲ **FIGURE 6**

b. In moving from *c* to *d*, in order to gain 60 units of guns, we must give up $160 - 100 = 60$ units of butter. The opportunity cost per unit of guns is

$$\frac{60 \text{ units butter}}{60 \text{ units guns}} = 1 \text{ unit butter per unit of guns}$$

c. In moving from *d* to *e*, in order to gain 40 units of guns, we must give up $100 - 40 = 60$ units of butter. The opportunity cost per unit of guns is

$$\frac{60 \text{ units butter}}{40 \text{ units guns}} = 1.5 \text{ unit butter per unit of guns}$$

d. The opportunity cost of producing more guns increases as the output of guns increases.

e. Likewise, the opportunity cost of producing more butter increases as the output of butter increases. Increasing opportunity costs imply that resources are not equally productive in gun and butter production; that is, they are nonhomogeneous.

f. Opportunity costs would always be constant, regardless of the output of guns or butter. The opportunity cost per unit of guns would be

$$200/220 = 10/11 \text{ units of butter}$$

The opportunity cost per unit of butter would be

$$220/200 = 1.1 \text{ units of guns}$$

Constant opportunity costs imply that resources are equally productive in gun and butter production; that is, they are homogeneous.

g. This combination is outside the *PPF* and therefore is not attainable. Since the economy cannot produce

this combination, the question of efficiency is irrelevant.

h. This combination is inside the *PPF* and is attainable. It is inefficient because the economy could produce more of either or both goods without producing less of anything else. Therefore some resources are not fully utilized.

3. a. Assuming that both goods require energy for their production, the entire *PPF* shifts out to the northeast as in Fig. 7(a).

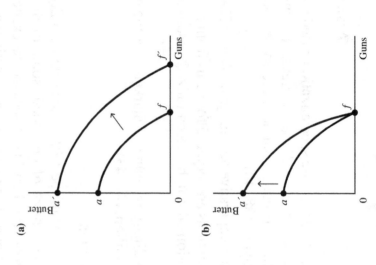

▲ **FIGURE 7**

b. Assuming that both goods use skilled labour in their production, the entire *PPF* shifts out to the northeast.

c. The *PPF* does not shift. An increase in the output of butter implies a movement along the *PPF* to the left, not a shift of the *PPF* itself.

d. The new invention implies that for every level of output of guns, the economy can now produce more butter. The *PPF* swings to the right, but remains anchored at point *f* as in Fig. 7(b).

e. The entire *PPF* shifts in toward the origin.

4. a. At the efficient quantity of output, marginal benefit = marginal cost. The Borg will produce 4 cubes (*MB* = *MC* = 4 transwarp coils/cube).

b. At 5 cubes, marginal benefit = 4 and marginal cost = 7. Since *MC* > *MB*, the Borg could better use their resources by shifting production out of cubes and into transwarp coils.

5. a. The situation for Quark is depicted in Fig. 8. Suppose Quark starts on *PPF*₁. If it continues to devote only 10 percent of its resources to the production of new capital goods, it is choosing to produce at a point like *a*. This will shift the *PPF* out in the next period, but only to the curve labelled 2 (where, presumably, Quark will choose to produce at point *b*).

b. Starting from the same initial *PPF*, if Quark now decides to increase the resources devoted to the production of new capital to 20 percent, it will be choosing to produce at a point like *c*. In this case, next period's *PPF* will shift further—to curve 3, and a point like *d*, for example.

Thus in comparing points *a* and *c*, we find the following costs and benefits: point *a* has the benefit of lowing costs and benefits: point *a* has the benefit of greater present consumption but at a cost of lower future consumption; point *c* has the cost of lower present consumption, but with the benefit of greater future consumption.

6. The lawyer has an absolute advantage in producing both legal and typing services relative to the secretary. Nevertheless, she has a comparative advantage in legal services, and the secretary has a comparative advantage in typing. To demonstrate these comparative advantages, we can construct Table 5 of opportunity costs.

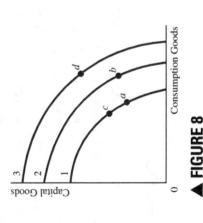

▲ **FIGURE 8**

TABLE 5

	Opportunity Cost of I Additional Hour ($)	
	Legal Services	Typing
Lawyer	200	200
Secretary	>200	15

Consider first the lawyer's opportunity costs. The lawyer's best forgone alternative to providing 1 hour of legal services is the $200 she could earn by providing another hour of legal services. If she provides 1 hour of typing, she is also forgoing $200 (1 hour) of legal services. What would the secretary have to forgo to provide 1 hour of legal services? He would have to spend 3 years in law school, forgoing 3 years of income in addition to the tuition he must pay. His opportunity cost is a very large number, certainly greater than $200. If he provides 1 hour of typing, his best forgone alternative is the $15 he could have earned at another secretarial job.

Thus Table 5 shows that the lawyer has a lower opportunity cost (comparative advantage) of providing legal services, and the secretary has a lower opportunity cost (comparative advantage) of providing typing services. It is on the basis of comparative advantage (not absolute advantage) that trade will take place from which both parties gain.

7. a. The completed table is shown here as Table 4 Solution.

TABLE 4 Solution

	Bottles Produced by I Unit of Labour		Opportunity Cost of I Additional Bottle	
	Wine	Beer	Wine	Beer
France	2	4	2.0 beer	0.50 wine
Germany	5	4	0.8 beer	1.25 wine

b. Germany, which can produce more wine (5 bottles) per unit of input, has an absolute advantage in wine production.

c. Neither country has an absolute advantage in beer production, since beer output (4 bottles) per unit of input is the same for both countries.

d. Germany, with the lower opportunity cost (0.8 beer), has a comparative advantage in wine production.

e. France, with the lower opportunity cost (0.5 wine), has a comparative advantage in beer production.

f. The incentive for trade depends only on differences in comparative advantage. Germany will specialize in wine production and France will specialize in beer production.

8. a. The individual *PPF*s for Tova and Ron are given by Fig. 9(a) and (b), respectively.

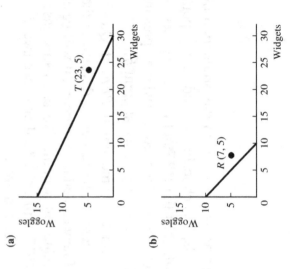

(a)

(b)

▲ **FIGURE 9**

b. The linear shape of the *PPF*s tells us that opportunity costs are constant along each frontier and that resources are equally productive in all activities, or are homogeneous.

These linear *PPF*s with constant opportunity costs abstract from the complexity of the real world. The world generally has increasing opportunity costs, but that fact is not essential for understanding the gains from trade, which is the objective of this problem. Making the model more complex by including increasing opportunity costs would not change our results, but it would make it more difficult to see them.

c. Individuals are self-sufficient if they consume only what they produce. This means there is no trade. Without trade, Tova's (maximum) consumption possibilities are exactly the same as her production possibilities—points along her *PPF*. Ron's (maximum) consumption possibilities are likewise the points along his *PPF*.

d. Tova has an absolute advantage in the production of both widgets and woggles. Her absolute advantage can be defined either in terms of greater output per unit of inputs or fewer inputs per unit of output. A comparison of the *PPF*s in Fig. 9 shows that, for given inputs of 30 hours, Tova produces a greater output of widgets than Ron (30 versus 10) and a greater output

of woggles than Ron (15 versus 10). The statement of the problem tells us equivalently that, per unit of output, Tova uses fewer inputs than Ron for both widgets (1 hour versus 3 hours) and woggles (2 hours versus 3 hours). Since Tova has greater productivity than Ron in the production of all goods (widgets and woggles), we say that overall she has an absolute advantage.

e. Tova has a comparative advantage in the production of widgets, since she can produce them at lower opportunity cost than Ron (1/2 woggle versus 1 woggle). On the other hand, Ron has a comparative advantage in the production of woggles, since he can produce them at a lower opportunity cost than Tova (1 widget versus 2 widgets).

f. Tova will produce widgets and Ron will produce woggles, yielding a total production between them of 30 widgets and 10 woggles.

g. After the exchange, Tova will have 23 widgets and 5 woggles (point *T*). Ron will have 7 widgets and 5 woggles (point *R*). These new post-trade consumption possibility points lie outside Tova's and Ron's respective pre-trade consumption (and production) possibilities. Hence trade has yielded gains that allow the traders to improve their consumption possibilities beyond those available with self-sufficiency.

3   Demand and Supply

Key Concepts

Markets and Prices

Competitive market—many buyers and sellers so no one can influence prices. **Relative price** of a good is

- its *opportunity cost*—the other goods that must be forgone to buy it.
- ratio of its **money price** to the money price of another good.
- determined by demand and supply.

Demand

The **quantity demanded** of a good is the amount consumers plan to buy during a given time period at a particular price. The **law of demand** states: "Other things remaining the same, the higher the price of a good, the smaller is the quantity demanded." Higher price reduces quantity demanded for two reasons:

- *substitution effect*—with an increase in the relative price of a good, people buy less of it and more of substitutes for the good.
- *income effect*—with an increase in the relative price of a good and unchanged incomes, people have less money to spend on all goods, including the good whose price increased.

The **demand curve** represents the inverse relationship between quantity demanded and price, *ceteris paribus*. The demand curve also is a willingness-and-ability-to-pay curve, which measures marginal benefit.

- A change in price causes movement along the demand curve. This is called a **change in the quantity demanded**. The higher the price of a good, the lower the quantity demanded.
- A shift of the demand curve is called a **change in demand**. The demand curve shifts from changes in

  - prices of related goods.
  - expected future prices.
  - income.
  - expected future income and credit.
  - population.
  - preferences.

- Increase in demand—demand curve shifts rightward.
- Decrease in demand—demand curve shifts leftward.
- For an increase in

  - price of a **substitute**—demand shifts rightward.
  - price of a **complement**—demand shifts leftward.
  - expected future prices—demand shifts rightward.
  - income (**normal good**)—demand shifts rightward.
  - income (**inferior good**)—demand shifts leftward.
  - expected future income or credit (**normal good**)—demand shifts rightward.
  - expected future income or credit (**inferior good**)—demand shifts leftward
  - population—demand shifts rightward.
  - preferences—demand shifts rightward.

Supply

The **quantity supplied** of a good is the amount producers plan to sell during a given time period at a particular price. The **law of supply** states: "Other things remaining the same, the higher the price of a good, the greater is the quantity supplied." Higher price increases quantity supplied because marginal cost increases with increasing quantities. Price must rise for producers to be willing to increase production and incur higher marginal cost.

The **supply curve** represents the positive relationship between quantity supplied and price, *ceteris paribus*. The supply curve is also a minimum-supply-price curve, showing the lowest price at which a producer is willing to sell another unit.

- A change in price causes movement along the supply curve. This is called a **change in the quantity supplied**. The higher the price of a good, the greater the quantity supplied.
- A shift of the supply curve is called a **change in supply**. The supply curve shifts from changes in

  - prices of factors of production.
  - prices of related goods produced.
  - expected future prices.
  - number of suppliers.
  - technology.
  - state of nature.

- Increase in supply—supply curve shifts rightward.
- Decrease in supply—supply curve shifts leftward.
- For an increase in

  - prices of factors of production—supply shifts leftward.
  - price of a *substitute in production*—supply shifts leftward.
  - price of a *complement in production*—supply shifts rightward.
  - expected future prices—supply shifts leftward.

- number of suppliers—supply shifts rightward.
- technology—supply shifts rightward.
- state of nature—supply shifts rightward.

Market Equilibrium

The **equilibrium price** is where the demand and supply curves intersect—where quantity demanded equals quantity supplied.

- Above the equilibrium price, there is a surplus (quantity supplied > quantity demanded), and price will fall.
- Below the equilibrium price, there is a shortage (quantity demanded > quantity supplied), and price will rise.
- Only in equilibrium is there no tendency for the price to change. The **equilibrium quantity** is the quantity bought and sold at the equilibrium price.

Predicting Changes in Price and Quantity

For a single change *either* in demand *or* in supply, *ceteris paribus*, when

- demand increases, *P* rises and *Q* increases.
- demand decreases, *P* falls and *Q* decreases.
- supply increases, *P* falls and *Q* increases.
- supply decreases, *P* rises and *Q* decreases.

When there is a simultaneous change *both* in demand *and* supply, we can determine the effect on either price or quantity. But without information about the relative size of the shifts of the demand and supply curves, the effect on the other variable is ambiguous. *Ceteris paribus*, when

- both demand and supply increase, *P* may rise/fall/remain constant and *Q* increases.
- both demand and supply decrease, *P* may rise/fall/remain constant and *Q* decreases.
- demand increases and supply decreases, *P* rises and *Q* may rise/fall/remain constant.
- demand decreases and supply increases, *P* falls and *Q* may rise/fall/remain constant.

Helpful Hints

1. When you are first learning about demand and supply, think of specific examples to help you understand how to use the concepts. For example, in analysing complementary goods, think about hamburgers and french fries; in analysing substitute goods, think of hamburgers and hot dogs. This will reduce the "abstractness" of the economic theory and make concepts easier to remember.

2. The statement "Price is determined by demand and supply" is a shorthand way of saying that price is determined by all of the factors affecting demand (prices of related goods, expected future prices, income, expected future income and credit, population, preferences) and all of the factors affecting supply (prices of factors of production, prices of related goods produced, expected future prices, number of suppliers, technology, state of nature). The benefit of using demand and supply curves is that they allow us to systematically sort out the influences on price of each of these separate factors. Changes in the factors affecting demand shift the demand curve and move us up or down the given supply curve. Changes in the factors affecting supply shift the supply curve and move us up or down the given demand curve.

   Any demand and supply problem requires you to sort out these influences carefully. In so doing, *always draw a graph*, even if it is just a small graph in the margin of a true/false or multiple-choice problem. Graphs are a very efficient way to "see" what happens. As you become comfortable with graphs, you will find them to be effective and powerful tools for systematically organizing your thinking.

   Do not make the common mistake of thinking that a problem is so easy that you can do it in your head, without drawing a graph. This mistake will cost you dearly on examinations. Also, when you do draw a graph, be sure to label the axes. As the course progresses, you will encounter many graphs with different variables on the axes. It is easy to become confused if you do not develop the habit of labelling the axes.

3. Another common mistake among students is failing to *distinguish* correctly between *a shift in a curve* and *a movement along a curve*. This distinction applies both to demand and to supply curves. Many questions in the Self-Test are designed to test your understanding of this distinction, and you can be sure that your instructor will test you

heavily on this. The distinction between "shifts in" versus "movements along" a curve is crucial for systematic thinking about the factors influencing demand and supply, and for understanding the determination of equilibrium price and quantity.

Consider the example of the demand curve. The quantity of a good demanded depends on its own price, the prices of related goods, expected future prices, income, expected future income and credit, population, and preferences. The term "demand" refers to the relationship between the price of a good and the quantity demanded, holding constant all of the other factors on which the quantity demanded depends. This demand relationship is represented graphically by the demand curve. Thus, the effect of a change in price on quantity demanded is already reflected in the slope of the demand curve; the effect of a change in the price of the good itself is given by a movement along the demand curve. This is referred to as a **change in quantity demanded**.

On the other hand, if one of the other factors affecting the quantity demanded changes, the demand curve itself will shift; the quantity demanded *at each price* will change. This shift of the demand curve is referred to as a **change in demand**. The critical thing to remember is that a change in the price of a good will not shift the demand curve; it will only cause a movement along the demand curve. Similarly, it is just as important to distinguish between shifts in the supply curve and movements along the supply curve.

To confirm your understanding, consider the effect (draw a graph!) of an increase in household income on the market for energy bars. First note that an increase in income affects the demand for energy bars and not supply. Next we want to determine whether the increase in income causes a shift in the demand curve or a movement along the demand curve. Will the increase in income increase the quantity of energy bars demanded even if the price of energy bars does not change? Since the answer to this question is yes, we know that the demand curve will shift rightward. Note further that the increase in the demand for energy bars will cause the equilibrium price to rise. This price increase will be indicated by a movement along the supply curve (an increase in the quantity supplied) and will not shift the supply curve itself.

Remember: It is shifts in demand and supply curves that cause the market price to change, not changes in the price that cause demand and supply curves to shift.

Notes:
_____

4. When analysing the shifts of demand and supply curves in related markets (for substitute goods like beer and wine), it often seems as though the feedback effects from one market to the other can go on endlessly. To avoid confusion, stick to the rule that each curve (demand and supply) for a given market can shift a maximum of *once*. (See Short Answer Problems **4** and **6** for further explanation and examples.)

5. The relationships between price and quantity demanded and supplied can be represented in three equivalent forms: demand and supply schedules, curves, and equations. Text Chapter 3 illustrates schedules and curves, but demand and supply equations are also powerful tools of economic analysis. The Mathematical Note to Chapter 3 (pages 76–77) provides the general form of these equations. The purpose of this Helpful Hint and the next is to further explain the equations and how they can be used to determine the equilibrium values of price and quantity.

Fig. 1 presents a simple demand and supply example in three equivalent forms: (a) schedules, (b) curves, and (c) equations. The demand and supply schedules in (a) are in the same format as used in the text. The price-quantity combinations from the schedules are plotted on the graph in (b), yielding linear demand and supply curves. What is new about this example is the representation of those curves by the equations in (c).

If you recall (Chapter 1 Appendix) the formula for the equation of a straight line ($y = a + bx$), you can see that the demand equation is the

(a) Demand and Supply Schedules

Price ($)	Q_D	Q_S	Shortage (–)/ Surplus (+)
1	4	0	–4
2	3	1	–2
3	2	2	0
4	1	3	+2
5	0	4	+4

(b) Demand and Supply Curves

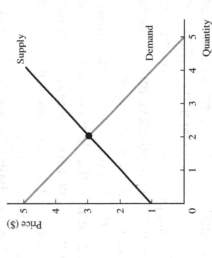

(c) Demand and Supply Equations

Demand: $P = 5 - 1Q_D$

Supply: $P = 1 + 1Q_S$

▲ **FIGURE 1**

equation of a straight line. Instead of y, P is the dependent variable on the vertical axis, and instead of x, Q_D is the independent variable on the horizontal axis. The intercept on the vertical axis a is $+5$, and the slope b is -1. The supply equation is also linear and graphed in the same way, but with Q_S as the independent variable. The supply curve intercept on the vertical axis is $+1$, and the slope is $+1$. The negative slope of the demand curve reflects the law of demand, and the positive slope of the supply curve reflects the law of supply.

You can demonstrate the equivalence of the demand schedule, curve, and equation by substituting various values of Q_D from the schedule into the demand equation, and calculating the associated prices. These combinations of quantity demanded and price are the coordinates (Q_D, P) of the points on the demand curve. You can similarly demonstrate the equivalence of the supply schedule, curve, and equation.

The demand and supply equations are very useful for calculating the equilibrium values of price and quantity. As the schedules and curves both show, two things are true in equilibrium: (1) the price is the same for consumers (the highest price they are willing to pay for the last unit) and producers (the lowest price they are willing to accept for the last unit) and (2) the quantity demanded equals the quantity supplied, so that there are no surpluses or shortages. In terms of the demand and supply equations, this means that, *in equilibrium*,

(1) the price in both equations is the same. We will denote the equilibrium price as P^*.

(2) $Q_D = Q_S =$ the equilibrium quantity bought and sold. We will denote the equilibrium quantity as Q^*.

In equilibrium, the equations become

$$\text{Demand: } P^* = 5 - 1Q^*$$
$$\text{Supply: } P^* = 1 + 1Q^*$$

These equilibrium equations constitute a simple set of simultaneous equations. Since there are two equations (demand and supply) and two unknowns (P^* and Q^*), we can solve for the unknowns.

Begin the solution by setting demand equal to supply:

$$5 - 1Q^* = 1 + 1Q^*$$

Collecting like terms, we find

$$4 = 2Q^*$$
$$2 = Q^*$$

Once we have Q^* (equilibrium quantity), we can solve for the equilibrium price using either the demand or the supply equations. Look first at demand:

$$P^* = 5 - 1Q^*$$
$$P^* = 5 - 1(2)$$
$$P^* = 5 - 2$$
$$P^* = 3$$

Alternatively, substituting Q^* into the supply equation yields the same result:

$$P^* = 1 + 1Q^*$$
$$P^* = 1 + 1(2)$$
$$P^* = 1 + 2$$
$$P^* = 3$$

Once you have solved for Q^*, the fact that substituting it into either the demand or the supply equation yields the correct P^* provides a valuable check on your calculations. If you make a mistake in your calculations, when you substitute Q^* into the demand and supply equations, you will get two different prices. If that happens, you know to recheck your calculations. If you get the same price when you substitute Q^* into the demand and supply equations, you know your calculations are correct.

6. Economists have developed the convention of graphing quantity as the independent variable (on the horizontal x-axis) and price as the dependent variable (on the vertical y-axis), and the foregoing equations reflect this. Despite this convention, economists

actually consider real-world prices to be the independent variables and quantities the dependent variables. In that case, the equations would take the form

$$\text{Demand: } Q_D = 5 - 1P$$

$$\text{Supply: } Q_S = -1 + 1P$$

You can solve these equations for yourself to see that they yield exactly the same values for P^* and Q^*. (*Hint:* First solve for P^* and then for Q^*.) Whichever form of the equations your instructor may use, the technique for solving the equations will be similar and the results identical.

Self-Test
True/False and Explain

Markets and Prices

1. In a competitive market, every single buyer and seller influences price.

2. The relative price of a good is the other goods that must be forgone to buy it.

3. A good's relative price can fall even when its money price rises.

Demand

4. The law of demand tells us that as the price of a good rises, demand decreases.

5. The demand curve is a willingness-and-ability-to-pay curve that measures marginal cost.

6. Hamburgers and fries are complements. If Burger Bar reduces the price of fries, the demand for hamburgers increases.

7. A decrease in income always shifts the demand curve leftward.

Supply

8. A supply curve shows the maximum price at which the last unit will be supplied.

9. If *A* and *B* are substitutes, an increase in the price of *A* always shifts the supply curve of *B* leftward.

10. When a cow is slaughtered for beef, its hide becomes available to make leather. Thus beef and leather are substitutes in production.

11. If the price of beef rises, there will be an increase in both the supply of leather and the quantity of beef supplied.

Market Equilibrium

12. When the actual price is above the equilibrium price, a shortage occurs.

Predicting Changes in Price and Quantity

13. If the expected future price of a good increases, there will always be an increase in equilibrium price and a decrease in equilibrium quantity.

14. Suppose new firms enter the steel market. *Ceteris paribus,* the equilibrium price of steel will always fall and the quantity will rise.

15. Suppose the demand for PCs increases while the cost of producing them decreases. The equilibrium quantity of PCs will rise and the price will always fall.

Multiple-Choice

Markets and Prices

1. A relative price is
   a. the ratio of one price to another.
   b. an opportunity cost.
   c. a quantity of a "basket" of goods and services forgone.
   d. determined by demand and supply.
   e. all of the above.

Demand

2. If an increase in the price of good *A* causes the demand curve for good *B* to shift leftward,
   a. *A* and *B* are substitutes in consumption.
   b. *A* and *B* are complements in consumption.
   c. *A* and *B* are complements in production.
   d. *B* is an inferior good.
   e. *B* is a normal good.

3. Which of the following could *not* cause an increase in demand for a commodity?
   a. an increase in income
   b. a decrease in income
   c. a decrease in the price of a substitute
   d. a decrease in the price of a complement
   e. an increase in preferences for the commodity

4. Some sales managers are talking shop. Which of the following quotations refers to a movement along the demand curve?
   a. "Since our competitors raised their prices our sales have doubled."
   b. "It has been an unusually mild winter; our sales of wool scarves are down from last year."
   c. "We decided to cut our prices, and the increase in our sales has been remarkable."
   d. "The Green movement has sparked an increase in our sales of biodegradable products."
   e. None of the above.

5. If Hamburger Helper is an inferior good, then, *ceteris paribus*, a decrease in income will cause

a. a leftward shift of the demand curve for Hamburger Helper.

b. a rightward shift of the demand curve for Hamburger Helper.

c. a movement up along the demand curve for Hamburger Helper.

d. a movement down along the demand curve for Hamburger Helper.

e. none of the above.

6. A decrease in quantity demanded is represented by a

a. rightward shift of the supply curve.

b. rightward shift of the demand curve.

c. leftward shift of the demand curve.

d. movement upward and to the left along the demand curve.

e. movement downward and to the right along the demand curve.

7. Which of the following "other things" are *not* held constant along a demand curve?

a. income

b. prices of related goods

c. the price of the good itself

d. preferences

e. all of the above

Supply

8. The fact that a decline in the price of a good causes producers to reduce the quantity of the good supplied illustrates

a. the law of supply.

b. the law of demand.

c. a change in supply.

d. the nature of an inferior good.

e. technological improvement.

9. A shift of the supply curve for rutabagas will be caused by

a. a change in preferences for rutabagas.

b. a change in the price of a related good that is a substitute in consumption for rutabagas.

c. a change in income.

d. a change in the price of rutabagas.

e. none of the above.

10. If a factor of production can be used to produce either good A or good B, then A and B are

a. substitutes in production.

b. complements in production.

c. substitutes in consumption.

d. complements in consumption.

e. normal goods.

11. Which of the following will shift the supply curve for good X leftward?

a. a decrease in the wages of workers employed to produce X

b. an increase in the cost of machinery used to produce X

c. a technological improvement in the production of X

d. a situation where quantity demanded exceeds quantity supplied

e. all of the above

12. Some producers are chatting over a beer. Which of the following quotations refers to a movement along the supply curve?

a. "Wage increases have forced us to raise our prices."

b. "Our new, sophisticated equipment will enable us to undercut our competitors."

c. "Raw material prices have skyrocketed; we will have to pass this on to our customers."

d. "We anticipate a big increase in demand. Our product price should rise, so we are planning for an increase in output."

e. "New competitors in the industry are causing prices to fall."

13. If an increase in the price of good *A* causes the supply curve for good *B* to shift rightward,
    a. *A* and *B* are substitutes in consumption.
    b. *A* and *B* are complements in consumption.
    c. *A* and *B* are substitutes in production.
    d. *A* and *B* are complements in production.
    e. *A* is a factor of production for making *B*.

Market Equilibrium

14. If the market for Twinkies is in equilibrium,
    a. Twinkies must be a normal good.
    b. producers would like to sell more at the current price.
    c. consumers would like to buy more at the current price.
    d. there will be a surplus.
    e. equilibrium quantity equals quantity demanded.

15. The price of a good will tend to fall if
    a. there is a surplus at the current price.
    b. the current price is above equilibrium.
    c. the quantity supplied exceeds the quantity demanded at the current price.
    d. all of the above are true.
    e. none of the above is true.

16. A surplus can be eliminated by
    a. increasing supply.
    b. government raising the price.
    c. decreasing the quantity demanded.
    d. allowing the price to fall.
    e. allowing the quantity bought and sold to fall.

17. A shortage is the amount by which quantity

  a. demanded exceeds quantity supplied.

  b. supplied exceeds quantity demanded.

  c. demanded increases when the price rises.

  d. demanded exceeds the equilibrium quantity.

  e. supplied exceeds the equilibrium quantity.

Predicting Changes in Price and Quantity

18. Which of the following will definitely cause an increase in the equilibrium price?

  a. an increase in both demand and supply

  b. a decrease in both demand and supply

  c. an increase in demand combined with a decrease in supply

  d. a decrease in demand combined with an increase in supply

  e. none of the above

19. Coffee is a normal good. A decrease in income will

  a. increase the price of coffee and increase the quantity demanded of coffee.

  b. increase the price of coffee and increase the quantity supplied of coffee.

  c. decrease the price of coffee and decrease the quantity demanded of coffee.

  d. decrease the price of coffee and decrease the quantity supplied of coffee.

  e. cause none of the above.

20. An increase in the price of Pepsi (a substitute for coffee) will

  a. increase the price of coffee and increase the quantity demanded of coffee.

  b. increase the price of coffee and increase the quantity supplied of coffee.

  c. decrease the price of coffee and decrease the quantity demanded of coffee.

  d. decrease the price of coffee and decrease the quantity supplied of coffee.

  e. cause none of the above.

21. A technological improvement lowers the cost of producing coffee. At the same time, preferences for coffee decrease. The *equilibrium quantity* of coffee will

  a. rise.

  b. fall.

  c. remain the same.

  d. rise or fall depending on whether the price of coffee falls or rises.

  e. rise or fall depending on the relative shifts of demand and supply curves.

22. Since 1980, there has been a dramatic increase in the number of working mothers. On the basis of this information alone, we can predict that the market for child-care services has experienced a(n)

  a. increase in demand.

  b. decrease in demand.

  c. increase in quantity demanded.

  d. decrease in quantity supplied.

  e. increase in supply.

23. If A and B are complementary goods (in consumption) and the cost of a factor of production used in the production of A decreases, the price of

  a. both A and B will rise.

  b. both A and B will fall.

  c. A will fall and the price of B will rise.

  d. A will rise and the price of B will fall.

  e. A will fall and the price of B will remain unchanged.

24. The demand curve for knobs is $P = 75 - 6Q_D$ and the supply curve for knobs is $P = 35 + 2Q_S$. What is the equilibrium price of a knob?

  a. $5

  b. $10

  c. $40

  d. $45

  e. none of the above

25. The demand curve for tribbles is $P = 300 - 6Q_D$. The supply curve for tribbles is $P = 20 + 8Q_S$. If the price of a tribble was set at $120, the tribble market would experience

a. equilibrium.

b. excess demand causing a rise in price.

c. excess demand causing a fall in price.

d. excess supply causing a rise in price.

e. excess supply causing a fall in price.

Short Answer Problems

Ⓔ 1. A tax on crude oil would raise the cost of the primary resource used in the production of gasoline. A proponent of such a tax has claimed that it will not raise the price of gasoline using the following argument: While the price of gasoline may rise initially, that price increase will cause the demand for gasoline to decrease, which will push the price back down. What is wrong with this argument?

2. Brussels sprouts and carrots are substitutes in consumption and, since they can both be grown on the same type of land, substitutes in production too. Suppose there is an increase in the demand for brussels sprouts. On the grid, trace the effects on price and quantity traded in both the brussels sprout and the carrot market. (Keep in mind Helpful Hint **4**.)

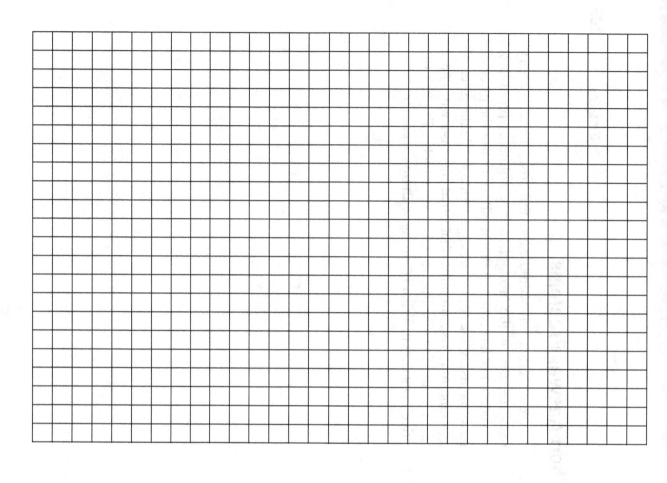

3. The information given in Table 1 is about the behaviour of buyers and sellers of fish at the market on a particular Saturday.

TABLE 1 Demand and Supply Schedules for Fish		
Price (per fish)	**Quantity Demanded**	**Quantity Supplied**
$0.50	280	40
$1.00	260	135
$1.50	225	225
$2.00	170	265
$2.50	105	290
$3.00	60	310
$3.50	35	320

a. On the grid, draw the demand curve and the supply curve. Be sure to label the axes. What is the equilibrium price?

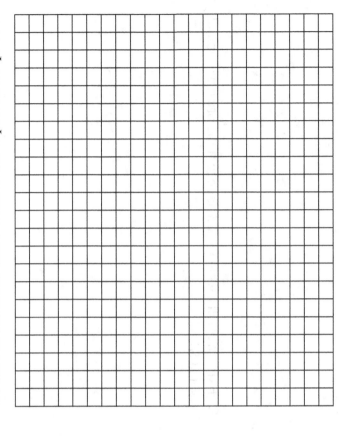

b. We will make the usual *ceteris paribus* assumptions about the demand curve so that it does not shift. List six factors that we are assuming do not change.

c. We will also hold the supply curve constant by assuming that six factors do not change. List them.

d. Explain briefly what would happen if the price was initially set at $3.

e. Explain briefly what would happen if the price was initially set at $1.

f. Explain briefly what would happen if the price was initially set at $1.50.

4. A newspaper reported, "Despite a bumper crop of cherries this year, the price drop for cherries won't be as much as expected because of short supplies of plums and peaches."

a. On the grid, use a demand and supply graph for the cherry market to explain the effect of the bumper crop alone.

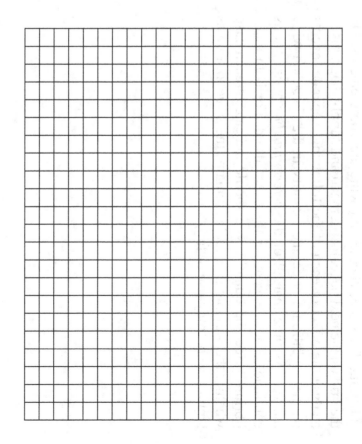

b. On the same graph, explain the impact on the cherry market of the short supplies of plums and peaches.

5. The market for wine in Canada is initially in equilibrium with supply and demand curves of the usual shape. Beer is a close substitute for wine; cheese and wine are complements. On the grid on the next page, use demand and supply diagrams to analyse the effect of each of the following (separate) events on the equilibrium price and quantity in the Canadian wine market. Assume that all of the *ceteris paribus* assumptions continue to hold except for the event listed. For both equilibrium price and quantity you should indicate in each case whether the variable rises, falls, remains the same, or moves ambiguously (may rise or fall).

   a. The income of consumers falls (wine is a normal good).

   b. Early frost (state of nature) destroys a large part of the world grape crop.

   c. A new churning invention reduces the cost of producing cheese.

   d. A new fermentation technique is invented that reduces the cost of producing wine.

   e. A new government study is published that links wine drinking and increased heart disease.

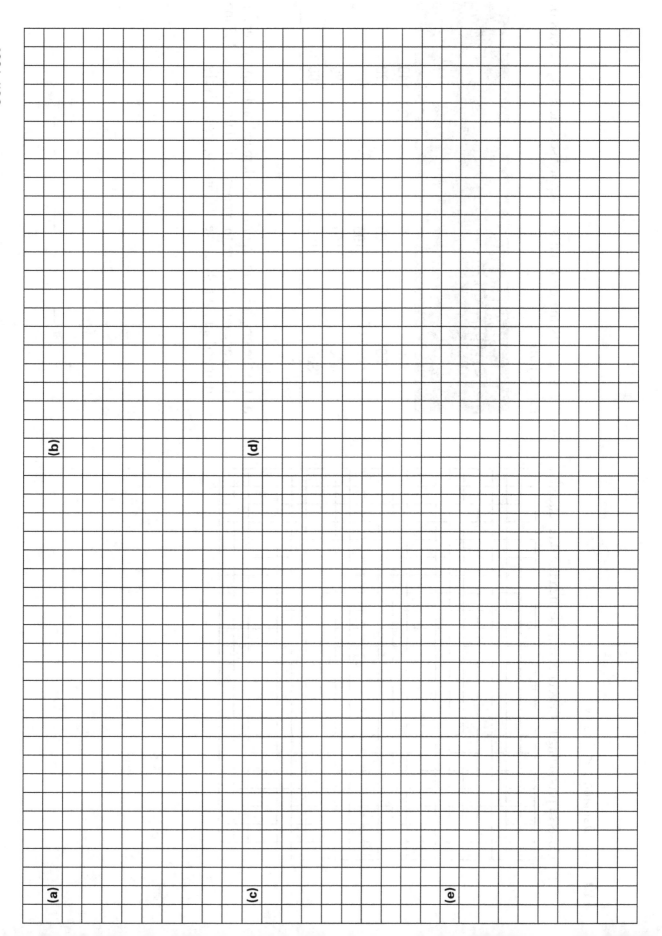

(b)

(d)

(a)

(c)

(e)

f. Costs of producing both beer and wine increase dramatically.

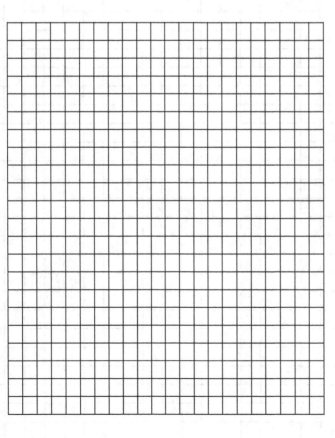

6. Table 2 lists the demand and supply schedules for cases of grape jam.

TABLE 2 Demand and Supply Schedules for Grape Jam Per Week		
Price (per case)	Quantity Demanded (cases)	Quantity Supplied (cases)
$70	20	140
$60	60	120
$50	100	100
$40	140	80
$30	180	60

a. On the graph in Fig. 2, draw the demand and supply curves for grape jam. Be sure to properly label the axes. Label the demand and supply curves D_0 and S_0 respectively.

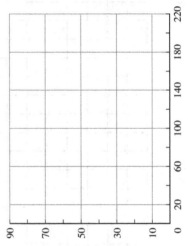

▲ **FIGURE 2**

b. What are the equilibrium price and quantity in the grape jam market? On your diagram, label the equilibrium point *a*.

c. Is there a surplus or shortage at a price of $40? How much?

d. The demand and supply schedules can also be represented by the following demand and supply equations:

Demand: $P = 75 - 0.25Q_D$

Supply: $P = 0.5Q_S$

Use these equations to solve for the equilibrium quantity (Q^*); equilibrium price (P^*). (*Hint:* Your answers should be the same as those in **6b.**)

e. Suppose the population grows sufficiently that the demand for grape jam increases by 60 cases per week at every price.

   i. In the space below, construct a table (price, quantity demanded) of the new demand schedule.

   ii. Draw the new demand curve on your original graph and label it D_1.

  iii. Label the new equilibrium point b. What are the new equilibrium price and quantity?

  iv. What is the new demand equation? (*Hints*: What is the new slope? What is the new price-axis intercept?)

7. The demand equation for dweedles is

$$P = 8 - 1Q_D$$

The supply equation for dweedles is

$$P = 2 + 1Q_S$$

where P is the price of a dweedle in dollars, Q_D is the quantity of dweedles demanded, and Q_S is the quantity of dweedles supplied. The dweedle market is initially in equilibrium and income is $300.

c. As a result of an increase in income to $500, the demand curve for dweedles shifts (the supply curve remains the same). The new demand equation is

$$P = 4 - 1Q_D$$

Use this information to calculate the new equilibrium quantity of dweedles; calculate the new equilibrium price of a dweedle.

a. What is the equilibrium quantity (Q^*) of dweedles?

b. What is the equilibrium price (P^*) of a dweedle?

d. On the graph in Fig. 3, draw and label: (1) the supply curve, (2) the initial demand curve, (3) the new demand curve.

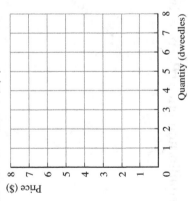

▲ **FIGURE 3**

e. Are dweedles a normal or inferior good? How do you know?

8. The demand equation for flubits is

$$P = 80 - 2Q_D$$

The supply equation for flubits is

$$P = 50 + 1Q_S$$

where P is the price of a flubit in dollars, Q_D is the quantity of flubits demanded, and Q_S is the quantity of flubits supplied. Assume that there are no changes in *ceteris paribus* assumptions.

a. If the price of flubits was set at $56, calculate the exact surplus or shortage of flubits.

b. Explain the adjustment process that will bring the situation above to equilibrium.

c. What is the equilibrium quantity (Q^*) of flubits?

d. What is the equilibrium price (P^*) of a flubit?

e. Now assume that as a result of technological advances, the supply curve for flubits shifts (the demand curve remains the same). The new supply equation is

$$P = 20 + 1Q_S$$

Use this information to calculate the new equilibrium quantity of flubits; calculate the new equilibrium price of a flubit.

Answers

True/False and Explain

1. **F** No single buyer or seller influences price. (55–56)

2. **T** Relative price is an opportunity cost. (55–56)

3. **T** If money prices of other goods rise even more, a good's relative price falls. If the price of gum rises from $1 to $2, but the price of coffee rises from $1 to $4, the opportunity cost of a pack of gum falls from 1 to 0.5 coffee forgone. (55–56)

4. **F** As price rises, *quantity demanded* decreases. (57–61)

5. **F** Measures marginal benefit. (57–61)

6. **T** Combined meal of hamburger and fries is now cheaper. (57–61)

7. **F** Leftward shift for normal good, rightward shift for inferior good. (57–61)

8. **F** Supply curve shows minimum price at which last unit supplied. (62–65)

9. **F** True if A and B are substitutes in production, but false if they are substitutes in consumption. (62–65)

10. **F** Beef and leather are complements in production because they are produced together of necessity. (62–65)

11. **T** For complements in production, a higher price for one good causes increased quantity supplied and increase in supply of the other good. (62–65)

12. **F** At $P >$ equilibrium P, there is surplus (quantity supplied $>$ quantity demanded). (66–67)

13. **F** Higher expected future prices cause a rightward shift in demand and leftward shift in supply. Price rises, but Δ quantity depends on relative magnitude of shifts. (68–65)

14. **T** Increased number of firms causes rightward shift in supply, leading to a fall in price and increased quantity. (68–75)

15. **F** Quantity will increase but Δ price depends on the relative magnitude of the shifts in demand and supply. (68–75)

Multiple-Choice

1. **e** Definitions. (55–56)

2. **b** For example, higher-priced fries cause decreased demand for hamburgers. (57–61)

3. **c** Both income answers could be correct if the commodity were normal (**a**) or inferior (**b**). (57–61)

4. **c** The other answers describe shifts of the demand curve. (57–61)

5. **b** Changes in income shift the demand curve rather than causing movement along the demand curve. (57–61)

6. **d** Decreased quantity demanded is movement up along the demand curve. Could also be caused by a leftward shift in supply. (57–61)

7. **c** "Other things" shift the demand curve. Only price can change along a fixed demand curve. (57–61)

8. **a** Question describes movement down along the supply curve. (62–65)

9. **e** Answers **a**, **b**, and **c** shift demand, while **d** causes movement along the supply curve. (62–65)

10. **a** Definition of a substitute in production. (62–65)

11. **b** Higher-priced factors of production shifts supply leftward. (62–65)

12. **d** The other answers describe shifts of the supply curve. (62–65)

13. **d** Definition of complements in production. Price changes of related goods in consumption shift demand. (62–65)

14. **e** At equilibrium price, plans producers and consumers match; quantity demanded = quantity supplied. (66–67)

15. **d** All answers describe price above the equilibrium price. (66–67)

16. **d** Other answers make surplus (excess quantity supplied) larger. (66–67)

17. **a** Shortage is horizontal distance between the demand and supply curves at a price below the equilibrium price. (66–67)

18. **c** Answers **a** and **b** have an indeterminate effect on price, while **d** causes a lower price. (68–75)

19. **d** Demand shifts leftward. (68–75)

20. **b** Demand shifts rightward. (68–75)

21. **e** Supply shifts rightward, demand shifts leftward, price definitely falls. (68–75)

22. **a** More working mothers increases preferences for child care, causing increased demand for child-care services. (68–75)

23. **c** Supply A shifts rightward causing lower-priced A. This increases demand for B, causing higher-priced B. (68–75)

24. **d** See Helpful Hint **5**. Set demand equal to supply, solve for $Q^* = 5$. Substitute $Q^* = 5$ into either demand or supply equation to solve for P^*. (68–77)

25. **b** At $P = \$120$, $Q_D = 30$, and $Q_S = 12.5$. There is excess demand so price will rise. (68–77)

Short Answer Problems

1. This argument confuses a movement along an unchanging demand curve with a shift in the demand curve. The proper analysis is as follows. The increase in the price of oil (the primary factor of production in the production of gasoline) will shift the supply curve of gasoline leftward. This will cause the equilibrium price of gasoline to increase and thus the quantity demanded of gasoline will decrease. Demand itself will not decrease—that is, the demand curve will not shift. The decrease in supply causes a movement along an unchanged demand curve.

2. The answer to this question requires us to trace through the effects on the two graphs in Fig. 4: (a) for the brussels sprout market and (b) for the carrot market. The sequence of effects occurs in order of the numbers on the graphs.

Look first at the market for brussels sprouts. The increase in demand shifts the demand curve rightward from D_0 to D_1 (1), and the price of brussels sprouts rises. This price rise has two effects (2) on the carrot market. Since brussels sprouts and carrots are substitutes in consumption, the demand curve for carrots shifts rightward from D_0

ket has now shifted once and the analysis must stop. We can predict that the net effects are increases in the equilibrium prices of both brussels sprouts and carrots, and indeterminate changes in the equilibrium quantities in both markets.

3. **a.** The demand and supply curves are shown in Fig. 5. The equilibrium price is $1.50 per fish.

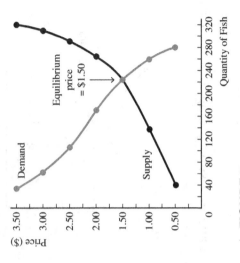

▲ **FIGURE 5**

b. Prices of related goods; expected future prices; income; expected future income and credit; population; preferences.

c. Prices of productive resources; prices of related goods produced; expected future prices; number of suppliers; technology; state of nature.

d. At a price of $3, quantity supplied (310) exceeds quantity demanded (60). Fish sellers find themselves with surplus fish. Rather than be stuck with unsold fish (which yields no revenue), some sellers cut their price in an attempt to increase the quantity of fish

---

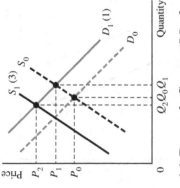

(a) Brussels Sprout Market

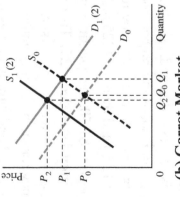

(b) Carrot Market

▲ **FIGURE 4**

to D_1. And, since brussels sprouts and carrots are substitutes in production, the supply curve of carrots shifts leftward from S_0 to S_1. Both of these shifts in the carrot market raise the price of carrots, causing feedback effects on the brussels sprout market. But remember the rule (Helpful Hint **4**) that each curve (demand and supply) for a given market can shift a maximum of *once*. Since the demand curve for brussels sprouts has already shifted, we can only shift the supply curve from S_0 to S_1 (3) because of the substitutes in production relationship. Each curve in each mar-

demanded. Competition forces other sellers to follow suit, and the price falls until it reaches the equilibrium price of $1.50, while quantity demanded increases until it reaches the equilibrium quantity of 225 units.

e. At a price of $1, the quantity demanded (260) exceeds the quantity supplied (135)—there is a shortage. Unrequited fish buyers bid up the price in an attempt to get the "scarce" fish. Prices continue to be bid up as long as there is excess demand, so the quantity supplied increases in response to higher prices. Price and quantity supplied both rise until they reach the equilibrium price ($1.50) and quantity (225 units).

f. At a price of $1.50, the quantity supplied exactly equals the quantity demanded (225). There is no excess demand (shortage) or excess supply (surplus), and therefore no tendency for the price or quantity to change.

4. a. The demand and supply curves for the cherry market are shown in Fig. 6.

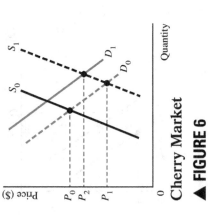

Cherry Market

▲ **FIGURE 6**

Suppose D_0 and S_0 represent the demand and supply curves for cherries last year. This year's bumper crop

increases supply to S_1. Other things being equal, the price of cherries would fall from P_0 to P_1.

b. But other things are not equal. Short supplies of plums and peaches (their supply curves have shifted leftward) drive up their prices. The increase in the prices of plums and peaches, which are substitutes in consumption for cherries, increases the demand for cherries to D_1. The net result is that the price of cherries only falls to P_2 instead of all the way to P_1.

5. The demand and supply diagrams for parts **a** to **e** are shown in Fig. 7.

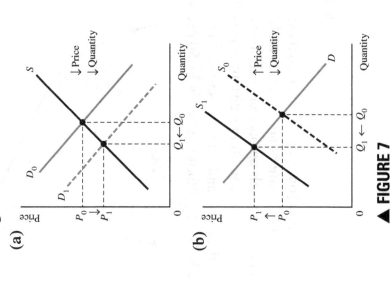

▲ **FIGURE 7**

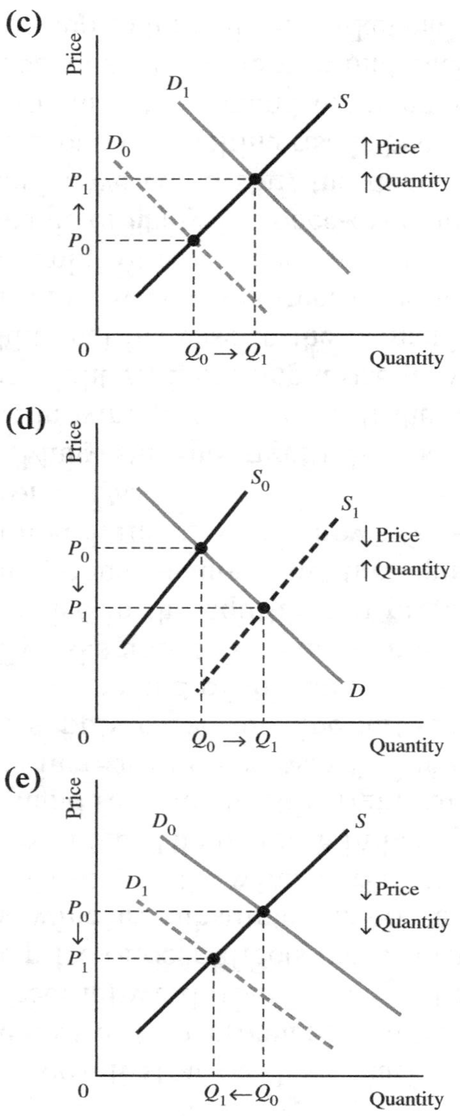

f. Questions like this require the examination of two separate but related markets—the beer and wine markets. Since this kind of question often causes confusion for students, Fig. 8 gives a more detailed explanation of the answer.

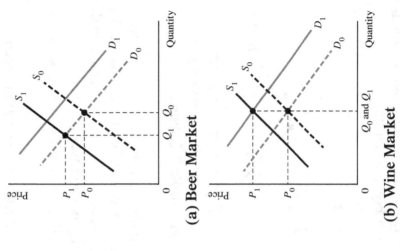

(a) Beer Market

(b) Wine Market

▲ **FIGURE 8**

▲ **FIGURE 7 (Continued)**

Look first at the beer market. The increase in the cost of beer production shifts the supply curve of beer leftward from S_0 to S_1. The resulting rise in the price of beer affects the wine market since beer and wine are substitutes (in consumption).

Turning to the wine market, there are two shifts to examine. The increase in beer prices causes the demand for wine to shift rightward from D_0 to D_1. The increase in the cost of wine production shifts the supply curve of wine leftward from S_0 to S_1. This is the end of the analysis, since the question only asks about the wine market. The final result is a rise in the equilibrium price of wine and an ambiguous change in the quantity of wine. Although the diagram shows $Q_1 = Q_0$, Q_1 may be $\geq$ or $\leq Q_0$.

Many students rightfully ask, "But doesn't the rise in wine prices then shift the demand curve for beer rightward, causing a rise in beer prices and an additional increase in the demand for wine?" This question, which is correct in principle, is about the dynamics of adjustment, and these graphs are only capable of analysing once-over shifts of demand or supply. We could shift the demand for beer rightward, but the resulting rise in beer prices would lead us to shift the demand for wine a *second time*. In practice, stick to the rule that each curve (demand and supply) for a given market can shift a maximum of *once*.

6. a. The demand and supply curves for grape jam are shown in Fig. 2 Solution.

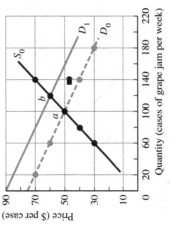

▲ **FIGURE 2 Solution**

b. The equilibrium is given at the intersection of the demand and supply curves (labelled point *a*). The equilibrium price is $50 per case and the equilibrium quantity is 100 cases per week.

c. At a price of $40 there is a shortage of 60 cases per week.

d. In equilibrium, the equations become:

$$\text{Demand: } P^* = 75 - 0.25Q^*$$
$$\text{Supply: } P^* = 0.5Q^*$$

To solve for Q^*, set demand equal to supply:

$$75 - 0.25Q^* = 0.5Q^*$$
$$75 = 0.75Q^*$$
$$100 = Q^*.$$

ii. The graph of the new demand curve, D_1, is shown in Fig. 2 Solution.

iii. The new equilibrium price is $60 per case and the quantity is 120 cases of grape jam per week.

iv. The new demand equation is $P = 90 - 0.25Q_D$. Notice that the slope of the new demand equation is the same as the slope of the original demand equation. An increase in demand of 60 cases at every price results in a rightward *parallel* shift of the demand curve. Since the two curves are parallel, they have the same slope. The figure of 90 is the price-axis intercept of the new demand curve, which you can see on your graph. *Remember:* The demand equation is the equation of a straight line ($y = a + bx$)—in this case, $a = 90$.

If you want additional practice in the use of demand and supply equations for calculating equilibrium values of price and quantity, you can use the new demand curve equation together with the supply curve equation to calculate the answers you found in **e iii.**

7. In equilibrium, the equations become

Demand: $P^* = 8 - 1Q^*$

Supply: $P^* = 2 + 1Q^*$

a. To solve for Q^*, set demand equal to supply:

$8 - 1Q^* = 2 + 1Q^*$

$6 = 2Q^*$

$3 = Q^*$

To solve for P^*, we can substitute Q^* into either the demand or supply equations. Look at demand first:

$P^* = 75 - 0.25Q^*$

$P^* = 75 - 0.25(100)$

$P^* = 75 - 25$

$P^* = 50$

Alternatively, substituting Q^* into the supply equation yields the same result:

$P^* = 0.5Q^*$

$P^* = 0.5(100)$

$P^* = 50$

e. i. Table 3 also contains the (unchanged) quantity supplied, for reference purposes.

TABLE 3 New Demand and Unchanged Supply Schedules for Grape Jam Per Week

Price (per case)	Quantity Demanded (cases)	Quantity Supplied (cases)
$70	80	140
$60	120	120
$50	160	100
$40	200	80
$30	240	60

b. To solve for P^*, we can substitute Q^* into either the demand or supply equations. Look first at demand:

$$P^* = 8 - 1Q^*$$
$$P^* = 8 - 1(3)$$
$$P^* = 8 - 3$$
$$P^* = 5$$

Alternatively, substituting Q^* into the supply equation yields the same result:

$$P^* = 2 + 1Q^*$$
$$P^* = 2 + 1(3)$$
$$P^* = 2 + 3$$
$$P^* = 5$$

c. In equilibrium, the equations are

Demand: $P^* = 4 - 1Q^*$
Supply: $P^* = 2 + 1Q^*$

To solve for Q^*, set demand equal to supply:

$$4 - 1Q^* = 2 + 1Q^*$$
$$2 = 2Q^*$$
$$1 = Q^*$$

To solve for P^*, we can substitute Q^* into either the demand or supply equations. Look first at demand:

$$P^* = 4 - 1Q^*$$
$$P^* = 4 - 1(1)$$
$$P^* = 4 - 1$$
$$P^* = 3$$

Alternatively, substituting Q^* into the supply equation yields the same result:

$$P^* = 2 + 1Q^*$$
$$P^* = 2 + 1(1)$$
$$P^* = 2 + 1$$
$$P^* = 3$$

d. The supply curve, initial demand curve, and new demand curve for dweedles are shown in Fig. 3 Solution.

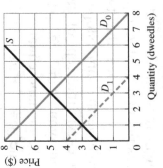

▲ **FIGURE 3 Solution**

e. Dweedles are an inferior good. An increase in income (from $300 to $500) caused a decrease in demand—the demand curve for dweedles shifted leftward.

8. a. Substitute the price of $56 into the demand and supply equations to calculate the quantities demanded and supplied at that price. This is the mathematical equivalent of what you do on a graph when you identify a price on the vertical axis, move your eye across to the demand (or supply) curve, and then move your eye down to read the quantity on the horizontal axis.

Substituting into the demand equation, we find

$$P = 80 - 2Q_D$$
$$56 = 80 - 2Q_D$$
$$2Q_D = 24$$
$$Q_D = 12.$$

Substituting into the supply equation,

$$P = 50 + 1Q_S$$
$$56 = 50 + 1Q_S$$
$$6 = Q_S$$

Quantity demanded exceeds quantity supplied by 6 (12 − 6), so there is a shortage of 6 flubits.

b. A shortage means the price was set below the equilibrium price. Competition between consumers for the limited number of flubits will bid up the price and increase the quantity supplied until we reach the equilibrium price and quantity.

c. In equilibrium, the equations are

Demand: $P^* = 80 - 2Q^*$
Supply: $P^* = 50 + 1Q^*$

To solve for Q^*, set demand equal to supply:

$$80 - 2Q^* = 50 + 1Q^*$$
$$30 = 3Q^*$$
$$10 = Q^*$$

d. To solve for P^*, substitute Q^* into the demand equation:

$$P^* = 80 - 2Q^*$$
$$P^* = 80 - 2(10)$$
$$P^* = 80 - 20$$
$$P^* = 60$$

You can check this answer yourself by substituting Q^* into the supply equation.

e. The new equilibrium equations are

Demand: $P^* = 80 - 2Q^*$
Supply: $P^* = 20 + 1Q^*$

To solve for Q^*, set demand equal to supply:

$$80 - 2Q^* = 20 + 1Q^*$$
$$60 = 3Q^*$$
$$20 = Q^*$$

To solve for P^*, substitute Q^* into the supply equations:

$$P^* = 20 + 1Q^*$$
$$P^* = 20 + 1(20)$$
$$P^* = 20 + 20$$
$$P^* = 40$$

You can check this answer yourself by substituting Q^* into the demand equation.

4 Measuring GDP and Economic Growth

Key Concepts

Gross Domestic Product

Gross domestic product (GDP) is the market value of all final goods and services produced within a country in given time period.

- Total production measured by market value of each good.

- Only new **final goods** (bought by final users) are measured, not **intermediate goods** (bought by firms from firms, used as inputs in production).

- GDP measures total production *and* total income *and* total expenditure.

Circular flow of expenditure and income shows four economic sectors (firms, households, governments, rest of world) operating in factor markets and goods (and services) markets.

- Households sell factor services to firms in return for income—total household income = aggregate income (Y).

- Firms produce goods and services, and sell **consumption expenditure** (C) to households.

- Firms' expenditures on **investment** (I = purchase of *new* capital + additions to inventory).

- Governments buy goods and services from firms (**government expenditures** (*G*)). Governments also collect taxes and make financial transfers to households and firms, but these not part of the circular flow.

- Rest of world buys our **exports** (*X*) and sells us **imports** (*M*): **net exports** = exports − imports.

Circular flow shows that aggregate income = aggregate production = aggregate expenditure:

$$Y = C + I + G + X - M$$

Capital stock is plant, equipment, buildings, and inventories used to produce goods and services.

- Investment (*I*) = purchase of *new* capital.
- **Depreciation** = decrease in value of firm's capital because of wear and tear.
- **Gross investment** = net investment + replacing depreciated capital.
- Δ capital stock = **net investment** = gross investment − depreciation.

Measuring Canada's GDP

Statistics Canada measures GDP two ways on the basis of equality:

$$\text{income} = \text{production} = \text{expenditure}$$

- *Expenditure approach* measures *C* + *I* + *G* + *X* − *M*.
- *Income approach* adds up all incomes paid from firms to households (with some adjustments).

- Net domestic income at factor cost = *wages, salaries, and supplementary income* + *other factor income* (profits + interest/investment income + farmers' income + non-farm unincorporated business income).

- Net domestic product at market prices = net domestic income + indirect taxes − subsidies.

Notes:

- GDP = net domestic product + depreciation.

- Gap between expenditure and income approaches is a statistical discrepancy, which arises due to measurement problems.

GDP increases from production of more goods and services, or from higher prices for goods and services.

- **Nominal GDP** is the value of final goods and services produced in a given year valued at that year's prices = sum of expenditures on goods and services.

- **Real GDP** is the value of final goods and services produced in given year when valued at prices of a reference base year. Real GDP measures changes in production only.

- Real GDP is calculated using quantities produced in each year, but valued with prices from the reference base year.

- In reference base year, real GDP = nominal GDP.

- To calculate real GDP in the current year, multiply current year quantity by base year price for each good, and sum resulting values.

The Uses and Limitations of Real GDP

Real GDP is used to compare standards of living over time and across countries.

- One method of comparison is **real GDP per person** (real GDP/population)—the value of goods and services enjoyed by the average person.

- Canada's real GDP per person over time shows growth of potential GDP per person (with slowdown after the 1960s) as well as fluctuations of real GDP around potential GDP.

 - **Potential GDP** is the maximum level of real GDP that can be produced while avoiding shortages of labour, capital, land, and entrepreneurial ability that would bring rising inflation.

- Lower growth rates of real GDP per person after the 1970s lead to an accumulated gap in real GDP (known as the Lucas wedge).

- **Business cycles** are fluctuations of the pace of expansion of real GDP.

  - Each cycle has two turning points (a peak and a trough), and two phases (**recession** when real GDP decreases for two or more quarters, and **expansion** when real GDP increases).

International comparisons of real GDP per capita are further flawed by currency conversion problems.

  - Using market exchange rates, U.S. real GDP per person is 15 times that of China.
  - Using purchasing power parity, or PPP, prices (prices prevailing in one country, such as the U.S.), U.S. real GDP per person is only 6.5 times China's.

Real GDP as a measure of economic well-being is flawed for the following reasons:

  - Real GDP does not include factors increasing economic well-being (household production, underground economic activity, health, life expectancy, leisure, security, political freedom, social justice).
  - Real GDP does not include factors that lower economic well-being (pollution).
  - The Human Development Index is a broader measure of economic well-being that includes health and education measures, as well as real GDP per person.

Appendix: Graphs in Macroeconomics

Graphs in macroeconomics focus on changes in variables over time.

- **Time-series graphs** show the relationship between time (measured on x-axis) and other variable(s) (measured on y-axis).

  - Reveals variable's level, direction of change, speed of change.
  - Also reveals **cycle** (tendency to alternate between upward and downward movements), and **trend** (tendency to move in one general direction).
  - A ratio scale is used on graphs to help see the growth rate of variables.

Notes:

Helpful Hints

1. Studying the circular flow and national accounts can be boring, but it is useful for several reasons. First, they provide crucial equalities that are the starting point for our economic model—studying this material will help you pass the course! Second, many current debates involve tradeoffs between economic growth and environmental damage. Understanding what GDP does and does not measure is crucial to this debate. Third, in macroeconomics we study how several markets operate simultaneously in a joint, interrelated equilibrium—the circular flow gives us our first taste of this interrelation.

2. One of the key equations in this and future chapters is

    $$Y = C + I + G + X - M$$

    which underlies Chapters 26 and 27.

    Macroeconomics tries to understand what affects GDP, and we start by measuring production (GDP). However, we cannot directly measure production easily. The circular flow helps us measure it indirectly. In the circular flow, production is purchased by the four economic decision makers (measured by expenditure), and money earned from these sales is used to pay incomes. Therefore, production can be measured in three equivalent ways:

    Therefore:

    $$\text{income} = \text{expenditure} = \text{value of production (GDP)}$$

    $$Y(\text{income}) = C + I + G + X - M(\text{expenditure})$$

3. Be sure to distinguish carefully between intermediate goods and investment goods. Both are goods sold by one firm to another, but they differ in terms of their use. Intermediate goods are processed and then resold, while investment goods are final goods. Also note that national income accounts include purchases of residential housing as investment because housing, like business capital stock, provides a continuous stream of value over time.

4. Note the difference between government expenditures on goods and services (*G*) and government transfer payments. Both involve payments by government, but transfer payments are not payments for currently produced goods and services. Instead, they are simply a flow of money, just like (negative) taxes.

5. It is important to understand the difference between real and nominal GDP. Nominal GDP is the value, *in current prices,* of the output of final goods and services in the economy in a year. Real GDP evaluates those final goods and services *at the prices prevailing in a base year (constant prices).*

Nominal GDP can rise from one year to the next, either because prices rise or because output of goods and services rises. A rise in real GDP, however, means that output of goods and services has risen.

If we had a simple economy that produced only pizzas, this rise in real GDP would be easy to measure—are there more pizzas to eat? In a multiple-good economy, we have a more complex task and must turn to a weighted average of goods and services we produce.

Notes:

Self-Test
True/False and Explain

Gross Domestic Product

1. GDP measures intermediate goods, not final goods.

2. Net investment gives the net addition to the capital stock.

3. In the aggregate economy, income is equal to expenditure and to GDP.

4. If exports currently equal imports, then GDP must equal consumption plus investment plus government expenditures.

5. Net exports are positive if expenditures by foreigners on goods and services produced in Canada are greater than expenditures by Canadian citizens on goods and services produced in other countries.

Measuring Canada's GDP

6. Real GDP is calculated by using the current year quantity and the base year price for each good.

7. If there were only households and firms and no government, market price and factor cost would be equal for any good.

8. Net exports are used in the income approach to measuring GDP.

9. If you are interested in knowing whether the economy is producing more output, you would look at real GDP rather than nominal GDP.

The Uses and Limitations of Real GDP

10. Potential GDP is the level of real GDP when labour, capital, land, and entrepreneurial ability are fully employed.

11. The Lucas wedge shows that business cycles lower economic well-being.

12. The Human Development Index shows the same ranking of countries as does real GDP per person.

13. If underground economic activity was included in GDP calculations, measured GDP levels would be higher.

Appendix: Graphs in Macroeconomics

14. A time-series graph shows the level of a variable across different groups at a point in time.

15. A ratio scale is used to distinguish a variable's level.

Multiple-Choice
Gross Domestic Product

1. For the aggregate economy, income equals
   a. expenditure, but these are not generally equal to GDP.
   b. GDP, but expenditure is generally less than these.
   c. expenditure equals GDP.
   d. expenditure equals GDP only if there are no government or foreign sectors.
   e. expenditure equals GDP only if there is no depreciation.

2. Which of the following is a consumption expenditure?
   a. spending by the CBC on children's programs
   b. welfare payments to single mothers
   c. the purchase of a new car by the IPSCO steel company
   d. the purchase of a new car by the Singh household
   e. the purchase of a computer by the IPSCO steel company

3. Danielle's Deliveries had $200,000 worth of delivery vans in 2012. During 2013, Danielle scrapped $20,000 worth of worn-out vans and bought $45,000 worth of new vans. What was Danielle's net investment in 2013?
   a. $20,000
   b. $25,000
   c. $45,000
   d. $65,000
   e. $225,000

4. Which of the following would be counted as investment expenditure in GDP calculations?
   a. The government builds a new building.
   b. The Hong household buys a computer.
   c. IPSCO Steel adds 1 million sheets to inventory.
   d. IPSCO Steel sells pipe to Alaska.
   e. Fred's Pizza Joint sells an old oven to Velma's Pizza Haven.

5. Which of the following adds to Canadian GDP?
   a. I shovel my own driveway.
   b. I sell my used Honda.
   c. the production and sale of flour to a bakery
   d. the purchase of a CD made in China
   e. the ice cream I buy from my grocery store

Measuring Canada's GDP

6. To obtain the factor cost of a good from its market price,
   a. add indirect taxes and subtract subsidies.
   b. subtract indirect taxes and add subsidies.
   c. subtract both indirect taxes and subsidies.
   d. add both indirect taxes and subsidies.
   e. subtract depreciation.

7. From the data in Table 1, what is net investment in Eastland?
   a. −$160
   b. $160
   c. $240
   d. $400
   e. $500

TABLE 1 Data From Eastland	
Item	Amount ($)
Wages, salaries, and supplementary labour income	800
Government expenditures on goods and services	240
Depreciation	240
Gross private domestic investment	400
Personal income taxes net of transfer payments	140
Indirect taxes	120
Net exports	80
Consumption expenditures	640

8. From Table 1, what additional data are needed to compute net domestic income at factor cost?

   a. income of nonfarm unincorporated businesses
   b. transfer payments
   c. subsidies
   d. depreciation
   e. net taxes

9. From the data in Table 1, what is GDP in Eastland?

   a. $1,120
   b. $1,180
   c. $1,360
   d. $1,420
   e. cannot be calculated with the given data

10. From the data in Table 2, compute Southton's nominal GDP in the current year.

    a. $197
    b. $198
    c. $208
    d. $209
    e. cannot be calculated with the given data

TABLE 2 Data From Southton

Item	Price ($)		Quantity	
	Base	Current	Base	Current
Rubber ducks	1.00	1.25	100	100
Beach towels	7.00	6.00	12	14

11. From the data in Table 2, compute Southton's nominal GDP in the base year.

    a. $184
    b. $197
    c. $198
    d. $209
    e. cannot be calculated with the given data

11. From the data in Table 2, compute Southton's real GDP in the base year.

a. $184

b. $197

c. $198

d. $209

e. cannot be calculated with the given data

13. From the data in Table 2, compute Southton's real GDP in the current year.

a. $184

b. $197

c. $198

d. $209

e. cannot be calculated with the given data

The Uses and Limitations of Real GDP

14. The underground economy is all economic activity that

a. produces intermediate goods or services.

b. is not taxed.

c. is legal but unreported or is illegal.

d. has negative social value.

e. is conducted underground.

15. Given that pollution is a byproduct of some production processes,

a. GDP accountants adjust GDP downward.

b. GDP accountants adjust GDP upward.

c. GDP accountants do not adjust GDP unless pollution is a serious problem.

d. GDP tends to overstate economic well-being.

e. GDP tends to understate economic well-being.

16. Which of the following is *not* a reason for GDP incorrectly measuring the value of total output?

a. leisure time

b. household production

c. underground economic activity

d. depreciation

e. environmental quality

17. Which of the following is the major reason China's measured GDP might be underestimated?

a. It includes replacement of depreciated capital stock.

b. It includes production processes that create pollution as a side-effect.

c. It ignores decreases in health and life expectancy.

d. It does not use purchasing power parity prices.

e. It ignores human rights and political freedoms.

18. Which of the following statements by politicians is talking about the business cycle?

a. "Canadian unemployment is falling due to the upturn in the economy."

b. "Crime rates increase every spring as the school year ends."

c. "An average of 220,000 new jobs are created each year in Canada."

d. "More capital investment will create more jobs."

e. "Business always rises just before Christmas."

19. In New Adanac, the average growth rates of potential GDP per capita were 4 percent in the 1980s, but fell to 1 percent in the 1990s. Which of the following statements about this change is true?

a. A strong recession must have started in the 1990s.

b. 1990 was a peak year for the business cycle.

c. The Lucas wedge equals 3 percent of GDP per person for each of the 10 years.

d. The Lucas wedge equals 1 percent of GDP per person for each of the 10 years.

e. The Lucas wedge equals 4 percent of GDP per person for each of the 10 years.

20. From the data in Table 3, in which year did Sudland's business cycle reach a peak?

a. 2009
b. 2010
c. 2011
d. 2012
e. 2013

TABLE 3 Data From Sudland

Year	Actual Real GDP	Potential Real GDP
2007	100	100
2008	107	105
2009	114	111
2010	113	118
2011	114	126
2012	122	134
2013	140	140

21. From the data in Table 3, in which year did Sudland's business cycle hit a trough?

a. 2009
b. 2010
c. 2011
d. 2012
e. 2013

22. From the data in Table 3, in which year(s) did Sudland have a recession?

a. 2010
b. 2010 and 2011
c. 2009, 2010, 2011
d. 2010, 2011, 2012
e. 2010, 2011, 2012, 2013

23. Why is the Human Development Index thought to be a better measure of economic well-being than real GDP per person?

a. It includes a measure of resource depletion.
b. It ignores health, which is hard to measure.
c. It includes leisure time and household production.
d. It includes health and education measures, as well as real GDP per person.
e. It includes only health and education measures, ignoring real GDP per person.

Short Answer Problems

ⓔ **1.** How can we measure gross domestic product by using either the expenditure or the income approach, when neither of these approaches actually measures production?

2. Suppose nominal GDP rises by 75 percent between year 1 and year 2.

    a. If the average level of prices has also risen by 75 percent between year 1 and year 2, what has happened to real GDP?

    b. If the average level of prices has risen by less than 75 percent between year 1 and year 2, has real GDP increased or decreased?

Appendix: Graphs in Macroeconomics

24. Fig. 1 is a time-series graph. The horizontal axis measures _____ and the vertical axis measures _____.

    a. time; the variable of interest

    b. time; slope

    c. the variable of interest in one year; the variable of interest in another year

    d. the variable of interest; time

    e. slope; time

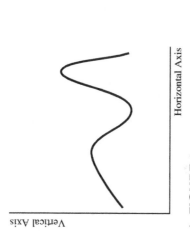

▲ **FIGURE 1**

25. The tendency for a variable to rise or fall over time is called its

    a. slope.

    b. trend.

    c. *y*-coordinate.

    d. level.

    e. correlation.

3. What *productive* activities are *not* measured and thus are *not* included in GDP? Is this lack of measurement a serious problem?

4. Use the data for Northland given in Table 4 to compute the following:

TABLE 4   **Data For Northland**

Item	Amount (billions of $)
Consumption expenditure (C)	600
Taxes (*Tax*)	400
Transfer payments (*TR*)	250
Exports (*X*)	240
Imports (*M*)	220
Government expenditure on goods and services (*G*)	200
Gross investment (*I*)	150
Depreciation (*Depr*)	60

a. GDP

b. net investment

c. net exports

5. Consider the data in Table 5 on potential and real GDP in $ for the country of Dazedland.

TABLE 5	Data For Dazedland	
Year	Actual Real GDP	Potential Real GDP
2007	200	200
2008	212	210
2009	211	220
2010	209	230
2011	240	240
2012	240	240
2013	248	248
2014	258	256
2015	254	264
2016	266	272

a. Identify the peaks and troughs of the business cycle for this economy.

b. In which years is this economy in recession?

c. What happened to productivity in 2011?

d. Calculate the Lucas wedge that resulted after 2011. (Assume the population stays constant, so that the changes in real GDP and potential GDP would be reflected in changes in real GDP per person and potential GDP per person.)

6. Fig. 2 shows the circular flow for Northweston. Aggregate income is $450 billion, exports are $40 billion, imports are $30 billion, consumption expenditure is $275 billion, government expenditure is $100 billion.

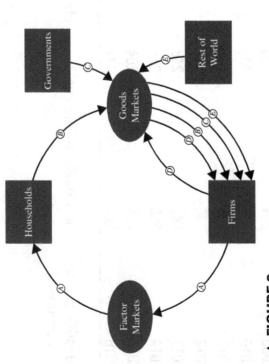

▲ FIGURE 2

a. Identify what each label A, B, C, D, and E represents as an economic value.

b. What is aggregate expenditure? Explain your steps.

c. What is GDP? Explain your steps.

d. What is investment? Explain your steps.

7. Consider the following economic activities. Identify to which of the markets in the circular flow each activity belongs. Give a one-line reason for each answer.

a. Fred of the Forest buys a new loincloth in preparation for his date with Angela.

8. Consider the list of economic activities in Short Answer Problem **7**. Identify whether the activity involves expenditures and, if so, to which component of expenditures each activity belongs (C, I, G, X, M).

b. Fred goes back to school at the University of Sandhurst to get his BA in Vine Swinging.

c. While in school, Fred goes on a Spring Break vacation in Florida.

d. Fred has graduated and is getting paid to knock down trees by Treetop City.

e. Fred buys his first house.

f. Fred and Angela open up Treetop Bed and Breakfast, catering only to Europeans.

Answers

True/False and Explain

1. **F** The opposite is true. (468)

2. **T** Net investment nets out depreciation (replacement of worn-out capital), leaving only new capital additions. (470)

3. **T** From the circular flow, firm production is sold (expenditure) and earnings are used to pay out incomes. (469)

4. **T** If $X = M$, then $X − M = 0$, and $Y = C + I + G + 0$. (469)

5. **T** By definition of exports (goods and services sold to the rest of the world) and imports (goods bought from the rest of the world), net exports = exports − imports. (468)

6. **T** Definition. (473)

7. **T** Market price = factor cost + taxes − subsidies. (471–472)

8. **F** They are an expenditure, used in the expenditure approach. (471)

9. **T** Real GDP measures the quantity of goods and services, while nominal GDP measures current dollar value and includes price level increases. (473)

10. **F** Shows impact of productivity slowdown. (474)

11. **F** There is a correlation between real GDP per person and real GDP per person, but rankings are different. (479)

12. **T** Since they are omitted, and they are a productive activity, real GDP would be higher if they were included. (478)

13. **F** Real GDP is an imperfect measure of standard of living; answer depends on factors such as exchange rates between each country's currency. (476–477)

14. **F** Definition of a cross-section graph. A time-series graph shows the relationship between time (on x-axis) and other variable(s) (on y-axis). (482)

15. **F** Shows when the *growth rate* changes. (483)

Multiple-Choice

1. **c** Expenditure = money earned by sales of produced goods, which is used to pay incomes (including profits). (470)

2. **d** **a** is government expenditure, **b** is transfer payment, **c** and **e** are investment. (468–470)

3. **b** Net investment = gross investment ($45,000) − replacement of depreciated capital ($20,000). (470)

4. **c** **a** is government expenditure, **b** is consumption, **d** is an export, and **e** is not current production. (468–470)

5. **e** **a** is household production, **b** is previous production, **c** is an intermediate good, **d** was produced outside Canada. (468)

6. **b** Market price = factor cost + indirect taxes − subsidies, so factor cost = market price − indirect taxes + subsidies. (471–473)

7. **b** Net investment = gross investment − capital consumption. (471–473)

8. **a** Table lists the other four components of factor incomes. (471–473)

9. **c** $Y = C + I + G + X - M = 640 + 400 + 240 + 80 = 1,360$. (471–473)

10. **d** Nominal GDP = sum of dollar value (= current price × current quantity) of all goods = ($1.25 × 100) + ($6 × 14) = 209. (473)

11. **a** Nominal GDP = sum of current price × current quantity of all goods = ($1 × 100) + ($7 × 12) = 184. (473)

12. **a** In base year, real GDP = nominal GDP. (473)

13. **c** Real GDP = sum of base price × current quantity of all goods = ($1 × 100) + ($7 × 14) = 198. (473)

14. **c** Definition. (477)

15. **d** No such adjustment occurs, so GDP overstates economic well-being. (478)

16. **d** Depreciation is part of GDP. (477–479)

17. **d** See text discussion. (476–477)

18. **a** Upturn implies expansion, which implies unemployment falls. **b** and **e** are irrelevant and seasonal, **c** is the average over the cycle, **d** is growth in potential GDP. (475–476)

19. **c** We cannot tell when year was, and low growth is not a recession. Lucas wedge = accumulated loss of output from slowdown in real GDP growth = 4% − 1% = 3%. (474–476)

20. **a** Growth turns from positive to negative. (475–476)

21. **b** Real GDP hits its lowest point. (475–476)

22. **a** Negative real GDP growth. (475–476)

23. **d** See text discussion. (479)

24. **a** Time is measured on the x-axis and the variable in which we are interested on the y-axis. (482)

25. **b** Definition. (482)

Short Answer Problems

1. The analysis of the circular flow showed that firms produce goods and services (what we wish to measure), and then use the proceeds to pay for factor incomes, rents, profits, etc. (what the income approach measures). Therefore expenditure = production = income.

2. **a.** Real GDP is unchanged. The increased value of goods and services is only because of increased prices.

   b. The fact that prices have risen less in proportion to the increase in nominal GDP means that real GDP has increased.

3. Activities that produce goods and services not included in GDP are underground economic activity and household production. Underground activities are not reported, because they are illegal or are legal but are not reported to circumvent taxes or government regulations. Household production includes productive activities that households perform for themselves. Because they do not hire someone else to mow the lawn or wash the car, they are not included in GDP. The seriousness of the problem depends on the actual size of the activity. The underground economy is estimated at about 5 to 15 percent of the Canadian economy.

4. **a.** GDP = $C + I + G + (X - M)$ = $970 billion.

   b. Net $I = I - Depreciation$ = $90 billion.

   c. Net exports = $X - M$ = $20 billion.

5. a. Peaks occur the year before percentage change in real GDP turns from positive to negative, 2008 and 2014. Troughs occur when percentage change in real GDP turns from negative to positive, 2010 and 2015.

b. The economy is in recession when the growth rate of real GDP is negative, 2009, 2010, and 2015.

c. Since growth in potential GDP slowed initially to zero and then continued at a slow rate, there is a productivity slowdown.

d. The Lucas wedge calculates the amount of difference between actual real GDP and what it would have been if real GDP had grown at the rate of potential GDP after the productivity slowdown. Since potential GDP was initially growing at $10 per year, that means the potential GDP would have been:

$250 in 2012
$260 in 2013
$270 in 2014
$280 in 2015
$290 in 2016

The shortfalls compared to actual real GDP are:

$10 in 2012
$12 in 2013
$12 in 2014
$26 in 2015
$24 in 2016

for a total Lucas wedge of $84.

6. a. A is aggregate income, B is consumption expenditure, C is government expenditure, D is investment, and E is net exports.

b. Aggregate income = aggregate expenditure = $450 billion.

c. Aggregate income = aggregate expenditure = GDP = $450 billion.

d. Investment is the only missing component of aggregate expenditure, and can be deduced from the equation $Y = C + I + G + X - M$, or $450 = $275 + I + $100 + $40 - 30, implying I = $65 billion. (Note that components of aggregate expenditure must all flow through the goods market.)

7. a. Goods and service market—purchase of a good.

b. Goods and service market—purchase of an educational service.

c. This is an expenditure, but money flows to the United States. Therefore, part of the domestic market.

d. Factor market—Fred is working for wage income.

e. Goods and service market—purchase of a good.

f. Goods and services market—purchase of a service.

8. a. Expenditure (C).

b. Expenditure (C).

c. Not a domestic expenditure (M).

d. Not an expenditure, a factor service purchase.

e. Expenditure (I—house purchases count as investment).

f. Expenditure (X).

5 Monitoring Jobs and Inflation

Key Concepts

Employment and Unemployment

Unemployment rises in recessions and falls in expansions.

- Unemployment creates problems from lost production/incomes of unemployed and damaged job prospects from lost human capital.

Statistics Canada surveys households on their job status.

- **Working-age population** = Number of people age 15 years and over.
- **Labour force** = employed + unemployed
  - Employed = those with full-time or part-time jobs.
  - Unemployed = without work, actively seeking within last four weeks, waiting to be called back after layoff, or waiting to start new job within four weeks.

- **Unemployment rate** = percentage of labour force unemployed. Increases during recessions.

- **Labour force participation rate** = percentage of working-age population in labour force. Strong upward trend until 1990; decreases during recessions, increases during expansions.

- **Employment-to-population ratio** = percentage of working-age population with jobs. Increased from 1960s to 1990 (many new jobs created); decreases during recessions, increases during expansions.

Measured unemployment rate excludes some underutilized labour (because they have not looked for a job within the last four weeks).

- **Marginally attached workers**—neither working nor looking for work, but available and want work.
- **Discouraged workers**—stopped looking for jobs because of repeated job search failures.

The most costly unemployment is long-term (it lasts more than 14 weeks), which fluctuates with the business cycle.

Unemployment and Full Employment

There is always some unemployment due to frictions, structural change, and cycles.

Frictional unemployment—due to normal labour turnover. Depends on the number of entrants/re-entrants and job creation/destruction.

- People become unemployed when they are laid off, voluntarily quit, or enter or re-enter the labour force to search for jobs.
- People end unemployment when they are hired, recalled, or withdraw from the labour force.

Structural unemployment—job losses due to technological change or international competition changing the skills need to perform jobs or the location of jobs.

- Lasts longer than frictional unemployment and is higher in slow-growing eastern provinces.

Cyclical unemployment—higher than normal unemployment at a business cycle trough and lower than normal at a peak.

Natural employment—only frictional and structural unemployment (no cyclical unemployment).

- **Natural unemployment rate** = natural unemployment as a percentage of the labour force.
- **Full employment**—unemployment rate equals natural unemployment rate.
- The natural unemployment rate is influenced by
  - the population age distribution—more younger workers means more frictional unemployment.
  - the scale of technological change.
  - the level of the real wage rate.
  - the level of unemployment benefits—higher benefits encourage more job search.
- Economists agree there is natural unemployment, but disagree about the size of the natural rate and the amount it fluctuates.

Actual unemployment rate fluctuates around the natural rate, as real GDP fluctuates around potential GDP over the business cycle.

- **Output gap**—the gap between real GDP and potential GDP.
  - When the output gap is positive, unemployment rate < the natural rate.
  - When the output gap is negative, unemployment rate > the natural rate.
- The natural unemployment rate is trending downward in Canada.

The Price Level, Inflation, and Deflation

Changes in **price level** (average level of prices) determines the value of future payments (loans, savings).

- **Inflation rate**—percentage change in price level.
- Unpredictable inflation

- creates winners/losers by creating unpredictable changes in the value of money, redistributing income and wealth.
  - lowers real GDP and employment.
  - leads to resources diverted from productive activities to predicting inflation.
- **Hyperinflation**—rapid inflation where money loses its value very quickly.

Consumer Price Index (CPI) measures average of prices paid for a fixed basket of consumer goods and services.

- CPI = 100 for reference base period (2002).
- CPI basket is constructed from monthly surveys of consumers' spending habits.

$$CPI = \frac{\text{Cost of CPI basket at current prices}}{\text{Cost of CPI basket at base-period prices}} \times 100$$

Inflation rate = percentage change in CPI.

- CPI overstates inflation rate (biased upward) because
  - new goods replace old goods.
  - quality improvements create some of price rises.
  - consumers change consumption toward cheaper goods not reflected in the fixed-basket price index.
  - consumers substitute toward discount outlets not covered in CPI surveys.
- Magnitude of CPI bias is probably low in Canada, but leads to distorted contracts, more government outlays, and incorrect wage bargaining.

Alternative price indexes include

- **GDP deflator** [(nominal GDP/real GDP) × 100], which measures all goods and controls for biases.

Notes:

- **chained price index for consumption** [(nominal consumption/real consumption) $\times 100$], which does not use fixed quantities.

Core inflation rate excludes volatile elements of CPI to reveal underlying trends.

Real variables (nominal variables divided by GDP deflator) are used to see what is "really" happening to key macroeconomic variables.

Helpful Hints

1. In a dynamic economy, some unemployment is efficient. There are economic benefits of frictional unemployment to individuals and to society. Younger workers typically experience periods of unemployment trying to find jobs that match their skills and interests. The benefit of the resulting frictional unemployment is a more satisfying and productive work life. Society benefits because the frictional unemployment that accompanies such a job search allows workers to find jobs in which they are more productive. As a result, total production of goods and services increases. (Compare this case with the case for graduates in the Republic of China up until the 1990s. They were assigned jobs upon graduation, with very little personal input about the type of job or location.)

   On the other hand, structurally unemployed workers will not get a new job without retraining or relocation. There is a greater cost to the worker and society—structurally unemployed workers are typically unemployed for longer time periods. These workers bear much of the cost of restructuring industries in our economy, although society gains in the long run from shifts of labour and other resources to new industries.

2. The term "full employment," or its equivalent "natural rate of unemployment," does not mean that everyone has a job. Rather, it means that the only unemployment is frictional and structural—there is no cyclical unemployment.

   It is possible for the actual rate of unemployment to be less than the natural rate of unemployment because it is possible for employment to exceed full employment levels. In these situations, people are spending too little time searching for jobs, and therefore less-productive job matches are being made.

3. There are three different types of unemployment, but defining these types does not explain them. Explanations of how unemployment occurs are a goal of the remaining chapters in the textbook!

Notes:

Self-Test

True/False and Explain

Employment and Unemployment

1. The employment-to-population ratio is the percentage of the working-age population in the labour force.

2. If the employment-to-population ratio increases, unemployment always decreases.

3. George was laid off last month, and is waiting to be recalled to his old job, so he is not actively seeking work. George is *not* counted as unemployed.

4. If the working-age population is 600,000, employment is 400,000, and unemployment is 30,000, then the unemployment rate is 7.0 percent.

5. A university student seeking a job is counted as unemployed.

6. If the number of discouraged workers decreases, the employment-to-population ratio decreases as they begin to look for jobs.

7. Discouraged workers are counted as unemployed but probably should not be.

Unemployment and Full Employment

8. Being unemployed for a few months after graduating from university always hurts the graduate.

9. A decline in the number of jobs in the automobile sector matched by an equal increase in the number of jobs offered in the banking sector will not alter the unemployment rate.

10. At full employment, there is no unemployment.

11. Bill has just graduated from high school and is looking for his first job. Bill is frictionally unemployed.

12. Fluctuations in unemployment over the business cycle create frictional unemployment.

The Price Level, Inflation, and Deflation

13. The CPI overstates the inflation rate because it ignores substitution toward higher-quality goods by households.

14. The market basket used in calculating the CPI changes each year.

15. The magnitude of the CPI bias in Canada is high.

Multiple-Choice

Employment and Unemployment

1. In a country with a working-age population of 20 million, 13 million are employed, 1.5 million are unemployed, and 1 million of the employed are working part time, half of whom wish to work full time. The size of the labour force is

   a. 20 million.

   b. 15.5 million.

   c. 14.5 million.

   d. 13 million.

   e. 11.5 million.

2. In a country with a working-age population of 20 million, 13 million are employed, 1.5 million are unemployed, and 1 million of the employed are working part time, half of whom wish to work full time. The labour force participation rate is

   a. 75.5 percent.

   b. 72.5 percent.

   c. 65 percent.

   d. 57.5 percent.

   e. none of the above.

3. In a country with a working-age population of 20 million, 13 million are employed, 1.5 million are unemployed, and 1 million of the employed are working part time, half of whom wish to work full time. The unemployment rate is

   a. 10 percent.

   b. 10.3 percent.

   c. 11.5 percent.

   d. 15.4 percent.

   e. none of the above.

4. Who of the following would be counted as unemployed in Canada?

   a. Doris only works five hours a week, but is looking for a full-time job.

   b. Kanhaya has stopped looking for work, since he was unable to find a suitable job during a two-month search.

   c. Sharon is a university student with no job.

   d. Maurice has been laid off from his job for 20 weeks, but expects a call back soon.

   e. Bogdan has been laid off from his job, but does not expect a call back and is not looking.

5. If the employment-to-population ratio increases,
   a. the unemployment rate *must* decrease.
   b. the labour force participation rate *must* increase.
   c. the labour force participation rate will be unaffected.
   d. aggregate hours worked *must* increase.
   e. none of the above.

6. The economic costs of unemployment include
   a. workers quitting and going to university.
   b. political problems for government.
   c. lost human capital of the unemployed.
   d. the creation of winners and losers due to job creation/ destruction.
   e. the diversion of resources from productive activities to predicting unemployment.

7. Including discouraged workers in the measured unemployment rate would
   a. not change the measured unemployment rate.
   b. lower the measured unemployment rate.
   c. raise the natural rate of unemployment.
   d. raise the full employment rate.
   e. raise the measured unemployment rate.

8. If the number of discouraged workers increases, all else unchanged, the
   a. unemployment rate will increase.
   b. employment-to-population ratio will decrease.
   c. labour force participation rate will increase.
   d. labour force participation rate will decrease.
   e. employment-to-population ratio will increase.

Unemployment and Full Employment

9. Which of the following events would raise cyclical unemployment?

a. Real GDP growth slows down or turns negative.

b. Unemployment benefits increase.

c. The pace of technological change increases.

d. Both job destruction and job creation increase.

e. All of the above

10. Unemployment will increase if there is an increase in the number of people

a. retiring.

b. withdrawing from the labour force.

c. recalled from layoffs.

d. leaving jobs to go to school.

e. leaving school to find jobs.

11. Who of the following would be considered structurally unemployed?

a. a Saskatchewan farmer who has lost her farm and is unemployed until retrained

b. a Nova Scotia fishery worker who is searching for a better job closer to home

c. a steelworker who is laid off but who expects to be called back soon

d. an office worker who has lost her job because of a general economic slowdown

e. none of the above

12. Who of the following would be considered cyclically unemployed?

a. a Saskatchewan farmer who has lost her farm and is unemployed until retrained

b. a Nova Scotia fishery worker who is searching for a better job closer to home

c. a steelworker who is laid off but who expects to be called back soon

d. an office worker who has lost her job because of a general economic slowdown

e. none of the above

13. Who of the following would be considered frictionally unemployed? A steelworker who

a. loses her job because of technological change.
b. is laid off but expects to be called back within a week.
c. gives up her job because she retires.
d. decides to leave the labour force and become a full-time ballet student.
e. becomes discouraged and stops looking for jobs.

14. In a recession, what is the largest source of the increase in unemployment?

a. people quitting jobs
b. people getting laid off
c. new entrants to the labour force
d. re-entrants to the labour force
e. involuntary part-time workers

15. At full employment, there is no

a. natural unemployment.
b. unemployment.
c. cyclical unemployment.
d. structural unemployment.
e. frictional unemployment.

16. Unemployment caused by permanently decreased demand for horse-drawn carriages is an example of

a. cyclical unemployment.
b. marginal unemployment.
c. frictional unemployment.
d. structural unemployment.
e. discouraged unemployment.

17. The natural rate of unemployment is

  a. the rate at which unemployment equals 0 percent.

  b. the same as cyclical unemployment.

  c. the rate at which cyclical unemployment equals 6 percent.

  d. the rate at which cyclical unemployment equals 0 percent.

  e. none of the above.

The Price Level, Inflation, and Deflation

18. Comparing the core inflation rate to the Consumer Price Index, the core inflation rate

  a. controls for the biases of the CPI.

  b. measures all goods produced, not just consumer goods.

  c. uses current-period quantities, not base-period quantities.

  d. excludes the volatile elements of the CPI.

  e. includes volatile elements not in the CPI.

19. If the inflation rate is positive, the price level in an economy is

  a. falling rapidly.

  b. rising.

  c. constant.

  d. falling slowly.

  e. zero.

20. From the data in Table 1, what is Southton's Consumer Price Index for the current year?

TABLE 1 Data from Southton

Item	Price ($) Base	Price ($) Current	Quantity Base	Quantity Current
Rubber ducks	1.00	1.25	100	100
Beach towels	9.00	6.00	12	14

  a. 112

  b. 105.6

  c. 100.5

  d. 100

  e. 94.7

21. Refer to the data in Table 1. Between the base year and the current year, the relative price of rubber ducks

a. remained unchanged.

b. fell.

c. rose.

d. cannot be determined with the given information.

e. depends on whether overall inflation was positive.

22. Which of the following is *not* a reason the Consumer Price Index overstates inflation?

a. New goods of higher quality and prices replace old goods.

b. Quality improvements create some part of price rises in existing goods and services.

c. Consumers change their consumption basket toward cheaper goods not reflected in the fixed-basket price index.

d. Consumers substitute toward using discount outlets not covered in CPI surveys.

e. It does not measure the underground economy.

23. The technique used to calculate the CPI implicitly assumes that consumers buy

a. relatively more of goods with relative prices that are increasing.

b. relatively less of goods with relative prices that are decreasing.

c. the same relative quantities of goods as in a base year.

d. goods and services whose quality improves at the rate of growth of real GDP.

e. more computers and CD players and fewer black-and-white TVs.

24. How does an unpredictable inflation rate cause problems?

a. Business cycles become more variable.

b. The stock market falls in value.

c. The value of money rises.

d. Resources are diverted from productive activities to tax evasion.

e. Resources are diverted from productive activities to fore-casting inflation.

25. In 2009 the Consumer Price Index measured 114.3. In 2010 it measured 118.0. What was inflation in 2010?

a. 1.18 percent

b. 3.1 percent

c. 3.2 percent

d. 3.7 percent

e. 18 percent

Short Answer Problems

Ⓒⓣ **1.** Explain why an economy does not have 0 percent unemployment when it has full employment.

Ⓒⓣ **2.** Should the government try to force the unemployment rate down as close to zero as possible? Discuss some problems such a policy might create.

3. Consider the following information about an economy: working-age population—20 million; full-time employment—8 million; part-time employment—2 million (1 million of whom wish they had full-time jobs); unemployment—1 million.

a. What is the labour force in this economy? What is the labour force participation rate?

b. What is the unemployment rate?

c. What is the involuntary part-time rate?

d. What is the employment-to-population ratio?

e. If 0.6 million of those unemployed are frictionally and structurally unemployed, what is the natural rate of unemployment?

f. What is the amount of cyclical unemployment?

g. Can you tell if this economy is in recession or expansion? Is the output gap positive or negative?

4. Are the costs of unemployment more severe for frictional or structural unemployment? Why?

5. Explain the difference between cyclical and structural unemployment. How would you tell a cyclically unemployed person from a structurally unemployed person?

6. Table 2 gives data for Southland, where there are three consumption goods: bananas, coconuts, and grapes.

TABLE 2 Data for Southland

Goods	Quantity in Base-Period Basket	Base Period Price ($)	Base Period Expenditure ($)	Current Period Price ($)	Current Period Expenditure ($)
Bananas	120	6		8	
Coconuts	60	8		10	
Grapes	40	10		9	

a. Complete the table by computing expenditures for the base period and expenditures for the same quantity of each good in the current period.

b. What is the value of the basket of consumption goods in the base period? in the current period?

c. What is the Consumer Price Index for the current period?

d. On the basis of the data in this table, would you predict consumers would make any substitutions between goods between the base period and the current period? If so, what kind of problems would this create for your measurement of the CPI?

7. Examine each of the following changes in John Carter's labour market activity, and explain whether they constitute unemployment, employment, or being out of the labour force. If unemployment, which of the three types of unemployment is represented?

a. John graduates from Barsoom High and starts looking for a job.

b. John has no luck finding the full-time job he wants and takes a part-time job cleaning out the canals.

c. Canal-cleaning doesn't work out for John because of unforeseen allergies, so he quits.

d. Discouraged by the lack of work, John stops looking and stays home watching his favourite soap opera, *As Mars Turns*.

e. John sees an advertisement on TV for the Barsoom Swordfighter School, and enrols to get his BSF.

f. John graduates at the top of his class and joins the Princess Dejah Thoris guards.

g. Barsoom University invents a new laser personal defence system, and the Princess disbands her guards—John spends a long time looking for work.

h. John sees an advertisement seeking someone to help explore the ruins of the lost city of Rhiannon and signs up as security—the six-armed tribes are particularly ferocious there.

⊕ **8.** Consider the data from 1995 in Table 3 on Canada as a whole and Newfoundland specifically.

TABLE 3

Economy	Labour Force Participation Rate	Unemployment Rate	Employment-to-Population Ratio
Canada	64.8	9.5	58.6
Newfoundland	53.1	18.3	43.3

Source: Statistics Canada, *Labour Force Review.*

Newfoundland has twice the unemployment of Canada, as well as a radically lower employment-to-population ratio and labour force participation rate. By examining these, can you get any insight into the impact of a high unemployment rate on the labour market in Newfoundland? Why is the gap in the employment-to-population ratio (15.3 points) so much bigger than the unemployment gap (8.8 points)?

Answers

True/False and Explain

1. **F** Percentage of working-age population with jobs. (494–495)

2. **F** True if participation decreases or doesn't increase much, otherwise false. (494–495)

3. **F** Since he is waiting for recall, he is counted. (493)

4. **T** Unemployment rate = [unemployment/(unemployment + employed)] × 100 = (30,000/430,000) × 100 = 7.0%. (494–495)

5. **F** Counted as out of labour force (not actively seeking work). (494–5)

6. **F** This change will only change the labour force participation. (495–496)

7. **F** Not counted as unemployed, but probably should be. (495–496)

8. **F** Depends on whether the time unemployed leads to a better job. (497)

9. **F** Workers retrain/relocate, leading to more structural unemployment. (497)

10. **F** Full employment still has frictional and structural unemployment. (497–498)

11. **T** Searching for jobs = frictionally unemployed. (497)

12. **F** Create *cyclical* unemployment. (497)

13. **T** See text discussion. (503–504)

14. **F** Changed every 10 years. (500)

15. **F** Low due to Statistics Canada's corrections. (504)

Multiple-Choice

1. **c** Employed + unemployed. (494–495)

2. **b** Labour force/working-age population = 14.5/20 = 72.5%. (494–495)

3. **b** Unemployed/labour force = 1.5/14.5 = 10.3%. (493–495)

4. **d** Doris is employed, Kanhaya isn't looking for work, Sharon is out of the labour force, Bogdan does not expect to be called back. (493)

5. **e** Any of **a** to **d** *might* occur, but they do not *have* to occur. (493–495)

6. **c** **a** is a gain, **b** is a real but not an economic cost, **d** is normal activity, **e** is nonsense. (492)

7. **e** It would add extra unemployed workers to the measured rate. (495–496)

8. **d** Discouraged workers were unemployed, but stop looking and exit the labour force, so unemployment rate decreases, labour force participation decreases, employment-to-population ratio is unchanged. (495–496)

9. **a** **b** to **d** raise frictional or structural unemployment, but if real GDP growth slows down, cyclical unemployment increases. (497)

10. **e** Others all lower unemployment. (497)

11. **a** Structural unemployment includes having the wrong skills. Others are frictional or cyclical unemployment. (497)

12. **d** Cyclical unemployment is due to economy-wide slowdowns. (497)

13. **b** **a** is structural and the rest are not officially unemployed. (497)

14. **b** See text discussion. (497)

15. **c** Definition. (497–498)

16. **d** Definition—unemployment caused by structural change. (497)

17. **d** Definition. (497–498)

18. **d** By construction. (504–505)

19. **b** Positive inflation implies current price level − past price level > 0, by definition. (503)

Ⓖ 20. **e** CPI = [(sum of current prices × base quantities)/(sum of base prices × base quantities)] × 100. (500–502)

21. **c** Ratio P(ducks)/P(towels) has risen. (500–504)

22. **e** This problem is for real GDP. (503–504)

23. **c** Because assumes a fixed basket. (503–504)

24. **e** Forecasting inflation becomes important because unpredictable inflation leads to unpredictable winners and losers because the value of money *falls*. (500)

25. **c** Inflation = (Δ price level/past price level) × 100 = [(118 − 114.3)/114.3] × 100 = 3.2%. (502)

Short Answer Problems

Ⓖ 1. An economy always has some unemployment, of people searching for jobs—frictional and structural unemployment. We define full employment as when there is zero cyclical unemployment, but still some frictional and structural unemployment.

Ⓖ 2. Pushing down the unemployment rate would eliminate frictional unemployment (which would reduce the number of good job matches) and structural unemployment (which would prevent the structural readjustment the economy needs). Therefore, it does not seem like a good idea to get unemployment as close to zero as possible!

3. **a.** The labour force is 11 million, the sum of employment and unemployment. Labour force participation rate = percentage of the working-age population who are in the labour force = 11/20 or 55 percent.

   b. The unemployment rate is 9.1 percent, the number of unemployed as a percentage of the labour force.

   c. It is 9.1 percent, the percentage of the labour force who are part time and want full time.

   d. It is 50 percent, the percentage of the working-age population with a job.

   e. Natural unemployment is frictional plus structural unemployment = 0.6 million. Natural rate of unemployment is 5.45% = (0.6 million/11 million) × 100.

   f. Cyclical unemployment is actual unemployment minus natural unemployment, or 0.4 million.

   g. Since there is positive cyclical unemployment, real GDP is below potential GDP and the output gap is negative. It is possible we have a recession (negative real GDP growth), but the economy could be expanding out of the recession.

4. The costs of unemployment include lost output of the unemployed, and deterioration of skills and abilities; in other words, human capital erodes. These costs are higher for structural unemployment because it lasts

longer, and often workers' human capital becomes worthless in the marketplace.

5. Cyclical unemployment is caused by a downturn in the economy, when there is a decrease in demand for all products. Structural unemployment is caused by structural changes in a specific industry or region and there is a decrease in demand for a certain type of labour whose skills are no longer desired.

Cyclical unemployment will end when the economy turns up. Structural unemployment will end when the workers retrain or move.

6. a. Table 2 is completed here as Table 2 Solution. Note that the base-period quantities are evaluated at current prices to find the value of quantities in the current period.

TABLE 2 Solution

Goods	Quantity in Base-Period Basket	Base Period Price ($)	Base Period Expenditure ($)	Current Period Price ($)	Current Period Expenditure ($)
Bananas	120	6	720	8	960
Coconuts	60	8	480	10	600
Grapes	40	10	400	9	360

b. The value of the basket of consumption goods in the base period is the sum of expenditures in that period: $1,600. The value of the basket of consumption goods in the current period is obtained as the sum of values of quantities in that period: $1,920.

c. The Consumer Price Index is the ratio of the value of quantities in the current period to the base period expenditure, times 100:

$$CPI = (1,920/1,600) \times 100 = 120.$$

d. Since the price of grapes has fallen relative to the prices of bananas and coconuts, we expect consumers to substitute toward the cheaper grapes and away from bananas and coconuts. This substitution means our CPI measure will be biased upward.

7. a. He is an entrant and is frictionally unemployed.
b. He is now employed, although he is also involuntarily part time.
c. He is a job leaver, and is frictionally unemployed.
d. He is a discouraged worker, but technically out of the labour force.
e. He is still out of the labour force.
f. He is employed.
g. He is structurally unemployed.
h. He is employed again.

8. The higher unemployment rate in Newfoundland has pushed many workers out of the labour force—they have become discouraged workers and are not even attempting to find work. (We can see this in the lower participation rate.) The bigger gap in the employment-to-population ratio reflects this exiting, because it includes measured unemployed and discouraged workers.

6 Economic Growth

Key Concepts

The Basics of Economic Growth

Economic growth is a sustained expansion of production possibilities, measured as the increase in real GDP.

- **Economic growth rate** = annual percentage change in real GDP =

$$\frac{\text{Real GDP this year} - \text{Real GDP last year}}{\text{Real GDP last year}} \times 100$$

- Standard of living depends on **real GDP per capita** (real GDP/population).
- Compounding leads to rapid growth—**rule of 70** states that the number of years it takes a variable to double in value = 70/(percentage growth rate).

Economic Growth Trends

Canada's growth rate was low in the 1950s, higher in the 1960s, average in the 1970s, slower in the 1980s, and below average after 1996.

- Internationally, between 1960 and now, Canada's real GDP per person has been similar to the United States, but Japan and other Asian countries have been catching up to both countries.

How Potential GDP Grows

Economic growth requires a sustained increase in potential GDP.

- More real GDP produced requires less leisure and more time spent working.
- Potential GDP is the level of real GDP at full-employment quantity of labour (with fixed amounts of land, entrepreneurial ability, capital).
- **Aggregate production function** (*PF*) shows the relationship between real GDP and the quantity of labour employed, all other influences constant.
  - Increase in quantity of labour employed creates movement up along the *PF*.

Aggregate labour market determines the quantity of labour hours employed and real GDP supplied.

- Demand for labour (*LD*)—quantity of labour demanded at each **real wage rate** = (money or nominal wage rate)/price level.
  - Firms hire labour as long as marginal product of labour > real wage rate.
  - Law of diminishing returns says that firms will hire more labour only if real wage rate falls.
- Supply of labour (*LS*)—quantity of labour supplied at each real wage rate.
  - Increase in real wage rate increases quantity of labour supplied because more people work and more people choose to work longer hours.
- Real wage rate adjusts to create full-employment labour market equilibrium where *LD* = *LS*, with real GDP = potential GDP.

Potential GDP increases if the labour supply increases or **labour productivity** (real GDP per hour of labour) increases.

- Labour supply increases if hours per worker increase, or employment-to-population ratio increases, or working-age population increases.

- Labour supply curve shifts right, real wage rate decreases, increasing hiring, causing movement along the *PF*, increasing potential GDP.

- Increase in labour productivity increases demand for labour—therefore, real wage rate increases, quantity of labour supplied increases, *PF* shifts upward, and potential GDP increases.

- Increases in population lower real GDP per person, but increases in labour productivity increase it.

Why Labour Productivity Grows

A fundamental precondition for labour productivity growth is an appropriate *incentive* system created by firms, markets, property rights, and money.

Given these preconditions, the pace of growth is affected by three things that increase labour productivity:

- Physical capital growth increases capital per worker.

- Human capital growth from education and training (including learning by repetitively doing tasks).

- Discovery of new technologies (often embodied in new capital).

Growth Theories, Evidence, and Policies

Classical growth theory argues that real GDP growth is temporary because it leads to population explosions that bring real GDP back to subsistence levels.

- It is also called Malthusian theory.

- Modern-day Malthusians argue that high population growth and climate change will eventually lower real GDP per person.

Neoclassical growth theory says that real GDP per person grows due to technological change inducing growth in capital per hour of labour.

- Assumes population growth rate is independent of economic growth.

- Driving force of economic growth is technological change and its interaction with capital accumulation.

- Ongoing *exogenous* technological advances increase the rate of return on capital, increasing saving and investment, increasing capital per person, creating real GDP growth.

- As capital per hour of labour increases, the rate of return on capital decreases due to diminishing returns, so capital accumulation and growth end unless new technological advances occur.

- Predicts growth rates and income levels per person in different countries should converge, but this convergence doesn't happen empirically.

New growth theory holds that real GDP per person grows indefinitely because of choices people make in pursuit of growth.

- New discoveries are sought for (temporary) profits, but once made discoveries are copied and benefits are dispersed throughout the economy *without* diminishing returns.

- Knowledge is a special kind of capital not subject to diminishing returns or decreasing rate of return.

- Inventions increase the rate of return to knowledge capital, resulting in increased capital per person and real GDP growth with *no automatic slowdown* because rate of return to capital does not diminish.

- New growth theory seems to fit the facts best (but not perfectly) with evidence that political stability, investment, and trade help economic growth.

Different growth theories lead to five main suggestions for increasing economic growth rates:

- Stimulate saving (and investment in capital) by tax incentives.

- Subsidize research and development and new technology.

- Improve education quality.

- Provide international aid to developing countries (but this suggestion has poor results empirically).

- Encourage international trade.

Notes:

Helpful Hints

1. Economic growth is a powerful force in raising living standards. Countries become rich by achieving high rates of growth in per person GDP and maintaining them over long periods of time. Compounding income can create startling effects. Consider the post-1973 productivity growth slowdown. Growth between 1960 and 1973 averaged 3.3 percent per year, but after 1973 was less than 2.1 percent per year. Between 1973 and 2007, real GDP per person rose by about 103 percent ($= [(1.021)^{34} - 1] \times 100$). However, if growth had continued at the pre-1973 rate of 3.3 percent, real GDP per person would have increased by about 202 percent ($= [(1.033)^{34} - 1] \times 100$). Even the worst recession over this period lowered real GDP per person by about 5 percent (see the discussion of the Lucas wedge in Chapter 20). Avoiding the productivity growth slowdown would clearly have had a big payoff!

2. The key to understanding different theories of growth is the role of "the law of diminishing returns" in each theory. This law states that adding more of one input, other inputs held constant, eventually leads to a diminishing returns to adding extra inputs.

   In neoclassical theory, the discovery of a new technology increases the rate of return on capital, increasing saving and investment, and increasing the amount of capital used. However, the increase in capital eventually leads to diminishing returns. Think of the introduction of new, more powerful computers. As the number of computers increases, holding constant the number of workers, the extra output of the nth computer will not be as high as the productivity of the first computer. Eventually, productivity of extra capital must decrease (decreasing the rate of return), and economic growth automatically slows down.

   New growth theory has a different idea of technology and capital, with no diminishing returns and no slowdown in economic growth. New growth theory examines "knowledge capital," a concept of technology that is not embodied in capital, but in ideas. These ideas might include new management techniques or new production processes (such as assembly lines) that can be copied from business to business without diminishing returns. Consider the introduction of new and better software (such as word processing software). As more copies of the software are introduced into different businesses around the country, we do not run into diminishing returns until the entire country has access to the new knowledge. Even then, improved software will be continually developed and introduced without diminishing returns (so that the rate of return does *not* decrease), and economic growth need not automatically slow down.

Notes:

Self-Test
True/False and Explain

The Basics of Economic Growth

1. The standard of living depends on the level of real GDP.

Economic Growth Trends

2. Canada's growth sped up in the 1990s, which was unusual in Canadian history.

3. Asian countries are catching up with Canada's real GDP per person.

How Potential GDP Grows

4. The aggregate production function shows the relationship between real GDP and labour inputs.

5. As the real wage rate increases, the quantity of labour demanded decreases, other things remaining constant.

6. An increasing population decreases the real wage rate and potential GDP.

7. An increase in labour productivity decreases real wages and increases potential GDP.

Why Labour Productivity Grows

8. Higher levels of human capital with the same physical capital per person will not raise per person income.

9. Rapid changes in technology create growth without the need for new capital.

10. The only way labour productivity can increase is if there is more physical capital.

Growth Theories, Evidence, and Policies

11. The empirical evidence is strongly in favour of classical growth theory.

12. Neoclassical growth theory argues that economic growth eventually slows down because the rate of return on capital diminishes as the amount of capital increases.

13. Classical growth theory argues that economic growth leads to a smaller population growth rate.

14. High economic growth has typically been accompanied by high saving rates.

15. In new growth theory, there are no diminishing returns for knowledge capital.

Multiple-Choice

The Basics of Economic Growth

1. Growthland's real GDP per capita was $112 billion in 2012 and $117 billion in 2013. What is the growth rate of Growthland's real GDP per capita?

   a. 4.3 percent
   b. 4.5 percent
   c. 5 percent
   d. 12 percent
   e. 17 percent

2. If Amazonia's growth rate of real GDP per capita is 7 percent, how many years before real GDP per capita doubles?

   a. Impossible to calculate without more data
   b. 3.5
   c. 7
   d. 10
   e. 14.3

Economic Growth Trends

3. Canada's economic growth rates were highest in which of the following decades?

   a. 1930s
   b. 1960s
   c. 1970s
   d. 1980s
   e. 1990s

4. Compared to growth in other countries, between 1960 and 2010 Canada

   a. fell behind most other countries.
   b. dramatically caught up to and passed other countries.
   c. worsened dramatically versus the United States, but did better versus other countries.
   d. did as well as or better than most countries except certain Asian countries.
   e. did none of the above.

5. Which of the following statements about Canada's long-term growth trends is *false?*

a. Economic growth rates have been steady, except for the business cycle.

b. Economic growth rates show periods of slow and high growth.

c. Economic growth rates were faster in the 1990s than in the 1980s.

d. Economic growth rates have generally been faster in Japan than in Canada.

e. African countries have fallen farther behind Canada in recent years.

How Potential GDP Grows

6. The aggregate production function shows

a. how much real GDP changes as capital stock changes, all else remaining the same.

b. how much real GDP changes as the price level changes, all else remaining the same.

c. how much labour demand changes as the real wage rate changes, all else remaining the same.

d. how much labour demand changes as the money wage rate changes, all else remaining the same.

e. none of the above.

7. The labour demand curve is

a. positively sloped and shifts with changes in the capital stock.

b. positively sloped and shifts with changes in the quantity of labour employed.

c. negatively sloped and shifts with changes in the capital stock.

d. negatively sloped and shifts with changes in the quantity of labour employed.

e. negatively sloped and shifts with changes in the real wage rate.

8. If the money wage rate is $12 per hour and the GDP deflator is 150, what is the real wage rate per hour?

a. $18

b. $15

c. $12

d. $8

e. $6

9. Which of the following quotations describes the upward-sloping labour supply curve?

a. "Recent higher wage rates have led to more leisure."

b. "The recent lower price level has induced people to work fewer hours."

c. "The recent higher real wage rate has induced people to work more hours."

d. "The recent high investment in capital equipment has raised hiring by firms."

e. "Adding extra workers leads to lower productivity of each additional worker."

10. *Ceteris paribus*, an increase in labour productivity results in a

a. higher real wage rate and higher potential GDP per hour of work.

b. lower real wage rate and higher potential GDP per hour of work.

c. higher real wage rate and lower potential GDP per hour of work.

d. lower real wage rate and lower potential GDP per hour of work.

e. constant real wage rate in the long run.

11. *Ceteris paribus*, an increase in population results in a

   a. higher level of labour employed and higher potential GDP per hour of work.

   b. lower level of labour employed and higher potential GDP per hour of work.

   c. higher level of labour employed and lower potential GDP per hour of work.

   d. lower level of labour employed and lower potential GDP per hour of work.

   e. constant level of labour employed and constant potential GDP per hour of work.

12. If the real wage rate is higher than the equilibrium wage rate,

   a. the real wage rate increases due to the labour surplus.

   b. the real wage rate decreases due to the labour surplus.

   c. labour supply decreases due to the high real wage rate.

   d. labour demand increases due to the high real wage rate.

   e. labour demand decreases due to the labour surplus.

13. If the capital stock increases, which of the following happens?

   a. The demand for labour increases.

   b. The supply of labour increases.

   c. Technology will improve.

   d. The level of real GDP decreases.

   e. The real wage rate decreases.

Why Labour Productivity Grows

14. Which of the following is *not* a source of economic growth?

   a. increasing stock market prices

   b. better-educated workers

   c. growing stock of capital equipment

   d. an appropriate incentive system

   e. advances in technology

15. Which of the following occurs with an improvement in technology?

a. The labour supply increases.

b. The capital stock increases.

c. The human capital stock decreases.

d. Real GDP growth decreases.

e. The real wage rate decreases.

16. Which of the following is an example of human capital?

a. The use of a laptop instead of pen and paper to take class notes.

b. A student being better at note-taking at the end of the fourth year than in the first year of university.

c. A student who records economics classes is doing better in a third-year business class than a student who does not.

d. Installing a software upgrade on your computer.

e. Falling asleep on your economics text while studying.

17. Which of the following would shift the aggregate production function upward?

a. a decrease in the stock of capital

b. a decrease in the real wage rate

c. an increase in labour employed

d. an increase in the price level

e. a technological discovery

Growth Theory, Evidence, and Policies

18. Which of the following is a suggestion for increasing Canadian economic growth rates?

a. Stimulate saving by taxing consumption.

b. Reduce the time period for patent protection to increase replication.

c. Put less public research funds into universities.

d. Protect our industries from foreign competition.

e. Tax education.

19. Government subsidies for research and development are justified

a. because there is too little private saving.

b. because it is too expensive for small firms.

c. because there are external benefits to research and development that firms ignore.

d. in order to take advantage of gains from specialization and exchange.

e. in order to overcome diminishing returns.

20. In neoclassical growth theory, if the rate of return on capital increases due to a technological advance, then

a. the rate of return on capital will eventually decline.

b. capital per hour of labour will decrease.

c. real GDP per hour of labour will decrease.

d. the rate of return on capital will never decline.

e. population growth will explode.

21. In new growth theory, if the rate of return on capital increases due to a technological advance, then

a. the rate of return on capital will eventually decline.

b. capital per hour of labour will decrease.

c. real GDP per hour of labour will decrease.

d. the rate of return on capital will never decline.

e. population growth will explode.

22. Incentives are important in the new growth theory because they

a. imply there are no diminishing returns.

b. lead to higher rates of saving.

c. imply that economic growth does not lead to population growth.

d. create specialization and exchange.

e. lead to profit-seeking searches for new discoveries.

23. In classical growth theory, economic growth eventually stops after a technological advance because

  a. of diminishing returns.

  b. knowledge capital is easily replicated.

  c. the rate of return on capital decreases back down to the target rate of savers.

  d. real GDP per person becomes too high.

  e. of high population growth resulting from increasing real GDP per person.

24. Compared to physical capital, knowledge capital

  a. can be replicated without diminishing returns.

  b. can be held in your hand.

  c. leads to an automatic slowdown in growth.

  d. cannot be replicated without diminishing returns.

  e. is none of the above.

25. The key difference between neoclassical growth theory and new growth theory is that

  a. capital is not subject to diminishing returns under new growth theory.

  b. capital is subject to diminishing returns under new growth theory.

  c. increases in technology increase the population, which drives workers' incomes back down to subsistence levels in neoclassical theory.

  d. technological advances are exogenous in new growth theory.

  e. the rule of 70 only holds in new growth theory.

Short Answer Problems

1. Pinkland has a population of 500 in 2012 and 525 in 2013. Its real GDP is $5,500,000 in 2012 and $6,050,000 in 2013.

   a. Calculate Pinkland's real GDP per capita in each year.

   b. Calculate the growth rates of real GDP and real GDP per capita between 2012 and 2013.

   c. If Pinkland's economic growth rate of real GDP per capita continues at this level, how many years will it take to double real GDP per capita?

2. Blueland's real GDP per capita is $100 and growing at 7 percent per year. Redland's real GDP per capita is $1,000 and growing at 3.5 percent per year. Use the rule of 70 to construct a table showing how many years it will take Blueland's real GDP per capita to catch up to Redland's if these growth rates remain constant.

3. Some economists speculate that the Asian miracle economies have achieved such fast growth at least partially because of their adeptness at replicating new technology from other countries. Explain how and why replicating is a good source of growth.

4. Paul Krugman and others argue that the Asian miracle economies' extra-high economic growth is mostly due to the mobilization of capital and labour resources that were previously underutilized, and that North American worries that these countries will surpass Canada and the United States are unfounded. Assuming it is true, explain why this argument implies these worries are unfounded.

5. Use an aggregate production function to explain why an increase in the amount of capital per hour of labour leads to economic growth.

6. An economy starts with the 2009 aggregate production function in Table 1, with 120 hours of labour hired in 2009.

TABLE 1

Labour (hrs/yr)	Real GDP (2009)	Real GDP per hour of labour (2009)	Real GDP (2010)	Real GDP per hour of labour (2010)
100	500	5.00		
110	540	4.91		
120	570	4.75		
130	590	4.54		
140	600	4.29		
150	605	4.03		

c. Where is the likely new 2010 production point for this economy? Explain briefly.

7. Consider the economy from Short Answer Problem **6**. The 2009 labour market equilibrium was at a real wage rate of $15, with 120 hours of labour hired. After the technological innovation, assuming no population increase, explain using a graph of the labour market for this country what has happened to labour demand, labour supply, amount of labour hired, and the real wage rate in 2010. Exact numbers are not needed, just an indication of the types of changes. Use the grid on the following page to draw your graph.

a. Graph this economy's 2009 aggregate production function.

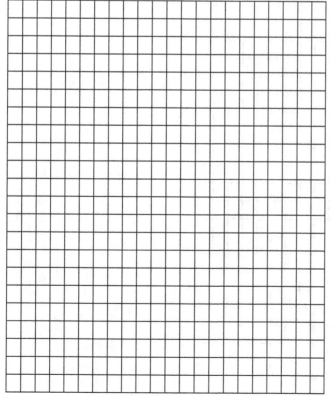

b. A technological innovation in 2010 increases labour productivity by 10 percent. Show the impact of this change in the remaining columns of Table 1, and on your graph from part **a**.

Economic Growth

8. Some commentators argue that, until recently, Japan had a higher growth rate than Canada or the United States because the Japanese people care more about the future and less about present consumption, leading to a higher Japanese saving rate. Explain within the context of growth theory whether this argument seems correct.

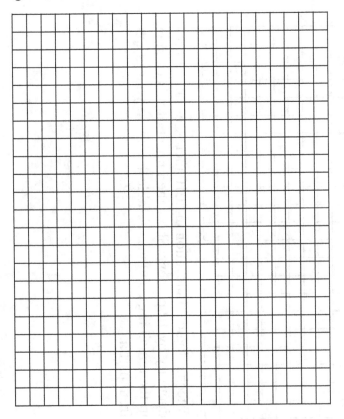

Answers

True/False and Explain

1. **F** Depends on real GDP *per capita*. (518)
2. **F** Growth was higher in the 1960s. (520)
3. **T** See text discussion. (521–522)
4. **T** Definition. (523)
5. **T** Definition of labour demand curve. (524)
6. **F** Increasing population increases the labour supply, decreases the real wage, but more labour is hired so potential GDP increases. (525–526)
7. **F** Shifts *LD* curve rightward, and increases real wage rate. (527)
8. **F** Human capital growth is part of advances in technology. (529)
9. **F** Rapid technological change is embodied in new human and physical capital. (530)
10. **F** Technological advances or increases in human capital also raise labour productivity. (521)
11. **F** New growth theory explains it better. (534–535)
12. **T** Due to law of diminishing returns. (532)
13. **F** Economic growth increases real GDP per hour, which increases population growth. (531)
14. **T** See discussion of East Asian economies. (535)
15. **T** Because knowledge capital can be duplicated at zero marginal cost. (532–534)

Multiple-Choice

1. **b** Growth rate = [(Δ real GDP per capita)/original level] × 100 = (5/112) × 100 = 4.5%. (518)
2. **d** By rule of 70: 70/7 = 10. (519)
3. **b** See text discussion. (520)
4. **d** See text discussion. (521–522)
5. **a** Growth rates have fluctuated. (521–522)
6. **e** Definition: how much real GDP changes as labour hired changes. (523–525)
7. **c** Negatively sloped due to diminishing marginal product. **d** and **e** imply movements along the demand curve. (523–525)
8. **d** Real wage = (money wage/price level) × 100. (519–523)
9. **c** Higher wages, higher quantity of labour supplied. **a** and **b** are opposite relationships, **d** and **e** refer to labour demand. (523–528)
10. **a** A productivity increase increases labour demand, raising the real wage rate. Potential GDP per hour of work = productivity, so it must have increased. (525–528)
11. **c** Labour supply shifts rightward, real wage falls, more people hired, but potential GDP per hour of work falls due to diminishing marginal productivity. (525–528)
12. **b** The labour surplus pushes down real wages. (524)
13. **a** Labour is more productive and therefore firms demand more. (526–527)

14. a Prices have no impact on productivity, others increase it. (526–527)

15. b New technology is typically embodied in new capital. (530)

16. b The student has learned (raised their human capital) by repetition. (529)

17. e Technological discovery increases the productivity of labour. (528–530)

18. a–b would lower return to and number of inventions, **c** would lower research and number of inventions, and trade and education should be encouraged. (535)

19. c See text discussion. (535)

20. a If rate of return on capital is high, saving increases supply of capital, increasing capital per hour of labour (and more real GDP per hour of labour). Eventually rate of return on capital decreases due to the law of diminishing returns. (531–532)

21. d If rate of return on capital is high, saving increases supply of capital, increasing capital per hour of labour (and more real GDP per hour of labour), but no change in rate of return on capital since the law of diminishing returns doesn't apply to knowledge capital. (532–534)

22. e This assumption makes technological change endogenous and continuous. (532–534)

23. e This growth leads to a decrease in real GDP per hour of labour. (531)

24. a Due to its nature—see text discussion. (534)

25. a Due to the different nature of knowledge capital. (531–534)

Short Answer Problems

1. a. Real GDP per capita = real GDP/population. In 2012, this equals $5,500,000/500 = $11,000. In 2013, this equals $6,050,000/525 = $11,524.

b. Growth rate of real GDP =

$$\frac{6,050,000 - 5,500,000}{5,500,000} \times 100\% = 10\%.$$

Growth rate of real GDP per capita =

$$\frac{11,524 - 11,000}{11,000} \times 100\% = 4.8\%.$$

c. From the rule of 70, 70/4.8 = 17.5 years.

2. The rule of 70 means that Blueland's real GDP per capita doubles every 10 years (= 70/7) while Redland's doubles every 20 years (= 70/3.5). Table 2 below shows the progress of each country's real GDP

TABLE 2

Year	Blueland Real GDP per Capita	Redland Real GDP per Capita
0	100	1,000
10	200	
20	400	2,000
30	800	
40	1,600	4,000
50	3,200	
60	6,400	8,000
70	12,800	
80	25,600	16,000

3. over several decades, and shows that Blueland will catch up to Redland in about 70 years.

Knowledge capital can be replicated without diminishing returns, so that the rate of return on capital increases after replication, which in turn brings more saving and investment. Capital per hour of labour can increase without limit, implying growth can increase without limit.

4. If Asian growth is due to increasing amounts of capital and labour, eventually these countries will run into diminishing returns to each of these inputs, so increases in productivity will slow down, meaning economic growth will also slow.

5. The aggregate production function illustrates how output increases as the amount of labour hired increases, holding constant labour productivity. Labour productivity increases with more physical capital, more human capital, or technological advances. If capital per hour of labour increases, the productivity of workers is increasing, so output per hour of labour is increasing—there is faster economic growth. This is illustrated graphically by an upward shift in the aggregate production function, reflecting more output for each amount of labour used.

6. a. Figure 1 below shows the graph of the 2009 production function, labelled PF_{2009}.

b. Table 1 Solution below shows the impact of the 10 percent increase in productivity as 10 percent higher real GDP at each level of labour, which translates into 10 percent higher real GDP per hour of labour hired.

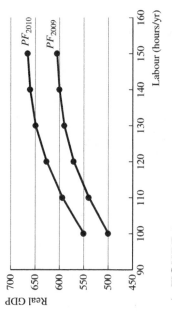

Real GDP

Labour (hours/yr)

▲ **FIGURE 1**

The new 2010 production function in Fig. 1 is labelled PF_{2010}.

c. If the original labour hired was 120, we know that the higher productivity (5.23 > 4.75) means firms want to hire more labour, not less. Therefore, we can assume labour hired is at least 120, if not higher. Reading off

TABLE 1 Solution

Labour (hrs/yr)	Real GDP (2009)	Real GDP per Hour of Labour (2009)	Real GDP (2010)	Real GDP per Hour of Labour (2010)
100	500	5.00	550	5.5
110	540	4.91	594	5.4
120	570	4.75	627	5.23
130	590	4.54	649	4.99
140	600	4.29	660	4.71
150	605	4.03	665.5	4.44

the PF_{2010} curve, production will at least be at real GDP of 627, if not higher.

7. Fig. 2 on the next page shows the original labour demand curve (LD_{2009}), labour supply curve (LS), and the original wage and quantity labour hired. As in the answer to Short Answer Problem 6c, labour demand will rise due to higher productivity. Labour supply is initially unchanged due to unchanged population, so the higher labour demand leads to a higher real wage rate, inducing a higher quantity of labour supplied, shown as a movement along the labour supply curve to a new, higher level of labour hired in the market equilibrium. Figure 2 shows this change. We cannot tell exactly how much the real wage rate increases, or how much more labour is hired, but it will be higher than the original levels for both.

8. If the Japanese people had a higher saving rate, this meant the increase in the supply of capital in Japan is higher in any situation. In general, Japan would have a higher capital stock per person than Canada, and it would be increasing each year at a higher rate, in turn leading to a higher growth rate of real GDP per person in Japan than in Canada. Thus this argument seems to hold true.

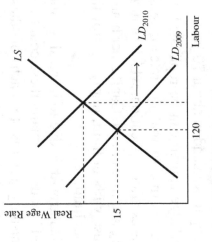

▲ **FIGURE 2**

7 Finance, Saving, and Investment

Key Concepts
Financial Institutions and Financial Markets

Financial markets channel saving from households to firms, who invest in new capital.

- *Finance*—activity of providing funds for capital expenditures. *Money*—used to pay for items and make financial expenditures.

- Physical capital is tools, instruments, machines, buildings used to produce goods and services. **Financial capital** is funds firms use to buy physical capital, which produces real GDP.

- **Gross investment** = amount spent on new capital. **Net investment** = Δ value of capital stock = gross investment − depreciation.

- **Wealth** = value of things people own. Δ wealth = **saving** (= income − net taxes − consumption) + capital gains/losses.

Three types of financial markets:

- Loan markets involve businesses or households borrowing from banks, including household **mortgages**—legal lending contracts giving lender ownership of house if borrower defaults.

- **Bond markets** involve firms, governments issuing/selling **bonds** (promise to make specified payments on specified dates).

- Bond terms can be months up to decades.

- **Mortgage-backed securities** are bonds paying income from a package of mortgages.

- Firms' **stock** shares (certificate of ownership and claim to profits) are traded in **stock markets.**

Financial markets are highly competitive from simultaneous borrowing and lending by **financial institutions** (firms operating on both sides of financial markets), including banks, trust and loan companies, credit unions, caisse populaires, pension funds, insurance companies.

- During the 2008 financial crisis, pension funds and financial institutions were hurt as investments in mortgage-backed securities collapsed in value when U.S. housing market collapsed.

- Companies become insolvent when **net worth** (total market value of lending − total market value of borrowing) is negative.

- Companies become illiquid if they are solvent but have insufficient cash to meet debt payments.

- Insolvent companies are forced to merge or are taken over by government.

- Interest rate on asset $= \dfrac{\text{interest received}}{\text{price of asset}} \times 100$

- Price of asset and interest rate are inversely related.

The Loanable Funds Market

Loanable funds market—aggregate of all financial markets.

- Adding financial flows from loanable funds to circular flow shows how investment is financed.

- Households' income spent on consumption or saving or **net taxes** (T = taxes − transfer payments received from governments): $Y = C + S + T.$

- Circular flow from Chapter 20 shows: $Y = C + I + G + X - M$.

- Combining above, I financed by private saving (S) + government saving ($T - G$) + borrowing from rest of world ($M - X$):

$$I = S + (T - G) + (M - X)$$

- If $T > G$, government can lend some of its surplus.

- If foreigners sell Canadians more goods than they buy from us ($M > X$), we must borrow from them to finance the difference, so foreign savings flows to Canada for investment purposes.

- I financed by **national saving** [$= S + (T - G)$] + foreign borrowing.

Nominal interest rate = dollars paid yearly in interest by borrower to lender as percent of dollars borrowed.

- **Real interest rate**—nominal rate adjusted for inflation ($\approx$ nominal interest rate − inflation rate).

- Real interest rate is the opportunity cost of loanable funds—determined in the market for loanable funds.

Quantity of loanable funds *demanded* to finance investment, government budget deficit, international lending.

- The higher the real interest rate, the lower is the quantity of loanable funds demanded—**demand for loanable funds** (*DLF* curve) has a negative relationship between the real interest rate and the quantity demanded.

- *DLF* shifts rightward if expected profit increases.

Quantity of loanable funds *supplied* from saving, government budget surplus, international borrowing.

- The higher the real interest rate, the higher is the quantity of loanable funds supplied—**supply of loanable funds** (*SLF* curve) has a positive relationship between the real interest rate and the quantity supplied.

- *SLF* curve shifts rightward if disposable income increases, expected future income falls, wealth falls, or default risk falls.

Real interest rate adjustments achieve equilibrium where quantity of loanable funds demanded = quantity supplied.

- Factors shifting *DLF* rightward lead to new equilibrium with higher real interest rate, and more loanable funds are supplied.

- Factors shifting *SLF* rightward lead to new equilibrium with lower real interest rate, and more loanable funds are demanded.

- Real interest rate has no trend over time.

Starting in 2001, U.S. Federal Reserve (the Fed) provided loanable funds (increasing *SLF*), leading to lower interest rates and large increases in house prices.

- In 2006, the Fed slowed *SLF* growth, interest rates rose, and many mortgage holders defaulted, pushing financial institutions into insolvency.

Government in the Loanable Funds Market

Government budget surplus increases the supply of loanable funds, lowering the real interest rate—investment increases more than private saving decreases.

- The **crowding-out effect** is when the budget deficit increases the real interest rate and investment decreases.

- The **Ricardo–Barro effect** holds that the government budget has no effect on the real interest rate or investment because rational taxpayers know increases in budget deficit (surplus) imply higher (lower) future taxes, so they adjust saving by an equivalent amount—no change in real interest rate.

The Global Loanable Funds Market

Loanable funds market is global—suppliers move to national markets with the highest real interest rates, demanders to markets with the lowest real interest rate.

- Flows in funds mean there will be one real interest rate globally (for assets with equal risk).

- Riskier assets will pay interest rate = rate on safe loan + risk premium.

- A country with a higher interest rate than the global rate will be a net borrower globally and have negative net exports as a result.

- A country with a lower interest rate than the global rate will be a net lender globally and have positive net exports as a result.

- Changes in demand and supply for small countries like Canada have no effect on the global interest rate. Changes for larger countries shift world *DLF* or *SLF* and affect the global interest rate.

Helpful Hints

1. Financial markets and financial institutions are at the centre of many economic activities. In Chapter 22 on economic growth, investment in physical capital plays a key role in creating economic growth. This chapter explains how household saving, government saving, and investment from foreigners are channelled via financial markets and institutions to firms that purchase capital goods to carry out investment.

   These concepts will reappear in Chapter 24 ("Money, the Price Level, and Inflation") and Chapter 30 ("Monetary Policy"), where we will see the role of the central bank in setting interest rates in financial markets (affecting investment and overall economic activity). Chapter 25 will highlight key relationships between interest rates, exchange rates, and the overall economy. Chapter 28 illustrates the impact of financial market problems on the business cycle, and Chapter 29 explains how government fiscal policy interacts with the financial markets to affect interest rates and investment.

   Financial markets and institutions are the key to understanding many other economic activities and policies. In the 2007–2008 financial crisis, a combination of external forces and loose monetary policy created a housing bubble. When the bubble started collapsing in 2007, this led to difficulties with financial institutions, difficulties that have spread to the goods and services markets and to the labour market. Over the next four years, governments of the western economies carried out massive monetary expansions and the largest fiscal stimuli in history in an attempt to avert a long recession. We will explore how these policies work in Chapters 29 and 30.

2. Although Canada is a strong developed country with a high standard of living, it is still a relatively small player on world financial markets. This means that the (risk-adjusted) real interest rate in Canada is set in the world market. Consequently, even though Canada has a strong financial sector without a housing crisis, we can still be affected by a U.S.-born financial crisis. The U.S. crisis has led to higher U.S. real interest rates (and higher aversion to risk), and these higher interest rates have spread to Canadian financial markets, creating negative effects for the Canadian economy.

Notes:

Self-Test

True/False and Explain

Financial Institutions and Financial Markets

1. When a household buys stock in a company, this is an example of gross investment.

2. A company is illiquid when it has negative net worth.

3. A mortgage is a bond paying income based on a package of house loans.

4. If a household has saving of $2,000 and a capital loss of $3,000, its net wealth will decrease.

5. If the interest rate on an asset increases, the price of the asset increases.

The Loanable Funds Market

6. The higher a household's expected future income, the more loanable funds they will supply.

7. If the nominal interest rate is 6 percent and the inflation rate is 4 percent, the real interest rate is 10 percent.

8. With no government and no international sector, if the demand for loanable funds is greater than the supply of loanable funds at the current real interest rate, the real interest rate will increase.

9. With no government and no international sector, an increase in the profits firms expect to earn will lead to a higher real interest rate in the loanable funds market.

10. $I = S + (G - T) + (M - X)$.

11. If the inflation rate increases and the nominal interest rate has increased, the real interest rate must be constant.

Government in the Loanable Funds Market

12. If there is no Ricardo–Barro effect, a higher government deficit lowers investment, other things being equal.

13. If there is a Ricardo–Barro effect, a higher government deficit lowers investment, other things being equal.

The Global Loanable Funds Market

14. If Calonia is a net lender to the rest of the world, it will have positive net exports.

15. Calonia is a small part of the global loanable funds market. If Calonia's demand for loanable funds is greater than Calonia's supply of loanable funds at the current real interest rate, the real interest rate will increase.

Multiple-Choice

Financial Institutions and Financial Markets

1. The capital stock does *not* include the

a. inventory of raw cucumbers ready to be made into pickles by the Smith Pickle Company.

b. Smith family holdings of stock in the Smith Pickle Company.

c. pickle factory building owned by the Smith family.

d. pickle-packing machine in the pickle factory building owned by the Smith family.

e. pickle inventories in the pickle factory building owned by the Smith family.

2. Eel Electronics has lent $10 million and borrowed $8 million. It has cash earnings per month of $100,000 and debt payments per month of $120,000. Eel Electronics is

a. solvent and liquid.

b. insolvent and illiquid.

c. solvent and illiquid.

d. insolvent and liquid.

e. solvent if interest rates are low enough.

3. On January 1, 2013, Bobcat Excavations had $50,000 worth of bobcat machines. During 2013, these machines fell in value by 50 percent. Bobcat also bought $35,000 worth of new machines. What was Bobcat's net investment in 2013?

a. $10,000

b. $25,000

c. $35,000

d. $60,000

e. $85,000

4. In which market would you find mortgage-backed securities?

a. stock market

b. bond market

c. housing market

d. capital market

e. loan market

5. Elena starts the year with $2,500 worth of stock and no other wealth. Her grandmother gives her a $5,000 Canada Savings Bond. Elena earns $15,000 in income, pays $1,000 in taxes, and spends $15,000 on consumption goods. Her stocks rise in value to $3,000. What is Elena's wealth at the end of the year?

    a. $6,500

    b. $7,000

    c. $7,500

    d. $8,000

    e. $9,000

6. Elena owns a Canada Savings Bond initially worth $5,000, which pays $500 per year. The value of the bond rises in the bond market to $7,500. What is the new interest rate on the bond?

    a. 5 percent

    b. 6.67 percent

    c. 10 percent

    d. 20 percent

    e. 500 percent

7. The key characteristic of financial institutions is that they

    a. are always liquid.

    b. will lend to anyone.

    c. buy a diversified portfolio of assets.

    d. simultaneously borrow and lend.

    e. provide risk-sharing services.

The Loanable Funds Market

8. Which of the following shifts the supply curve of loanable funds leftward?

    a. increase in current disposable income

    b. decrease in current disposable income

    c. decrease in expected future income

    d. increase in the real interest rate

    e. decrease in the real interest rate

9. Which of the following is *false*?

a. $Y = C + I + G + M - X$
b. $I = S + (T - G) + (M - X)$
c. $Y = C + S + T$
d. $Y + M = C + I + G + X$
e. $Y = C + I + G + X - M$

10. Saving can be measured as income minus

a. taxes.
b. transfer payments.
c. net taxes minus consumption expenditure.
d. consumption expenditure.
e. net taxes plus subsidies.

11. In Canada's economy, investment is financed by

a. $C + I + G + X - M$.
b. $C + S + T$.
c. $S + T + M$.
d. $S + (T - G) + (X - M)$.
e. $S + (T - G) + (M - X)$.

12. Which of the following causes a household to increase the amount it saves?

a. decrease in current disposable income
b. increase in expected future income
c. increase in net taxes
d. decrease in expected future income
e. none of the above

13. Investment will be higher if

a. the government deficit is higher.

b. national saving is higher.

c. net exports are higher.

d. the real interest rate is higher.

e. government spending is higher.

14. Southton has investment of $100, household saving of $90, net taxes of $25, government spending of $30, exports of $25, and imports of $10. What is national saving?

a. $85

b. $90

c. $95

d. $100

e. $105

15. If the inflation rate increases by 3 percent and the nominal interest rate increases by 2 percent, the

a. real interest rate increases.

b. opportunity cost of borrowing increases.

c. opportunity cost of borrowing decreases.

d. opportunity cost of spending increases.

e. level of spending decreases.

16. Table 1 shows the initial market for loanable funds in Northland. The prime minister of Northland gives a brilliant speech, convincing firms in Northland of future strong economic growth in the country. The likely new equilibrium has a real interest rate of _____ with a quantity of loanable funds of _____.

a. 6 percent; $100 billion

b. 7 percent; $100 billion

c. 7 percent; $120 billion

d. 5 percent; $120 billion

e. 5 percent $80 billion

TABLE 1 Data From Northland

Real Interest Rate	Demand for Loanable Funds ($ billions)	Supply of Loanable Funds ($ billions)
3%	160	40
4%	140	60
5%	120	80
6%	100	100
7%	80	120
8%	60	140

17. Table 1 shows the initial market for loanable funds in North-land. Disposable income then increases. The likely new equilibrium has a real interest rate of ____ with a quantity of loanable funds of ____.

a. 6 percent; $100 billion

b. 7 percent; $100 billion

c. 7 percent; $120 billion

d. 5 percent; $120 billion

e. 5 percent; $80 billion

Government in the Loanable Funds Market

18. Table 1 shows the initial market for loanable funds in North-land. There is no Ricardo–Barro effect. If the government moves from a balanced budget to a surplus of $20 billion, the new equilibrium has a real interest rate of ____ and quantity of loanable funds traded equal to ____.

a. 6.5 percent; $110 billion

b. 6.5 percent; $90 billion

c. 5.5 percent; $90 billion

d. 5.5 percent; $110 billion

e. 6 percent; $120 billion

19. In the market for loanable funds, if the Ricardo–Barro effect does not hold, a higher government surplus leads to

a. increased real interest rate and increased investment.

b. increased real interest rate and decreased investment.

c. decreased real interest rate and increased investment.

d. decreased real interest rate and decreased investment.

e. no effect on real interest rate or investment.

20. Fig. 1 shows the loanable funds market for a country that is not part of the global market. Currently the country has a government budget balance = 0. There is no Ricardo–Barro effect. If the government introduces a deficit of $20 billion, the new real interest rate = _____ and the new level of investment = _____.

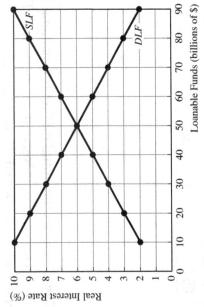

▲ FIGURE 1

a. 7 percent; $40 billion
b. 5 percent; $60 billion
c. 7 percent; $50 billion
d. 5 percent; $50 billion
e. 6 percent; $50 billion

The Global Loanable Funds Market

21. Fig. 1 shows the loanable funds market for a country that is part of the global market, with no government budget deficit or surplus. If the world interest rate is 4 percent, we have net _____ and investment of _____.

a. lending of $40 billion; $40 billion
b. borrowing of $40 billion; $30 billion
c. borrowing of $0 billion; $50 billion
d. borrowing of $40 billion; $70 billion
e. lending of $40 billion; $70 billion

22. Which of the following newspaper quotations describes a situation where Canada would end up with lower investment?

a. "A rise in the U.S. government budget deficit is forcing up world interest rates."

b. "World lenders are worried about Canada's government budget deficit."

c. "The booming Chinese economy is dramatically raising its spending on new investment projects."

d. All of the above

23. In the global economy, investment is financed by

a. $S + (T - G)$.

b. $S + (T - G) - (X - M)$.

c. $S + (G - T)$.

d. $S + (T - G) + (X - M)$.

e. $S + (T - G) + (M - X)$.

24. In Canada's economy, the real interest rate is determined by

a. national investment.

b. national saving.

c. the government budget deficit/surplus.

d. all of the above.

e. none of the above.

25. Calonia is a small country in the global loanable funds market, and is currently an international borrower. If there is no Ricardo–Barro effect, what will happen in Calonia's loanable funds market if the government deficit increases?

a. Less borrowing from the rest of the world.

b. Investment will increase.

c. In the circular flow, consumption expenditure will fall.

d. Investment will not change.

e. Investment will decrease.

Short Answer Problems

1. The Athabasca Oil Exploration Company starts the year with $1 million worth of equipment. It has debts of $500,000, for a beginning net worth of $500,000. During the year, the following events occur:

   - Athabasca borrows $2.5 million to buy $2 million worth of new equipment plus $500,000 worth of stock in another company.

   - The stock in the other company increases in value to $600,000.

   - Athabasca's old equipment depreciates in value to a worth of $250,000.

   a. Calculate Athabasca's gross and net investment for the year, and the end of year value of its physical capital stock.

   b. At the end of the year, what is Athabasca's net worth? Is it solvent?

2. In an interview in the late 1990s, the Governor of the Bank of Canada argued that Canada's interest rates had fallen drastically in the late 1990s because the federal and provincial governments had drastically reduced the size of their budget deficits, and that this would increase investment spending. Assume initially that Canada does not participate in the global loanable funds market. With the help of a graph, explain if the explanation makes sense.

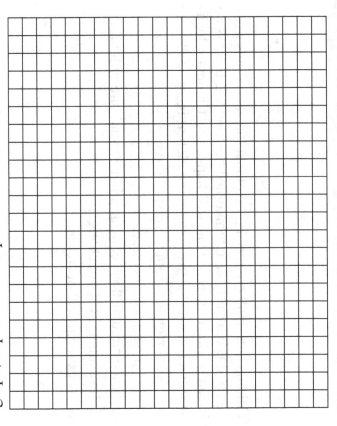

3. Return to the statements made by the governor in question **2.** In reality, Canada does participate in the global loanable funds market and was a net borrower in the late 1990s. In this case, would Canada's lower budget deficits lead to lower interest rates? Once again, draw a (new) graph of the loanable funds market as part of your answer.

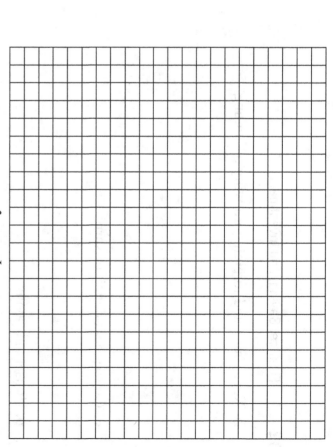

4. Consider the following data on Calonia:

TABLE 2 Data For Calonia	
Item	**Amount (billions of $)**
Consumption expenditure (C)	600
Net taxes (T)	300
Exports (X)	240
Imports (M)	220
Government expenditure on goods and services (G)	200
Net investment (I)	150
Depreciation	60
Household income (Y)	1030

Use this data to calculate Calonia's:

a. Gross investment

b. Net exports and foreign borrowing or lending

c. Government deficit or surplus

d. Household saving

e. National saving

f. Total funds available for investment

5. Marie started the year with $100,000 of stock. During the year, the following events occurred:
  • Marie's stocks rose in value to $128,000. She sold $20,000 of stock at the end of the year to use as a down payment on her new house.
  • Marie borrowed $172,000 from the bank, and with her stock sale proceeds as the difference, bought a house for $192,000.
  • Marie earned $35,000 and paid $12,000 in taxes.
  • Marie consumed $22,000.
  Showing all steps, calculate Marie's wealth at the end of the year.

6. Opar is an isolated economy that does not trade with the world. It has constant real GDP of 100 million opals, government expenditure is constant at $12 million opals, and the government deficit is constant at 2 million opals. Consider the values of consumption and investment shown in Table 3.

b. Pellucidar is another isolated economy that does not trade with the world. It has constant real GDP of 120 million opals, government expenditure is constant at 15 million opals, and the government deficit is constant at 4 million opals. Consider the values of consumption and investment shown in Table 4.

Calculate and fill in the two blank columns of the table using the space below for your calculations. What is the real interest rate and quantity of loanable funds in Pellucidar in equilibrium?

TABLE 4 Data From Pellucidar

Real Interest Rate	C	Supply of Loanable Funds (Saving)	I	Demand for Loanable Funds
3%	100		32	
4%	95		28	
5%	90		24	
6%	85		20	
7%	80		16	
8%	75		12	

TABLE 3 Data From Opar

Real Interest Rate	C	Supply of Loanable Funds (Saving)	I	Demand for Loanable Funds
3%	75		22	
4%	70		18	
5%	65		14	
6%	60		10	
7%	55		6	
8%	50		2	

a. Calculate and fill in the two blank columns of the table using the space below for your calculations. What is the real interest rate and quantity of loanable funds in Opar in equilibrium?

7. An enterprising entrepreneur builds a machine that drills through the earth and connects Opar to Pellucidar. International trade opens up, and so does a loanable funds market between the two countries.

Table 5 below shows the total *world* loanable funds market.

TABLE 5	World Data		
Real Interest Rate	Supply of Loanable Funds (Saving) *C*	*I*	Demand for Loanable Funds
3%	175		54
4%			
5%			
6%			
7%			
8%			

a. Using your data from Tables 3 and 4, fill in the remaining information and find the world equilibrium real interest rate and quantity of loanable funds traded.

b. For Opar after world trade, what is the level of domestic saving, domestic investment, net exports, and international lending or borrowing?

c. For Pellucidar after world trade, what is the level of domestic saving, domestic investment, net exports, and international lending or borrowing?

8. Suppose that a technological innovation dramatically raises expected profits in Canada. Assuming that Canada is initially neither a net lender nor a net borrower on the global loanable funds market, draw a graph of Canada's loanable funds market and show the impact (if any) of the innovation on the demand for loanable funds, the supply of loanable funds, the real interest rate, investment, net exports, and foreign borrowing or lending.

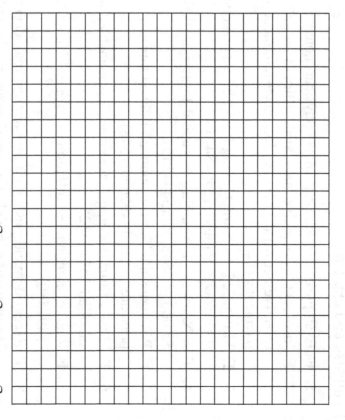

Answers

True/False and Explain

1. **F** Example of financial capital, not physical capital. (544)

2. **F** Insolvent = negative net worth. Illiquid = solvent (positive net worth) but insufficient cash to meet debt payments. (547)

3. **F** Mortgage is a contract giving lender house ownership if borrower defaults. (545–546)

4. **T** Δ Net wealth = saving − capital loss = $2,000 − $3,000 = −$1,000. (544–545)

5. **F** With constant interest payment, interest rate and asset price are inversely related. (548)

6. **F** Higher future income, less saving, less loanable funds supplied. (551–552)

7. **F** Real ≈ nominal − inflation = 6% − 4% = 2%. (549–550)

8. **T** Excess demand pushes up real interest rate, decreasing quantity demanded, increasing quantity supplied until equal at new equilibrium real interest rate. (552)

9. **T** Higher expected profits lead to higher demand for loanable funds, creating a shortage and raising real interest rates. (552–553)

10. **F** $I = S + (T − G) + (M − X)$. (548–549)

11. **F** Real = nominal − inflation. Depends on how much nominal rate and inflation rate have increased. (549–550)

12. **T** Higher deficit means more government borrowing, shifting *DLF* rightward, increasing real interest rate, and lowering investment. (556)

13. **F** Effect from True/False **12** is countered by rational taxpayers saving for higher future tax payments— *SLF* shifts rightward. (556)

14. **T** When Calonia lends, the rest of the world is using the funds to pay for Calonia's positive net exports = rest of world's negative net exports. (557)

15. **F** Real interest rate is determined by the global rate. If Calonia's demand is greater than supply, Calonia borrows from the rest of world. (557–558)

Multiple-Choice

1. **b** Definition. (544)

2. **c** Net worth = $10 million − $8 million > 0 (solvent), and cash payments < debt payments (illiquid). (547)

3. **a** Net investment = gross investment − depreciation = $35,000 − $25,000 (0.50 × $50,000) = $10,000. (544)

4. **b** Bonds paying income from package of mortgages. (545)

5. **b** New wealth = original wealth + Δ wealth = original wealth + saving + capital gain/loss + stock gift = original wealth + after-tax income − consumption + capital gain/loss + stock gift = $2,500 + $15,000 − $1,000 − $15,000 + $500 + $5,000 = $7,000. (544)

6. **b** Interest rate = (interest payment)/value × 100 = $500/$7,500 × 100 = 6.67%. (548)

7. **d** Definition. (546)

8. **b** Less income available for saving. (551–552)

9. **a** Should be $X - M$ and not $M - X$. (548–549)

10. **c** From $S = (Y - T) - C$. (548–549)

11. **e** Definition. (548–549)

12. **d** Lower future income means more saving for future. (551–552)

13. **b** $I = S + (T - G) + (M - X)$ tells us **a**, **c**, **e** are false and **b** is true. Higher real interest rate discourages investing; **d** is false. (548–551)

14. **a** National saving = $S + (T - G) = \$90 + \$25 - \$30 = \$85$. (548–549)

15. **c** Real interest rate decreases since increase in inflation rate > increase in nominal interest rate. Opportunity cost of spending decreases, so spending increases. Real interest rate decreases, opportunity cost of borrowing decreases. (549–550)

16. **c** Expected future profits increase and shifts *DLF* rightward, raising real interest rate and quantity of loanable funds. (552–553)

17. **d** Higher disposable income shifts *SLF* rightward, real interest rate falls, quantity of loanable funds increases. (552–553)

18. **a** Deficit shifts *DLF* rightward by $20 billion at every level. New equilibrium is where new *DLF* and old *SLF* intersect. (556)

19. **c** *SLF* shifts rightward— real interest rate decreases, increasing investment. (556)

20. **a** *DLF* shifts rightward by $20 billion— real interest rate increases to 7 percent, decreasing investment along old *DLF*. (556)

21. **d** Imagine a flat *SLF* at 4 percent, borrow difference between domestic *DLF* and *SLF*. (557–559)

22. **d** **a** shifts world *SLF* leftward, **b** raises the risk premium (adds a risk premium to the world interest rate when Canada borrows), **c** shifts world *DLF* rightward. (557–559)

23. **a** In global economy $X = M$. (557–559)

24. **e** It is determined by the world real interest rate. (557–558)

25. **d** *SLF* is horizontal at global real interest rate. More funds will flow in to finance the deficit. With no change in real interest rate, there is no change in investment. (557–558)

Short Answer Problems

1. **a.** Gross investment = total spending on (physical) capital equipment = $2 million.
Net investment = gross investment – depreciation = $2 million – $750,000 = $1.25 million.
Capital stock = old capital stock + net investment = $1 million + $1.25 million = $2.25 million.

   b. Net worth = total market value of (physical and financial) assets – total market value of borrowing = $2.25 million + $600,000 – $3 million = –$150,000.
It has negative net worth; it is insolvent.

2. Fig. 2 shows the effects the governor is talking about in action. DLF_0 is the original demand for loanable funds, with r_0 the original real interest rate.

   Deficit reduction causes a decline in the demand for loanable funds—a shift to DLF_1. With no global markets, this leads to a lower real interest rate, r_1. The lower real interest rate increases the quantity of investment demand, shown as the movement along the *DLF* curve. Assuming deficits are now zero, the quantity of investment demand goes from I_0 to I_1. (Assuming no Ricardo–Barro effect.)

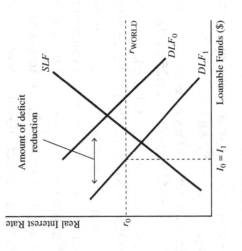

▲ **FIGURE 2**

3. Fig. 3 shows the situation with a global market. Since Canada was initially a net borrower, we know the world interest rate (r_{WORLD}) is initially lower than a Canadian-only equilibrium, and at this interest rate the demand for loanable funds is greater than the supply.

With the deficit reduction comes a decline in the demand for loanable funds, the leftward shift to DLF_1. With global markets, this does not change the real interest rate, and there is also no change in the level of investment (still measured on DLF_1).

In reality, another change occurred. The lower Canadian deficit reduced the perception of the riskiness of Canadian assets. The risk premium fell, and the r_{WORLD} that Canada pays did fall a bit, and the quantity of investment demanded did increase a bit.

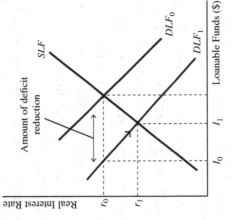

▲ **FIGURE 3**

4. **a.** Gross investment = net investment + depreciation = $150 + $60 = $210 billion.

b. Net exports = $X − M$ = $240 − $220 = $20 billion. Since net exports are positive, we are lending to foreigners; foreign lending = $20 billion.

c. $G − T$ = $200 − $300 = −$100 billion, a government surplus.

d. Household saving = $Y − C − T$ = $1,030 − $600 − $300 = $130 billion.

e. National saving = $S + (T − G)$ = $130 + $100 = $230 billion.

f. I = national saving − foreign lending = $230 − $20 = $210 billion.

5. First, we must calculate Marie's saving, which is income − consumption − net taxes = $35,000 − $12,000 − $22,000 = $1,000. This will be added to her wealth.

Second, value of the stocks = $128,000 − $20,000 in sales = $108,000.

Third, she has a house worth $192,000.

So, assets = $1,000 + $108,000 + $192,000 = $301,000. However, we must deduct her debts of $172,000 for net wealth of $129,000.

6. a. Table 3 Solution is filled in below. Saving is calculated as $S = Y − C − T$, where income is constant at 100 million opals, and taxes are 10 million opals given the deficit of 2 million opals and government expenditure of 12 million opals. The demand for loanable funds = I + the deficit of 2 million opals.

TABLE 3 Solution

Real Interest Rate	Supply of Loanable Funds			Demand for Loanable Funds
	C	(Saving)	I	
3%	75	15	22	24
4%	70	20	18	20
5%	65	25	14	16
6%	60	30	10	12
7%	55	35	6	8
8%	50	40	2	4

Equilibrium occurs when quantity demanded equals quantity supplied of 20 million opals at 4 percent.

b. Table 4 Solution is filled in below, using the same method as in Short Answer Problem **6a**. Equilibrium occurs at an interest rate of 6 percent with 24 million opals traded.

TABLE 4 Solution

Real Interest Rate	Supply of Loanable Funds			Demand for Loanable Funds
	C	(Saving)	I	
3%	100	9	32	36
4%	95	14	28	32
5%	90	19	24	28
6%	85	24	20	24
7%	80	29	16	20
8%	75	34	12	16

7. a. Table 5 Solution is calculated first by adding the consumption of each country at each real interest rate, etc. The world real interest rate occurs when world quantity supplied equals world quantity demanded at 44 million opals and real interest rate of 5 percent.

TABLE 5 Solution

Real Interest Rate	Supply of Loanable Funds			Demand for Loanable Funds
	C	(Saving)	I	
3%	175	24	54	60
4%	165	34	46	52
5%	155	44	38	44
6%	145	54	30	36
7%	135	64	22	28
8%	125	74	14	20

b. At a real interest rate of 5 percent, in Opar the quantity supplied of loanable funds is 25 million opals and the quantity demanded is 16 million opals. This leaves a surplus of 9 million opals that are lent internationally (foreigners borrow 9 million opals), so that net exports equal +9 million opals.

c. At a real interest rate of 5 percent, in Pellucidar the quantity supplied of loanable funds is 19 million opals, the quantity demanded is 28 million opals. This leaves a shortage of 9 million opals that are borrowed internationally (foreigners lend 9 million opals), so that net exports equal −9 million opals.

8. Fig. 4 shows the loanable funds market. Since Canada is neither a net lender nor a net borrower, the Canadian quantity demanded and supplied of loanable funds is initially equal at the world real interest rate.

The initial impact of the increased profits is increased investment by firms, leading to a rightward shift in the demand for loanable funds to DLF_1, with a resulting increase in the quantity of loanable funds traded from LF_0 to LF_1 (the difference equals the additional investment) and no change in the real interest rate. There is no change in the Canadian supply, so extra loanable funds come from the global market by borrowing internationally, the difference between LF_0 and LF_1. As a net international borrower, Canada must now have negative net exports equal to that amount.

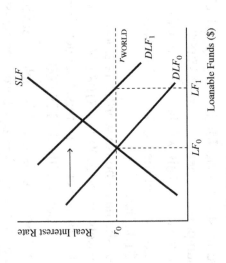

▲ **FIGURE 4**

8 Money, the Price Level, and Inflation

Key Concepts

What Is Money?

Money is something acceptable as a **means of payment** (method of settling a debt) and has three functions:

- Medium of exchange—accepted in exchange for goods and services.
  - Better than **barter** (direct exchange of goods for goods)—guarantees double coincidence of wants.
- Unit of account—agreed measure for prices.
- Store of value—exchangeable at a later date.

Two official measures of money:

- **M1**—currency held by individuals and businesses + chequable deposits of individuals and businesses.
- **M2**—M1 + all other deposits.

Money is **currency** (coins + Bank of Canada notes) and deposits (convertible into currency, used to pay debts).

- Cheques are only an instruction to banks.

- Credit cards are ID cards for loans, not money.
- Currency plus some deposits are means of payments; other deposits are not, but have liquidity.

The Banking System

The banking system consists of depository institutions and the Bank of Canada.

- **Depository institutions** take deposits from households and firms and make loans to others.

  - **Chartered banks** (chartered under the Bank Act), **credit unions** and caisses populaires, and **trust and mortgage loan companies.**

- Banks and other depository institutions provide services for fees and earn income lending out deposits. Banks have four assets:

  - **reserves** (cash + deposits at Bank of Canada), held to meet demand for currency
  - liquid assets (short-term government and commercial bills)
  - securities (longer-term bonds)
  - loans to corporations and households

- Banks make profits by paying depositors low interest rates and lending at high rates in return for services of

  - creating liquidity
  - pooling risks
  - lowering cost of borrowing funds
  - lowering cost of monitoring borrowers

Bank of Canada is Canada's **central bank**—supervises financial institutions, markets, payments system, and conducts monetary policy.

- Acts as banker to other banks and government, and as **lender of last resort** (makes loans to the banking system when there is a reserve shortage).

- Bank of Canada is the sole issuer of bank notes.

- Bank of Canada balance sheet shows assets (government securities and loans to banks, usually zero) and liabilities (bank notes and deposits of banks and government).

- **Monetary base** (Bank of Canada notes/coins + depository institutions' deposits at the Bank) can be changed using **open market operation** (purchase or sale of government securities by Bank).

- If Bank of Canada buys government bonds, this increases banking system reserves, increasing the monetary base.

- If Bank of Canada sells government bonds, this decreases banking system reserves, decreasing the monetary base.

How Banks Create Money

Banks create money (deposits) when they lend out excess reserves (**reserves** = notes/coins in vaults + deposits at the Bank of Canada).

- Quantity of deposits that can be created is limited by the monetary base, the level of desired reserves, and the desired currency holding.

- People desire to hold some money as currency—**currency drain ratio** = currency/deposits.

- If a bank gets a new deposit, it creates **excess reserves** (actual reserves − desired reserves).

  - **Desired reserve ratio** = ratio of reserves to total deposits banks wish to hold.

- Banks loan out excess reserves.

  - Borrower spends loan (and keeps some as currency), recipient of spent money deposits it at her bank.

  - New bank has more reserves, some are desired but some are excess reserves, leading to further steps in the deposit multiplier process.

- Total Δ quantity of money = increase in currency + increase in deposits.
- **Money multiplier** = (Δ quantity of money)/(Δ monetary base).

The Market for Money

People choose money holdings based on price level, nominal interest rate, real GDP, financial innovation.

- People hold money for its buying power.
  - Increase in price level (P) causes equal increase in nominal money demanded (M), so no change in real money demanded (M/P).
- Interest rate = opportunity cost of holding money.
  - Higher interest rate decreases quantity of real money demanded.
  - **Demand for money** is the relationship between the quantity of real money demanded and the nominal interest rate, holding constant other factors.
- Increase in real GDP shifts MD curve rightward.
- Financial innovation has an ambiguous effect on MD curve—decreases demand for currency and some deposits, increases demand for other deposits.

Money market equilibrium occurs when the quantity of money demanded equals the quantity of money supplied.

- Short-run equilibrium is determined by the quantity of money supplied (determined by actions of banks and the Bank of Canada).
- Changes in interest rate create a new equilibrium in the money market.
  - If the Bank of Canada increases the quantity of money, people find themselves with excess money holdings.
  - Therefore, they buy financial assets, increasing the price of financial assets and decreasing the interest rate toward equilibrium.

Notes:

- In the long run, supply and demand of loanable funds determines real interest rate, nominal interest rate = real interest rate + expected inflation rate.

The Quantity Theory of Money

Quantity theory of money predicts an increase in quantity of money leads to equal percentage increase in price level.

- Quantity theory starts with **velocity of circulation** (the average number of times a dollar is used annually to buy goods and services).
- $(V = PY/M)$, which leads to equation of exchange: $(MV = PY)$.
  - Assumes velocity is unaffected by ΔM.
  - Then, % ΔP = % ΔM − % ΔY.
- Historical evidence suggests the money growth rate is correlated with the inflation rate, but greater than the inflation rate.

Mathematical Note: The Money Multiplier

The money multiplier (mm) is the ratio of money (M) to the monetary base (MB): $mm = M/MB$.

- M = deposits + currency = $D + C$.
- MB = bank reserves + currency = $R + C$.
- Therefore $mm = (D + C)/(R + C)$.
- Divide all variables on right-hand side by D to get $mm = (1 + C/D)/(R/D + C/D)$.
- C/D is the currency ratio, R/D is the banks' reserve ratio.

Helpful Hints

1. What is money? Whatever meets the functions of money is money. For example, cigarettes functioned as money in prisoner-of-war camps. However, you should be able to answer this question on several levels. First, as a general definition, money is a medium of exchange. Second, as a classification, chequable deposits are money but savings deposits are not. Third, as more specific definitions, M1 and M2 are official definitions of money.

   We refer to our income earnings as the "money we make working." However, in economics, money means the *stock* of money we are holding in currency plus deposits (M1 or M2). Money does *not* mean the *flow* of income earnings—be careful of this distinction.

   Distinguish between the act of holding money and the act of consumption spending. Holding money means dealing with money markets, not goods and services markets. The choice for households in this chapter is between holding bonds and holding money. The choice for consumer spending involves saving versus spending.

2. Become thoroughly familiar with the money multiplier process by which banks create money.

   Two fundamental facts allow banks to create money. First, banks create money by creating new chequable deposits. Second, banks hold fractional reserves. Fractional reserves mean that when a bank receives a deposit, it only holds part of it as reserves and lends the rest. The bank is not indulging in a scam—it is still maintaining assets (reserves plus loans) to match its liabilities (deposits). When that loan is spent, at least part of the proceeds will likely be deposited in another bank, creating a new deposit (money).

   The deposit multiplier process follows from this last fact: banks make loans when they receive new deposits. These loans are spent—some leaves the process as currency drain, and the rest returns to another bank, creating another new deposit. The process repeats itself, adding more deposits (but in progressively smaller amounts) in each round. Practise going through examples until the process becomes second nature. As you go, note the role played by the profit-seeking behaviour of banks. Profit-seeking leads them to turn reserves, which earn no revenues, into loans, which earn revenues.

Notes: _____

3. Be careful to avoid a common error when working through open market operations. When the Bank of Canada buys or sells securities, private bank reserves at the Bank of Canada change. Many students automatically put the changed bank reserves at the Bank of Canada under assets in the Bank's balance sheet, because they are an asset on the *private bank's balance sheet*. However, this is an error—the reserves are a deposit at the Bank of Canada, and therefore a *liability* to the Bank of Canada.

4. The important equation of exchange states:

$$\begin{matrix} \text{Quantity} \\ \text{of money} \end{matrix} \times \begin{matrix} \text{Velocity of} \\ \text{circulation} \end{matrix} = \begin{matrix} \text{Price} \\ \text{level} \end{matrix} \times \begin{matrix} \text{Real} \\ \text{GDP} \end{matrix}$$

The quantity of money times the average number of times each dollar is spent (equalling total expenditure) is equal to the dollar value of the goods and services on which it was spent. The equation is always true by definition—it is an identity. By further assuming that both the velocity of circulation and potential GDP are independent of the quantity of money in the long run, we get the quantity theory of money. The assumptions imply that when the quantity of money increases by 10 percent, in the long run the price level increases by 10 percent to maintain equality between the two sides of the equation.

Self-Test

True/False and Explain

What Is Money?

1. Money is anything generally acceptable as a means of payment.

2. A fixed term deposit at a chartered bank is part of M1.

3. If the public shifts deposits from chequing accounts to non-chequing accounts, M1 will decrease and M2 increase.

The Banking System

4. One of the key economic functions of banks is acting as a lender of last resort.

5. Individual households are generally better at pooling risk than are depository institutions.

6. A bank's reserves consist of cash in its vault plus its deposits at the Bank of Canada.

How Banks Create Money

7. The size of the monetary base limits the amount of deposit creation in the money creation process.

8. If a depositor uses a debit card to buy something, her bank's reserves decline.

The Market for Money

9. If the price level increases, the quantity of real money people want to hold increases.

10. If interest rates increase, the quantity of real money demanded decreases.

11. The development of near-money deposits and growth in the use of credit cards in the 1970s caused the demand for M1 to shift leftward.

12. If households or firms have more money than they want to hold, they will buy financial assets, causing asset prices to increase and the interest rate to decrease.

13. If the price of a bond increases, the interest rate earned on the bond decreases.

The Quantity Theory of Money

14. If the quantity of money is $50 billion and nominal GDP is $200 billion, the velocity of circulation is 1/4.

15. The international data does not support the quantity theory of money.

Multiple-Choice

What Is Money?

1. Which of the following is a function of money?
   a. medium of exchange
   b. measure of liquidity
   c. pooling risk
   d. store of exchange
   e. reducing transactions costs

2. Which of the following is a component of M2 but *not* of M1?
   a. currency in circulation
   b. personal chequing deposits
   c. personal nonchequing deposits
   d. currency in bank vaults
   e. Canada Savings Bonds

3. Which of the following is *most* liquid?
   a. chequing deposits
   b. real estate
   c. government bonds
   d. savings deposits
   e. cheques

4. Which of the following is *not* a store of value?
   a. credit cards
   b. personal chequing deposits
   c. term deposits
   d. other chequable deposits
   e. nonchequing deposits

The Banking System

5. Which of the following statements about depository institutions is *false*?

  a. They maximize their owner's wealth, ignoring all else.

  b. They keep reserves to meet cash withdrawals.

  c. A credit union is a depository institution.

  d. They pool and therefore reduce risk.

  e. They borrow at low interest rates and lend at higher interest rates.

6. Which of the following is an economic service provided by a depository institution?

  a. borrowing low and lending high

  b. keeping cash reserves

  c. pooling liquidity

  d. lowering the cost of borrowing funds

  e. creating liquid liabilities

7. When a bank receives short-term deposits and issues long-term loans, this is an example of

  a. being a lender of last resort.

  b. lowering the cost of borrowing.

  c. creating liquidity.

  d. taking unnecessary risks.

  e. pooling risk.

8. Which of the following is an asset of the Bank of Canada?

  a. currency in circulation

  b. government securities held in the Bank of Canada

  c. deposits of chartered banks at the Bank of Canada

  d. coins in circulation

  e. deposits of governments at the Bank of Canada

9. Which balance sheet in Table 1 shows the initial impact on the banking sector of an open market purchase by the Bank of Canada of $100 million of government securities from the banking sector?

   a. (a)
   b. (b)
   c. (c)
   d. (d)
   e. none of the above

How Banks Create Money

10. The Bank of Speedy Creek currently has actual (and desired) reserves of $40, loans of $460, and deposits of $500. What is its desired reserve ratio?

    a. 4 percent
    b. 8 percent
    c. 12.5 percent
    d. 25 percent
    e. 40 percent

TABLE 1 Banking System Balance Sheet (Millions)

(a)

Assets		Liabilities
Reserves	+100	
Securities	−100	

(b)

Assets		Liabilities
Reserves	−100	
Securities	+100	

(c)

Assets		Liabilities	
Reserves	+100	Deposits +100	

(d)

Assets	Liabilities	
	Deposits	+100
	Securities	−100

11. The Bank of Speedy Creek currently has actual (and desired) reserves of $40, loans of $460, and deposits of $500. Huck Finn comes along and deposits $10. After Huck's deposit, but before any other actions have occurred, the total amount of *monetary base* in the economy

   a. is unchanged, with currency $10 higher and deposits $10 lower.

   b. has increased by $10.

   c. has decreased by $10.

   d. is unchanged, with deposits $10 higher and currency $10 lower.

   e. depends on if Huck deposited his money in a savings deposit or a demand deposit.

12. The Bank of Speedy Creek currently has actual (and desired) reserves of $40, loans of $460, and deposits of $500. Huck Finn comes along and deposits $10. After Huck's deposit, but before any other actions have occurred, the total amount of *money* in the economy has

   a. stayed the same, with currency and deposits unchanged.

   b. stayed the same, with currency falling and deposits rising.

   c. decreased, with currency falling and deposits staying the same.

   d. increased, with currency unchanged and deposits rising.

   e. decreased, with currency falling and deposits unchanged.

13. The Bank of Speedy Creek currently has actual (and desired) reserves of $40, loans of $460, and deposits of $500. Huck Finn comes along and deposits $10. After Huck's deposit, but before any other actions have occurred, the Bank of Speedy Creek will have excess reserves of

   a. zero.

   b. $9.

   c. $9.20.

   d. $10.

   e. $40.

14. The Bank of Speedy Creek currently has actual (and desired) reserves of $40, loans of $460, and deposits of $500. Huck Finn comes along and deposits $10. After Huck's deposit, given that the Bank of Speedy Creek is profit-seeking, what amount of new loans will it make?

   a. zero

   b. $9

   c. $9.20

   d. $10

   e. $40

15. The Bank of Speedy Creek currently has actual (and desired) reserves of $40, loans of $460, and deposits of $500. Huck Finn comes along and deposits $10. After Huck's deposit, and after the Bank of Speedy Creek has lent the amount it wishes to lend, the total amount of reserves in the bank will be $_____, the total amount of loans will be $_____, and the total amount of deposits will be $_____.

   a. 40.80; 469.20; 510

   b. 40; 460; 500

   c. 50; 470; 520

   d. 41; 469; 510

   e. 42.50; 467.50; 510

16. If new deposits are made in the banking system, which of the following will limit the amount of the new money created?

   a. the desired reserve ratio only

   b. the currency drain ratio only

   c. the monetary base only

   d. the desired reserve ratio and the currency drain ratio, but not the monetary base

   e. the desired reserve ratio, the currency drain ratio, and the monetary base

17. Which of the following steps in the description of the money multiplier process is *wrong*?

  a. Banks lend out excess reserves.

  b. Bank deposits increase.

  c. The deposits are spent.

  d. Some new spending returns as deposits, and currency comes in as new deposits.

  e. Banks once again have excess reserves, and the process continues.

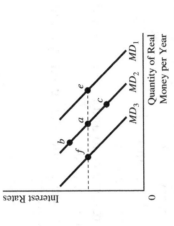

▲ **FIGURE 1 The Demand for Real Money Balances by an Individual House Hold**

The Market for Money

18. Consider Fig. 1. Which of the following best describes the response of this household to an *increase* in their annual income?

  a. movement from *a* to *f*

  b. movement from *a* to *c*

  c. movement from *e* to *a*

  d. movement from *b* to *a*

  e. movement from *a* to *e*

19. Which of the following could cause the demand curve for M1 to shift leftward?

  a. increase in real GDP

  b. decrease in interest rates

  c. expanded use of credit cards

  d. increase in quantity of money supplied

  e. increase in the price level

20. Real money is equal to nominal money

  a. divided by real GDP.

  b. minus real GDP.

  c. divided by the price level.

  d. minus the price level.

  e. divided by velocity.

21. If the interest rate is above the equilibrium rate, how is equilibrium achieved in the money market?

  a. People buy goods to get rid of excess money, lowering the price of goods, and lowering the interest rate.

  b. People sell goods to get rid of excess money, lowering the price of goods, and lowering the interest rate.

  c. People sell bonds to get rid of excess money, lowering the price of bonds, and lowering the interest rate.

  d. People sell bonds to get rid of excess money, raising the price of bonds, and lowering the interest rate.

  e. People buy bonds to get rid of excess money, raising the price of bonds, and lowering the interest rate.

22. Money market equilibrium occurs

  a. when interest rates are constant.

  b. when the level of real GDP is constant.

  c. when quantity of real money supplied equals quantity of real money demanded.

  d. only under a fixed exchange rate.

  e. when bond prices are constant.

The Quantity Theory of Money

23. The quantity theory of money begins with the equation of exchange, $MV = PY$, and then adds the assumptions that

  a. velocity varies inversely with the rate of interest, and the price level is independent of the quantity of money.

  b. velocity and the price level are independent of the quantity of money.

  c. potential GDP and the quantity of money are independent of the price level.

  d. potential GDP and the price level are independent of the quantity of money.

  e. velocity and potential GDP are independent of the quantity of money.

24. According to the quantity theory of money, in the long run

   a. V/M is constant.
   b. Y/M is constant.
   c. Y/P is constant.
   d. M/P is constant.
   e. M/V is constant.

25. According to the quantity theory of money, an increase in the quantity of money will increase the price level

   a. but will have no effect on real GDP or velocity of circulation.

   b. as well as increase both real GDP and velocity of circulation.

   c. as well as increase real GDP but decrease velocity of circulation.

   d. as well as decrease real GDP but increase velocity of circulation.

   e. but have no effect on real GDP while decreasing velocity of circulation.

Short Answer Problems

1. Banks can no longer issue their own paper money, but can create deposit money by crediting people's deposits. Since there is no paper money deposited to back up this creation, is this created money real? Is it acceptable in society? Why or why not?

2. Briefly explain how and why banks create new money during the deposit multiplier process (in a multibank system).

4. There is only one chartered bank in the country of Adanac, and it has the following assets and liabilities:

Currency reserves	$20 million
Reserves held at the Bank of Adanac	$10 million
Loans	$700 million
Securities	$20 million
Deposits	$750 million

a. Assuming that the bank has freely chosen its reserves, what is its desired reserve ratio?

b. If the amount of currency in circulation is $50 million, what is the monetary base? What is the money supply?

c. What is the currency drain ratio?

3. Why do people care about the quantity of real money they hold rather than the quantity of nominal money?

5. Consider the balance sheets in Table 2 for the Bank of Canada and the Bank of Speedy Creek:

TABLE 2

Bank of Speedy Creek

Assets		Liabilities	
Reserves	60	Deposits	1,000
Securities	100		
Loans	840		
	1,000		

Bank of Canada

Assets		Liabilities	
Government securities	9,000	Bank of Canada notes	10,000
Loans to banks	500	Chartered banks' deposits	1,000
Other net assets	2,000	Government deposits	500
	11,500		11,500

Suppose that the Bank of Canada buys all $100 of securities from the Bank of Speedy Creek. Show what happens to the balance sheets of the Bank of Speedy Creek and the Bank of Canada as a result of this action, explaining as you go. What does this action do to the reserves in the banking system?

6. Assume the central bank adjusts the quantity of money to keep the quantity of real money supplied constant.
   a. Describe what happens to the money supply in this situation.

Using the grid, show on a graph and briefly explain what each of the following will do (in sequence) to the demand for real money (defined as M1) and therefore the equilibrium interest rate. Assume that the real money supply remains constant.

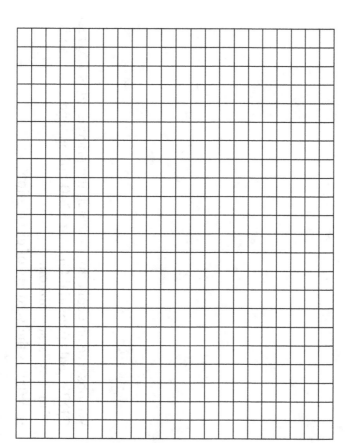

b. The price level rises.

c. There is a financial innovation (widespread adoption of electronic funds transfers) that reduces the need to use chequing accounts.

d. Real GDP falls during a recession.

7. Briefly explain the role of the Bank of Canada in the banking system.

8. We observe an economy in which the price level is 1.5, real GDP equals potential GDP at $240 billion, and the quantity of money is $60 billion.

a. What is the velocity of circulation?

b. According to the quantity theory of money, what is the long-run result of an increase in the quantity of money to $80 billion?

Answers

True/False and Explain

ⓒ 1. **T** Basic function of money. (568)

2. **F** See definition of M1. (569–570)

3. **F** M1 decreases as chequing accounts decrease, but chequing and nonchequing accounts are both part of M2, so no change in M2. (569–570)

4. **F** This is function of a central bank. (572–573)

5. **F** Large size allows banks to pool risk. (571–572)

6. **T** Definition. (571)

7. **T** Limits the amount available for desired reserves and desired currency holdings. (576)

8. **T** Withdrawal decreases deposits = decrease in reserves. (576–577)

9. **F** Real money demand is independent of the price level. (578–579)

10. **T** Increase in interest rate increases the opportunity cost of holding money and decreases the quantity of money demanded. (578–579)

11. **T** Shift toward M2—see text discussion. (580)

12. **T** Agents substitute toward bonds, increasing bond demand and bond prices, which implies a decrease in bond interest rate. (581)

13. **T** Price of bond and its interest rate are inversely related. (581)

14. **F** $V = PY/M = 200/50 = 4$. (582)

15. **F** Correlation between money growth and inflation is not perfect, but it is strong. (583)

Multiple-Choice

1. **a** See text discussion. (568)

2. **c** Definition. (569)

3. **a** Most readily changed into currency. (570)

4. **a** Credit cards are not guaranteed for future purchases—credit card company might cancel your card. (569)

5. **a** Must be prudent about risk, too. (571)

6. **d** See text discussion. (572)

7. **c** Short-term deposits are more liquid for depositors than lending long-term themselves. (572)

8. **b** Definition. (573)

9. **a** Buying government bonds increases reserves. (575)

10. **b** Desired reserve ratio = chosen reserves/deposits = $40/500 = 0.08$. (576)

11. **d** Decrease in currency in circulation = increase in bank reserves. (576–577)

12. **b** Decrease in currency as deposit made = increase in deposits. (576–577)

13. **c** Excess = actual ($50) − desired ($40.80 = 0.08 × $510). (576–577)

14. **c** Banks will lend the amount of excess reserves. (576–577)

ⓒ 15. **a** The $10 deposit is divided between the new desired reserves ($0.08 × $10) and new loans. (576–577)

16. e The monetary base limits possible amount of new reserves and new currency in circulation. The higher the desired reserve ratio, the more money banks hold back at each stage. The higher the currency drain ratio, the more households hold back at each stage. (576)

17. d Some of the new spending is kept back as currency and not deposited. (579)

18. e a to f, e to a are decreases in income, others are Δ interest rates. (579)

19. c Financial innovation means people use less money. Other changes create rightward shift or no shift. (579)

20. c Definition. (578)

21. e If interest rate > equilibrium, this implies too much money, which implies buying bonds, leading to increase in price of bonds and therefore decrease in interest rates. (581)

22. c Definition. (581)

23. e See text discussion. (582–583)

24. d Because theory assumes Y/V ($= M/P$) is constant. (582–583)

25. a Due to assumption that neither GDP nor velocity affected by Δ quantity of money. (582–583)

Short Answer Problems

1. This created money is real, because it is backed by the assets of the bank, which consist of the bank's reserves, loans, and holdings of securities.

   Deposit money is generally accepted in society (you can buy goods, pay debts, etc., with it) because people know that the banks will provide currency upon demand.

2. Banks create money by making new loans. When banks get a new deposit, this leaves them with excess reserves. The desire to make profits leads banks to lend out excess reserves, creating a matching deposit, which is new money. When these loans are spent, the person receiving the money deposits much of it in a bank deposit, creating excess reserves, and the process continues.

3. Nominal money is simply the number of dollars, while real money is a measure of what money will buy. Real money decreases if the price level rises while the number of dollars is constant. What matters to people is the quantity of goods and services that money will buy, not the number of dollars. If the price level rises by 10 percent, people will want to hold 10 percent more dollars (given a constant real income and interest rates) to keep the same purchasing power.

4. **a.** Desired reserve ratio = desired reserves/deposits = $30/750 = 0.04$.

   b. Monetary base = reserves + currency in circulation = $80 million. Money supply = currency in circulation + deposits = $800 million.

   c. Currency drain ratio = currency in circulation/deposits = $50/750 = 1/15 = 0.0667$.

5. The impact of the purchase on the balance sheets is shown in Table 3.

   The Bank of Canada increases its securities by 100, and pays for it by increasing the Bank of Speedy Creek's deposits at the Bank of Canada by 100, which is an increase in this bank's reserves by 100 (matching the decrease in security holdings). The balance sheets in Table 3 show the changes, and then the new positions.

The increase in banks' deposits of 100 also increases the reserves of the banking system by 100.

TABLE 3

Changes in Balance Sheets

Bank of Speedy Creek

Assets		Liabilities	
Reserves	+100	Deposits	0
Securities	−100		
Loans	0		
	0		

Bank of Canada

Assets		Liabilities	
Government securities	+100	Bank of Canada notes	0
Loans to banks	0	Ch. banks' deposits	+100
Other net assets	0	Government deposits	0
	+100		+100

6. **a.** If the central bank is targeting the quantity of money, quantity of money supplied is fixed and money supply curve is vertical (at MS in Fig. 2).

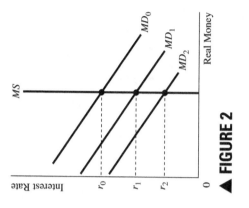

▲ **FIGURE 2**

b. A change in price level has no impact on real money demand, so no impact on equilibrium interest rate (r). In Fig. 2, demand for real money remains at MD_0, and interest rate remains at r_0.

c. This financial innovation reduces the need to use chequing accounts, which are part of M1. Therefore demand for real money falls to MD_1, and equilibrium interest rate falls to r_1 in Fig. 2.

d. Decrease in real GDP lowers demand for real money to MD_2, and the equilibrium interest rate falls to r_2 in Fig. 2.

7. The Bank of Canada supervises financial institutions and markets and the financial system, and conducts monetary policy. It acts as banker to other banks and to the government, and acts as lender of last resort by making loans to the banking system when there is a shortage of reserves. It is also the sole issuer of bank notes.

8. a. The velocity of circulation is

$$\text{Velocity of circulation} = \frac{\text{Price level} \times \text{Real GDP}}{\text{Quantity of money}}$$

With the given values for the price level, real GDP, and quantity of money, we have

$$\text{Velocity of circulation} = \frac{1.5 \times 240}{60} = 6$$

b. The quantity theory of money predicts that in the long run an increase in quantity of money causes an equal percentage increase in the price level. An increase in money from $60 billion to $80 billion is a one-third (33 percent) increase. Thus the quantity theory of money predicts the price level will increase by a third (33 percent). Since the initial price level is 1.5, the predicted price level will be 2.0. (Can also be calculated using the equation of exchange.)

9 The Exchange Rate and the Balance of Payments

Key Concepts

The Foreign Exchange Market

To buy foreign goods/assets, Canadians need **foreign currency** (foreign notes, coins, bank deposits); to buy Canadian goods/assets, foreigners need Canadian dollars.

- Currencies of one country are exchanged for the currency of another in the **foreign exchange market**.

- **Exchange rate** = price at which one currency exchanges for another.

- Currency depreciation (appreciation) is the decrease (increase) in value of the Canadian dollar in terms of another currency.

The exchange rate is determined by supply and demand in the foreign exchange market.

- Demand for Canadian dollars = supply of foreign currency; supply of Canadian dollars = demand for foreign currency.

- Quantity of Canadian dollars demanded in foreign exchange market = planned amount to buy at a given price, based on demands for Canadian exports and assets; depends on:

  - exchange rate
  - world demand for Canadian exports
  - interest rates in Canada and other countries
  - expected future exchange rate

- Increase in exchange rate decreases quantity demanded of Canadian dollars (movement up to the left along the demand curve), because

  - exports become more expensive for foreigners, decreasing demand for exports and therefore demand for dollars.

  - expected profits decrease from buying Canadian dollars to hold until they appreciate.

- Quantity of Canadian dollars supplied in foreign exchange market = planned amount to sell at a given price = planned purchases of foreign currencies to buy imports and foreign assets; depends on:

  - exchange rate
  - Canadian demand for imports
  - interest rates in Canada and other countries
  - expected future exchange rate

- Increase in exchange rate increases the quantity supplied of Canadian dollars (movement up to the right along the supply curve), because

  - imports become cheaper for Canadians, increasing demand for imports/demand for foreign currency = increase in supply of Canadian dollars.

  - expected profits increase from buying foreign currency to hold until it appreciates, increasing demand for foreign currency = increase in supply of Canadian dollars.

- Market equilibrium is determined by demand and supply—exchange rates adjust instantly as required to achieve equilibrium for all exchange rates.

Exchange Rate Fluctuations

Demand curve for Canadian dollars shifts *rightward* if

- world demand for Canadian exports increases.
- **Canadian interest rate differential** (Canadian interest rate − foreign interest rate) increases, increasing demand for Canadian assets.

- expected future exchange rate increases, increasing expected profits from buying Canadian dollars and holding them until they appreciate.

Supply curve of Canadian dollars shifts *leftward* if

  - Canadian demand for imports decreases.
  - Canadian interest rate differential increases.
  - expected future exchange rate increases.

Expected changes in exchange rates are strongly affected by arbitrage behaviour (buying in one market and selling at a higher price in another), which in turn creates

- **purchasing power parity** (two currencies have the same value or purchasing power)—if no parity, and a Canadian dollar buys more than a U.S. dollar, demand for the Canadian dollar increases, supply decreases, and Canadian dollar appreciates.

- **interest rate parity** (two currencies earn the same rate of return, adjusted for expected Δ exchange rate)—if parity does not hold (adjusted for risk), and if returns are higher in Canada, increased demand for Canadian dollar instantly increases the exchange rate.

Real exchange rate (*RER*) is the relative price of Canadian-produced goods and services versus foreign-produced—$RER = (E \times P)/P^*$ where $P/P^* =$ Canadian/foreign price level and $E =$ nominal exchange rate = foreign currency per Canadian dollar.

- Nominal exchange rate is determined by purchasing power parity and interest parity, and in the short run this also determines the real exchange rate.

- In the long run the nominal exchange rate and price levels are determined together, and the real exchange rate does not change.

Exchange Rate Policy

Three different exchange rate policies:

- Current policy is **flexible exchange rate**— exchange rate is determined by supply and demand, changes in interest rates influence exchange rate.

- **Fixed exchange rate** policy pegs the exchange rate at a target value—if Δ exchange rate, Bank of Canada must buy/sell Canadian dollars to change demand/supply—works only as long as foreign currency reserves last.

- **Crawling peg** policy intervenes to meet selected target *path* for the exchange rate.

Financing International Trade

Balance of payments accounts measure Canada's international trading, borrowing, and lending.

- **Current account** = net exports + net interest income + net transfers.
- **Capital account** = foreign investment in Canada − Canadian investment abroad.
- **Official settlements account** = net changes in Canada's **official reserves** (government's holdings of foreign currency). If official reserves increase, official settlement balance is negative.

- Current account balance + capital account balance + official settlements balance = 0.
- To pay a current account deficit we must borrow from abroad or decrease official reserves.

Net borrower country borrows more from rest of world than lends in current year (capital account surplus).

- **Net lender**—lending more to rest of world than borrowing in current year (capital account deficit).

- **Debtor nation**—has borrowed more than lent to rest of world over history; **creditor nation** is the reverse.

Current account balance is primarily determined by **net exports** ($X - M$).

- From circular flow, net exports = **private sector balance** ($S - I$) + **government sector balance** ($T - G$).

- In the short run, the nominal exchange rate affects net exports; in the long run it has no effect.

Notes:

Helpful Hints

1. There is an important difference between trade within a single country and trade between countries—currency. Individuals trading in the same country use the same currency, and trade is straightforward. International trade (to be examined in detail in Chapter 31) is complicated by the fact that individuals in different countries use different currencies. A Japanese vendor selling goods wants payment in Japanese yen, but a Canadian buyer is likely holding only Canadian dollars. This chapter addresses this complication by examining the foreign exchange market.

2. The exchange rate is volatile because supply and demand often shift in a reinforcing manner, since they are both affected by the same changes in expectations. These changes in expectations are driven by two forces: purchasing power parity and interest rate parity. Each of these is a version of the law of one price, which states that anytime there is a difference in the price of the same good in two markets, natural economic forces (unless restricted) will eliminate that discrepancy and establish a single price. Suppose that the price in market 1 increases relative to the price in market 2. Individuals will now buy in market 2 (lower price) and not in market 1 (higher price). This increase in demand in market 2 and decrease in demand in market 1 will cause the two prices to come together. This principle also applies to international markets: natural market forces result in a single world price for the same good (allowing for effects of tariffs, transport costs, etc.).

   Suppose that purchasing power parity does not hold. For example, suppose that the wholesale price of an MP3 player in Canada is $100, and in Japan it is 10,000 yen, and that the exchange rate is currently 125 yen per dollar. The dollar price of the player in Japan is $80 (10,000 yen/125 yen per dollar). People expect the demand for the player in Canada to decrease (= a decrease in demand for Canadian dollars) and the demand for the player in Japan to increase (= supply of dollars rising), which would lead to the exchange rate depreciating toward 100 yen per dollar (purchasing power parity level). Expectations will lead to a decrease in demand for the Canadian dollar and an increase in supply of the Canadian dollar, so that the exchange rate will depreciate even before demand for the player adjusts!

The law of one price also holds for prices of assets like bonds. Recall from Chapter 23 that bond prices are inversely related to interest rates; interest rate parity is a version of the law of one price. Consider a situation where, taking into account the expected depreciation of the Canadian dollar, the Canadian interest rate was higher than the U.S. rate (which implies the price of bonds is lower in Canada). Buyers would demand Canadian bonds, raising their price and lowering Canadian interest rates. In addition, they would be selling U.S. bonds, lowering their price and raising U.S. interest rates. These actions occur until the interest rate differential between the two countries has shrunk to a level where it just reflects the expected depreciation of the Canadian dollar—interest rate parity holds.

Self-Test

True/False and Explain

The Foreign Exchange Market

1. If the exchange rate between the Canadian dollar and the Japanese yen changes from 130 yen per dollar to 140 yen per dollar, the Canadian dollar has appreciated.

2. If the Canadian dollar can buy $0.75 U.S., the U.S. dollar can buy $1.25 Canadian.

3. The demand for Canadian dollars by foreigners is automatically matched by Canadian demand for foreign currency.

4. A decrease in the exchange rate increases the quantity demanded for Canadian dollars because exports become cheaper for foreigners.

5. The expected profits effect says that an increase in the exchange rate will decrease the quantity supplied of Canadian dollars.

Exchange Rate Fluctuations

6. An increase in Canadian interest rates increases demand for the Canadian dollar.

7. The demand and supply of Canadian dollars tend to move independently of each other.

8. Countries with currencies expected to appreciate will have higher interest rates than countries with currencies expected to depreciate.

9. If the yen price of the dollar is 100 yen per dollar and the price of a traded good is $10 in Canada, purchasing power parity implies that the price in Japan will be 1,000 yen.

10. If the foreign exchange value of the Canadian dollar is expected to increase, the supply of Canadian dollars increases.

Exchange Rate Policy

11. If the Bank of Canada sets a target exchange rate and demand for the Canadian dollar increases, the Bank of Canada will sell Canadian dollars.

12. Under a flexible exchange rate, Bank of Canada policy will not affect the exchange rate.

Financing International Trade

13. There can be no such thing as a balance of payments surplus/deficit, because by definition a *balance* of payments must always *balance*.

14. If a nation is a net borrower from the rest of the world it must be a debtor nation.

15. If Canada borrows more from the rest of the world than it lends to the rest of the world, Canada has a capital account surplus.

Multiple-Choice

The Foreign Exchange Market

1. The exchange rate between the Canadian dollar and the British pound is 0.5 pounds per dollar. If a radio sells for 38 pounds in Britain, what is the dollar price of the radio?

   a. $19
   b. $25
   c. $38
   d. $57
   e. $76

2. Consider Table 1. Between 2009 and 2010, the Canadian dollar _____ versus the euro and _____ versus the yen.

   a. appreciated; depreciated
   b. appreciated; appreciated
   c. depreciated; depreciated
   d. depreciated; appreciated
   e. has not changed; has not changed

3. Consider Table 1. Between 2009 and 2010, the yen

   a. must have depreciated in value versus the euro.
   b. must have appreciated in value versus the euro.
   c. may or may not have appreciated in value versus the euro.
   d. will have appreciated in value versus the euro if the euro has a high weight in CERI.
   e. will have appreciated in value versus the euro if the euro has a lower weight in CERI.

4. If the demand for Canadian dollars increases, this is matched by a(n)

   a. increase in demand for foreign exchange.
   b. increase in supply of foreign exchange.
   c. increase in supply of Canadian dollars.
   d. decrease in demand for foreign exchange.
   e. decrease in supply of foreign exchange.

TABLE 1

Currency	2009 Exchange Rate	2010 Exchange Rate
EU euro	2 euros/dollar	3 euros/dollar
Japanese yen	120 yen/dollar	90 yen/dollar

5. The quantity of Canadian dollars demanded depends on all of the following *except*

  a. the exchange rate.

  b. the interest rate in Canada.

  c. interest rates in the rest of the world.

  d. the Canadian demand for imports.

  e. the expected future exchange rate.

6. A decrease in the exchange rate increases the quantity demanded of Canadian dollars because

  a. exports become more expensive for foreigners.

  b. imports become more expensive for Canadians.

  c. expected profits from buying Canadian dollars increase.

  d. expected profits from buying foreign currency decrease.

  e. cross exchange rates adjust quickly.

7. Which of the following best describes the expected profit effect?

  a. A lower exchange rate leads to importers using the forward market to lower exchange rate risk.

  b. A lower exchange rate leads to buying foreign currency to hold until it appreciates.

  c. A higher exchange rate leads to buying foreign currency to hold until it appreciates.

  d. A higher exchange rate leads to buying Canadian dollars to hold until they appreciate.

  e. A higher exchange rate leads to exporters using the forward market to lower exchange rate risk.

8. An increase in the exchange rate increases the quantity supplied of Canadian dollars because

  a. imports become cheaper for Canadians, increasing demand for imports and therefore demand for foreign currency, which equals an increase in quantity supplied of Canadian dollars.

  b. imports become more expensive for Canadians, increasing demand for imports and therefore demand for foreign currency, which equals an increase in quantity supplied of Canadian dollars.

  c. our exports become cheaper for foreigners, increasing demand for exports and therefore demand for foreign currency, which equals an increase in quantity supplied of Canadian dollars.

  d. expected profits increase from buying and holding Canadian dollars until they appreciate in value, which increases the quantity supplied of Canadian dollars.

  e. expected profits increase from selling and holding foreign currency until it appreciates in value, which increases the quantity supplied of Canadian dollars.

9. If the exchange rate is too high in the foreign exchange market,

  a. there is a surplus and the exchange rate will increase.

  b. there is a surplus and the exchange rate will decrease.

  c. exports are cheap, and the demand curve for Canadian dollars will shift rightward.

  d. there is a shortage and the exchange rate will decrease.

  e. there is a shortage and the exchange rate will increase.

Exchange Rate Fluctuations

10. Which of the following quotations best describes purchasing power parity?

  a. "The recent high Canadian interest rate has increased demand for the Canadian dollar."

  b. "The market feeling is that the Canadian dollar is over-valued and will likely depreciate."

  c. "The price of bananas is the same in Canada and the United States, adjusting for the exchange rate."

  d. "The expected depreciation of the Canadian dollar is currently lowering demand for it."

  e. None of the above.

11. When would the exchange rate decrease in value the most?
   a. Supply and demand of dollars both increase.
   b. Supply of dollars increases, and demand decreases.
   c. Supply of dollars decreases, and demand increases.
   d. Supply and demand of dollars both decrease.
   e. When the Bank of Canada intervenes.

12. Which of the following shifts the supply curve of Canadian dollars rightward?
   a. Increase in demand for foreign goods by Canadian citizens.
   b. Decrease in demand for Canadian goods by foreigners.
   c. The dollar is expected to appreciate.
   d. U.S. interest rates decrease.
   e. None of the above

13. Which of the following shifts the demand curve for Canadian dollars rightward?
   a. Increase in demand for foreign goods by Canadian citizens.
   b. Decrease in demand for Canadian goods by foreigners.
   c. The dollar is expected to appreciate.
   d. The dollar is expected to depreciate.
   e. U.S. interest rates increase.

14. If interest rates in Canada are greater than interest rates in Japan, interest rate parity implies that
   a. the inflation rate is higher in Japan.
   b. Japanese financial assets are poor investments.
   c. the yen is expected to depreciate against the dollar.
   d. the yen is expected to appreciate against the dollar.
   e. Canadian financial assets are poor investments.

15. Consider Fig. 1. Which graph best shows the impact of an increase in demand for Canadian exports?

a. (a)

b. (b)

c. (c)

d. (d)

e. (e)

16. Consider Fig. 1. Which graph best shows the impact of an increase in the Canadian interest rate differential?

a. (a)

b. (c)

c. (d)

d. (e)

e. (f)

17. Consider Fig. 1. Which graph best shows the impact of a decrease in Canadian demand for imports?

a. (a)

b. (b)

c. (c)

d. (d)

e. (f)

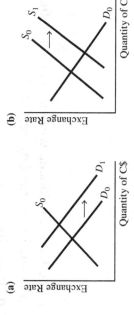
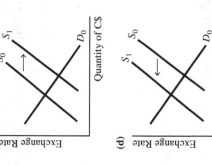
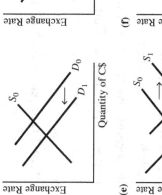
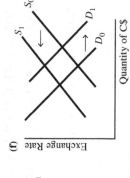
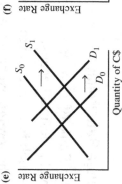

▲ **FIGURE 1**

Exchange Rate Policy

18. The Bank of Canada cannot set the exchange rate at any level it desires because

a. such intervention violates international law.

b. the foreign exchange market is unregulated.

c. doing so would make Canada a debtor nation.

d. doing so would require unlimited foreign currency reserves.

e. interest rate parity forbids it.

19. If the Bank of Canada wishes to increase the exchange rate to maintain its crawling peg, it should

a. lower interest rates.

b. increase the quantity of money.

c. buy foreign exchange.

d. sell Canadian dollars.

e. buy Canadian dollars.

Financing International Trade

20. Suppose Canada initially has all balance of payments accounts in balance (no surplus or deficit). Then Canadian firms increase imports from Japan, financing that increase by borrowing from Japan. There will now be a current account

a. surplus and a capital account surplus.

b. surplus and a capital account deficit.

c. deficit and a capital account surplus.

d. deficit and a capital account deficit.

e. deficit and a capital account balance.

21. The country of Mengia came into existence at the beginning of year 1. Given the information in Table 2, in year 4 Mengia is a

   a. net lender and a creditor nation.
   b. net lender and a debtor nation.
   c. net borrower and a creditor nation.
   d. net borrower and a debtor nation.
   e. net lender and neither a creditor nor a debtor nation.

TABLE 2

Year	Borrowed from Rest of World (billions of dollars)	Lent to Rest of World (billions of dollars)
1	60	20
2	60	40
3	60	60
4	60	80

22. Assuming that Mengia's official settlement account is always in balance, in which year or years in Table 2 did Mengia have a current account surplus?

   a. year 1
   b. year 2
   c. years 1, 2, and 3
   d. years 1 and 2
   e. year 4

23. If Mengia's official settlement balance was in deficit every year, for which year or years in Table 2 can you say for sure there was a current account surplus?

   a. year 1
   b. year 2
   c. years 2 and 3
   d. years 1 and 2
   e. years 3 and 4

24. Suppose a country's government expenditures are $400 billion, net taxes are $300 billion, saving is $300 billion, and investment is $250 billion. This country has a government budget

a. surplus and a private sector surplus.
b. surplus and a private sector deficit.
c. deficit and a private sector surplus.
d. deficit and a private sector deficit.
e. surplus and a private sector balance.

25. The distinction between a debtor or creditor nation and a net borrower or net lender nation depends on the distinction between

a. the level of saving and the saving rate.
b. the level of saving and the rate of borrowing.
c. the stock of net debt and the flow of net borrowing.
d. exports and imports.
e. nothing really; they are the same.

Short Answer Problems

1. Suppose there is an increase in demand for Canadian exports. Using the grids, illustrate and explain with a graph of the foreign exchange market what this change will do when there is a
   a. flexible exchange rate.

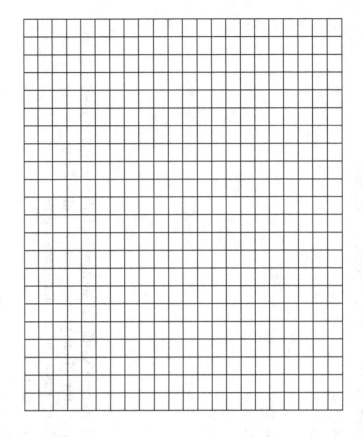

b. fixed exchange rate.

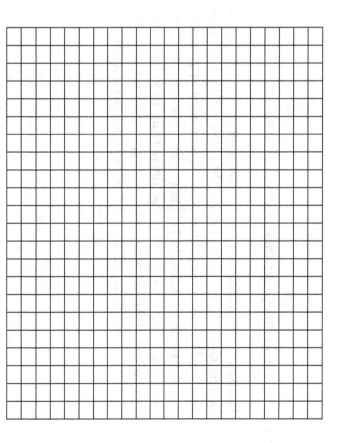

2. What determines the value of the nominal exchange rate in the short run, in a market with no government intervention?

ⓔ **3.** Consider this headline from the December 12, 1997, issue of *The Globe and Mail*: "Dollar Hits New 11-½ Year Low: Interest Rate Hike Expected After Recurrence of Asian Flu Forces Bank of Canada to Intervene." Clearly the Canadian dollar's exchange rate was decreasing in value during December 1997. Explain why an increase in interest rates by the Bank of Canada would help reverse this decrease.

ⓔ **4.** Explain how an expected increase in the exchange rate can be a self-fulfilling prophecy.

ⓔ **5.** Table 3 shows some exchange rates for the Canadian dollar.

TABLE 3	Exchange Rates		
	USD	**JPY**	**CAD**
USD	—	0.78	?
JPY	?	—	?
CAD	1.06	0.83	—

Note: USD = U.S. dollar, JPY = 100 Japanese yen, CAD = Canadian dollar.

a. Fill in the missing values in Table 3 (indicated by the question marks), showing all calculations in the space below.

b. If you were a trader, could you make money by starting with $100 Canadian, buying some USD, using your USD to buy some Japanese yen, and then use your yen to buy Canadian dollars? (Ignore minor rounding errors of 1 percent or less.)

6. Suppose that the nominal exchange rate between the Canadian dollar and the euro is 2 euros per dollar, that the price level in Canada is 122.7, and the price level in Europe is 200.5.

    a. What is the real exchange rate expressed as units of Eurozone real GDP per unit of Canadian real GDP?

    b. Does purchasing power hold?

c. If purchasing power does not hold, explain what will happen in the long run to the foreign exchange market in the long run to create purchasing power parity.

b. If there is a profit opportunity, where would you resell it if you wanted to make a profit? (Ignore any taxes, tariffs, transportation costs, and differences in quality.)

c. Does purchasing power parity hold?

7. You are trying to decide whether to buy some laptops for your business in either Canada or the United States. Looking at identical machines on the Dell Canada and the Dell U.S. websites, you find that they sell for US$750 in the United States and CAD$1,000 in Canada.

a. Where would you buy the laptop if the exchange rate between the Canadian dollar and the U.S. dollar was US$0.80 per C$?

8. The international transactions of a country for a given year are reported in Table 4.

TABLE 4	
Transaction	Amount (billions of dollars)
Exports of goods and services	100
Imports of goods and services	130
Transfers to the rest of the world	20
Loans to the rest of the world	60
Loans from the rest of the world	?
Increases in official reserves	10
Net interest income	0

a. What is the official settlements balance?

b. What is the amount of loans from the rest of the world?

c. What is the current account balance?

d. What is the capital account balance?

Answers

True/False and Explain

1. **T** Dollar is more valuable—takes more yen to buy one dollar. (594)

2. **F** Inverting $0.75 USD/CAD yields $1.33 = 1/0.75. (594)

3. **F** Automatically matched by the *supply* of foreign currency. (595)

4. **T** If $CAD is cheaper, takes less foreign currency to buy each $CAD, making our exports cheaper, increasing demand for exports, which increases quantity demanded of $CAD. (595–596)

5. **F** The expected profits lead to *increased* selling of Canadian dollars. (597)

6. **T** Increases the interest rate differential, making Canadian assets more attractive to foreigners. (599)

7. **F** Both are affected by expected future exchange rate and interest rates, so they move together. (599–601)

⊕ 8. **F** Expected appreciation implies increased earnings in foreign currency terms, which increases demand for foreign bonds, which decreases interest rates until interest rate parity holds. (602)

9. **T** Under purchasing power parity, the yen price is identical in each country. $10 × 100 yen/$ = 1,000 yen. (602)

10. **F** Expected increase in foreign exchange value of dollar implies a profit opportunity from holding dollars, which increases demand for dollars. (599–602)

11. **T** Shifts supply curve of $CAD rightward, offsetting shift in demand. (604–605)

12. **F** Will not affect it intentionally, but might unintentionally, since changes in monetary policy affect interest rates, which affect demand and supply of Canadian dollars. (604)

⊕ 13. **F** Overall flow of money in/out of country = sum of the three balances of payment must balance. Each of the three balances may be in deficit/surplus/balance. (607–609)

14. **F** May or may not be true. For net borrower, *current* net borrowing > 0. For debtor nation, sum of *all* net borrowing > 0. (609)

15. **T** Definition—note which way the money is flowing. Surplus = net $ flow in. (607–609)

Multiple-Choice

1. **e** $76 = £38 × ($2 per £). (594)

2. **a** Takes more euros to buy CAD$1 (increase in value) and less yen (decrease in value). (594)

⊕ 3. **b** 2009: 1/60 euro/yen = (2 euros/$)/(120 yen/$). 2010: 1/30 euro/yen = (3 euros/$)/(90 yen/$). Takes more euros in 2010 to buy 1 yen, so yen has appreciated. (594)

4. **b** Buyers of Canadian $ must supply foreign exchange to buy it. (595)

5. d Affects supply of Canadian $. (595–597)

6. c Expected profits effect—low Canadian $ is likely to appreciate. (596)

7. c High Canadian $ value = low foreign currency value, which is then more likely to appreciate and make a profit. (597)

8. a Imports effect. (596–597)

9. b If exchange rate is high, there is a surplus (quantity supplied > quantity demanded) and therefore downward pressure on price (exchange rate). (598)

10. c Two currencies have the same purchasing power. (602)

11. b Draw a graph. (599–601)

12. a Increased demand for foreign currency increases supply of Canadian dollars. (600)

13. c **a** has no impact on demand, **b**, **d**, and **e** shift demand leftward. (599)

14. d Therefore Canadian dollar expected to depreciate, offsetting the interest rate differential. (601–602)

15. a Greater demand for exports = greater demand for Canadian $ to buy exports. (599–602)

16. e Higher interest rate differential makes Canadian assets more desirable, increasing demand for these assets (and therefore increasing demand for Canadian $) and decreasing demand for foreign assets (and therefore decreasing demand for foreign currency = decrease in supply of Canadian currency). (602)

17. d Lower Canadian demand for imports means lower Canadian demand for foreign currency = decrease in supply of Canadian currency. (599–600)

18. d Such intervention requires buying/selling Canadian dollars, which changes foreign currency reserves, which cannot occur forever. (604–606)

19. e This increases demand for CAD. **a** decreases demand, **b–d** increase supply. (605–606)

ⓒ **20. c** Imports > exports implies current account deficit. Borrowing > lending implies capital account surplus. (Think about which direction money is flowing.) (607–609)

21. b Current lending > borrowing implies net lender. Sum of past borrowing > sum of lending implies debtor nation. (609)

22. e Official settlements balance = 0 implies current account surplus = capital account deficit, which occurs only when lending > borrowing. (607–609)

ⓒ **23. e** Since current account + capital account + official settlements account = 0, when official settlements is a deficit, to be sure current is a surplus, it must be the case that capital is 0 or a deficit. (607–609)

24. c Government sector deficit = $T - G = 300 - 400 = -100$. Private sector surplus = $S - I = 300 - 250 = +50$. (610–611)

25. c Debtor/creditor depends on stock of accumulated net debt. Borrower/lender depends on current year flow. (609)

Short Answer Problems

1. a. Under a flexible exchange rate, the government does not intervene. Therefore, the exchange rate will adjust to find the new equilibrium. An increase in demand for Canadian exports leads to an increase in demand for

The Exchange Rate and the Balance of Payments

Canadian dollars to buy those exports, shown in Fig. 2 as a rightward shift in the demand curve. The result is a new equilibrium with a higher exchange rate (ER_1) and a higher quantity of Canadian dollars exchanged ($C\$_1$) each day in the foreign exchange market.

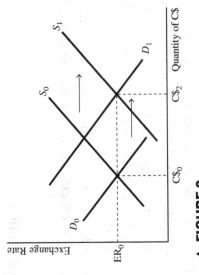

▲ **FIGURE 2**

b. Under a fixed exchange rate, the government intervenes to keep the exchange rate fixed at the target (original) value. Therefore, the exchange rate will *not* adjust to find the new equilibrium. As above, an increase in demand for Canadian exports leads to an increase in demand for Canadian dollars to buy those exports, shown in Fig. 3 as a rightward shift in the demand curve. However, now the Bank of Canada supplies Canadian dollars to match this increase (buying foreign currency), so there is also a rightward shift in the supply curve. The result is a new equilibrium with the same exchange rate (ER_0) and an even higher quantity of Canadian dollars exchanged ($C\$_2$) each day in the foreign exchange market.

2. The value of the exchange rate is determined by supply and demand. The supply of the Canadian dollar is affected by three things—changes in the Canadian interest rate differential, changes in the expected future exchange rate, and the Canadian demand for imports. The demand for the Canadian dollar is also affected by the first two factors, as well as by the world demand for Canadian exports. Finally, changes in the interest rate differential and in the expected future exchange rate are driven by purchasing power parity and interest rate parity.

3. An increase in Canadian interest rates increases the Canadian interest rate differential, which increases the desirability of Canadian assets relative to foreign assets. This increases demand for Canadian dollars by foreigners, and decreases demand for foreign exchange by Canadians, which decreases the supply of the Canadian dollar. These shifts in demand and supply increase the exchange rate.

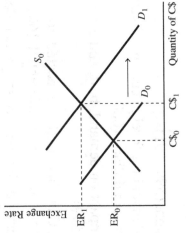

▲ **FIGURE 3**

4. If the exchange rate is expected to increase, there will be an increase in demand for Canadian dollars to try and make a profit from the increase. In addition, there will be a decrease in supply of Canadian dollars because the expected increase implies a decrease in the value of foreign currency and therefore a decrease in the demand for foreign currency, which is matched by a decrease in supply of Canadian dollars. The impact of these two changes is a shift leftward in the supply curve and a shift rightward in the demand curve for Canadian dollars, which both put upward pressure on the Canadian exchange rate!

5. a. Table 3 Solution shows the appropriate values. Values are calculated by inverting the existing values: e.g., $1.28 = 1/0.78$.

TABLE 3 Solution

	USD	JPY	CAD
USD	—	0.78	0.94
JPY	1.28	—	1.21
CAD	1.06	0.83	—

b. The columns for each currency tell us what they buy. CAD$100 will buy US$94. Going to the USD column, we can see that US$94 will buy 120 (= 94 × 1.28) hundreds of yen. Going to the JPY column, we can see that 120 hundreds of yen can buy CAD$100 (= 120 × 0.83). Therefore, there is no profit opportunity; the rates are aligned.

6. a. The real exchange rate is calculated with the formula

$$RER = E \times (P_{CAN}/P_{EURO})$$
$$= 2 \times (122.7/200.5) = 1.224$$

The real exchange rate is 1.224 units of Eurozone real GDP per unit of Canadian real GDP.

b. No, purchasing power parity does not hold. When it holds, the real exchange rate = 1. If we bought the "average" Eurozone good at 200.5 euros, this converts to CAD$100.25 (= 200.5/2), which is less than the price of the average Canadian good (122.7).

c. There is a profit opportunity to be made by moving relatively cheaper Eurozone goods from Europe to Canada. Traders carrying out this arbitrage will be buying up European goods and demanding euros to do so. The extra demand for euros will raise the value of the euro and lower the value of the Canadian dollar (lower the nominal exchange rate) to something less than 2 euros per CAD. This in turn will eventually erase the profit opportunity, as the real exchange rate converges on 1.

7. a. The Canadian laptop costs US$800 = CAD$1,000 × US$0.80 per CAD. Therefore, it is cheaper to buy from the U.S. website.

b. It is profitable to buy it in the United States for US$750 and sell it in Canada for US$800.

c. No, the two currencies do not have the same purchasing power—U.S. dollars buy more.

8. a. Because official reserves increased, the official settle-ments balance is -10.

  b. Current account balance $-$ capital account balance $+$ official settlements balance $= 0$, or $(100 - 130 - 20) - (\text{Loans from rest of world} - 60) + (-10) = 0$, so loans from rest of world $- 120$.

  c. Current account balance is a $50 billion deficit: exports $-$ imports $-$ transfers to the rest of the world $-$ net interest income to the rest of the world.

  d. Capital account balance is a surplus of $60 billion: loans from the rest of the world $-$ loans to the rest of the world.

10 Aggregate Supply and Aggregate Demand

Key Concepts
Aggregate Supply

The *AS–AD* model explains how equilibrium real GDP and the price level are determined and fluctuate.

Quantity of *real GDP supplied* depends on quantities of labour, physical and human capital, state of technology.

- At a given time, only quantity of labour can vary.
- Labour market can be at full employment, above full employment, or below full employment.
- Potential GDP is the quantity of real GDP supplied at full employment.
  - Over the business cycle, employment fluctuates around full employment, as real GDP fluctuates around potential GDP.

Two *AS* concepts: long-run (*LAS*) and short-run (*SAS*).

- **Long-run aggregate supply** (*LAS*) is relationship between quantity of real GDP supplied (*Y*) and price level when money wage rate changes in step with price (*P*) level to achieve full employment.
  - *LAS* curve is vertical at potential GDP—increase in *P* leads to equivalent percentage increase in resource prices, which means profits and real wages remain constant—no Δ employment, no Δ quantity supplied *Y*.

- *LAS* shifts rightward when potential GDP increases due to increase in full employment quantity of labour, increase in capital stock, and technological advance.

- **Short-run aggregate supply (SAS)** is relationship between quantity of real GDP supplied and price level when the money wage rate, other resource prices, and potential GDP are held constant.

  - *SAS* curve is upward sloping—increase in *P* leads to an increase in profits and employment and an increase in quantity supplied *Y*.

- *SAS* shifts along with *LAS*, but also shifts if Δ resource prices.

- Money wage changes due to expected changes in inflation and departures from full employment creating changes in labour market.

Aggregate Demand

Quantity of real GDP demanded is the total amount of final goods and services produced in Canada that economic agents plan to buy. It depends on price level, expectations, fiscal/monetary policy, and world economy.

- **Aggregate demand (AD)** is total quantity of real GDP demanded ($Y = C + I + G + X - M$) at a given price level (*P*).

- Increase in *P* decreases quantity of real GDP demanded, represented by movement up along the *AD* curve because of *wealth and substitution effects*.

- Changes in other factors shift the *AD* curve.

- If **fiscal policy** cuts taxes (which increases **disposable income**) or increases government expenditure, *AD* increases.

- If monetary policy decreases interest rates or increases quantity of money, *AD* increases.

- If exchange rate decreases or foreign income increases, *AD* increases.

- Increase in expectations of future disposable income or future inflation or future profits increases *AD*

Explaining Macroeconomic Trends and Fluctuations

There are two different types of macroeconomic equilibrium. Long-run equilibrium is the state toward which the economy is heading. Short-run equilibrium is the normal state of the economy, and occurs at each point in time along the path to long-run equilibrium.

- **Long-run macroeconomic equilibrium** occurs when real GDP = potential GDP—when $AD = SAS = LAS$.

- **Short-run macroeconomic equilibrium** occurs when real GDP demanded = real GDP supplied (where $AD = SAS$), with P adjusting to achieve equilibrium.

- Economic growth results from LAS shifting rightward on average, due to increase in labour, capital, and technology advances.

- Persistent inflation occurs when AD grows faster than LAS—quantity theory of money says money supply growth is the most likely source.

- Growth in Y is not steady, but goes in cycles because AD and SAS do not shift at the same pace.

- Over the business cycle, short-run equilibrium may occur at
  - **full-employment equilibrium**, where real GDP = potential GDP.
  - **below full-employment equilibrium**—$AD = SAS$ left of LAS; real GDP < potential GDP by amount of **recessionary gap** (= **output gap**—gap between real GDP and potential GDP).
  - **above full-employment equilibrium**—$AD = SAS$ right of LAS; real GDP > potential GDP by amount of **inflationary gap**.

- Economy fluctuates in the short run because of fluctuations in AD and SAS.

- If AD increases so Y > potential, the economy does not stay in above full-employment equilibrium—upward pressures on the money wage rate shifts SAS leftward toward long-run equilibrium.

- If resource prices increase so SAS shifts leftward and Y < potential, then **stagflation** results (inflation and falling real GDP).

Macroeconomic Schools of Thought

Economist have different views about business cycles.

- **Classical** macroeconomists believe the economy is self-regulating and always at full employment.

  - **New classical** economists believe business cycles are efficient responses of the economy to uneven technological change.

- **Keynesian** macroeconomists believe the economy is rarely at full employment and needs active monetary and fiscal policy.

  - **New Keynesian** economists agree with Keynesians that money wage is sticky *and* other prices are, too.

- **Monetarists** believe the economy is self-regulating and normally at full employment, provided monetary policy is not erratic.

Notes: _____

Helpful Hints

1. The aggregate demand and aggregate supply model introduced in this chapter (and developed throughout this book) is an insightful method of analyzing complex macroeconomic events. To sort out these complex events, it is helpful if you *always draw a graph*—even a small graph in the margin of a multiple-choice question. Graphs are powerful and effective tools for analyzing economic events.

2. When using graphs, two factors often confuse students:

   a. Sometimes graphs are based on explicit numerical or algebraic models, where the intercepts, slopes, sizes of shifts, etc., have explicit values. Often these numbers are based on real-world values, but sometimes they are just "made-up" numbers that the instructor has picked to illustrate the point (although they are still economically logical). Do *not* get caught up in the exact values of the numbers. Concentrate on the basic economic results—for example, an increase in AD leads to an increase in the price level and real GDP.

   b. One common student mistake is failing to *distinguish between a shift in a curve versus a movement along a curve.* This distinction is crucial in understanding the factors that influence AD and AS, and you can be sure that your instructor will test you on it! The slope of the AD curve reflects the impact of a change in the price level on aggregate demand. A change in the price level produces a *movement along the AD curve.* A change in one of the factors affecting the AD curve other than the price level *shifts* the entire AD curve. Similarly, a change in the price level produces a *movement along* the SAS or the LAS curve and does not lead to a shift in the curves.

3. A change in the price level will not shift the AD or the AS curves. To cement the previous point, consider Fig. 1. The initial long-run equilibrium is at the point a. (For the moment, ignore the SAS_1 curve.)

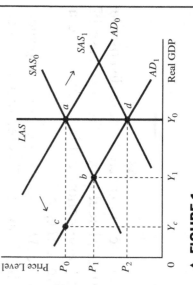

▲ **FIGURE 1**

What happens in our model when there is a decrease in expected future disposable income and profits (such as happened in the 1990–1991 recession)? This decrease in expected income and profits leads to a decrease in consumption and investment, and a decrease in aggregate demand, shown as the shift from AD_0 to AD_1.

To understand what happens next, imagine that the AD_0 and SAS_1 curves are peeled off the page (remember, we are ignoring SAS_1 for the moment). This removal leaves us with the curves SAS_0 and AD_1, and with a price level of P_0. At P_0, there is a surplus of goods and services (the quantity of real GDP supplied is Y_0 [at a], greater than the quantity of real GDP demanded of Y_c [at c]). Firms find their inventories piling up, so they cut prices and decrease production.

This decrease in price eliminates the surplus in two ways. First, as price decreases, firms supply fewer goods and services: a movement down along the SAS curve from a to b. (Be careful—the price change does *not* shift the SAS curve.) Second, the decrease in price increases the quantity demanded: a movement down along AD_1 from c to b. (Note there is no shift in the AD curve as price changes.)

The result is the new, below full-employment equilibrium at b, with a lower price level (P_1) and a lower level of real GDP (Y_1).

4. In Fig. 1, point b is a short-run, below full-employment equilibrium, but it is not a long-run equilibrium, since $Y_1 < Y_0$ (potential). There are two possible adjustments back from Y_1 to Y_0. First, the government or central bank could intervene with an expansionary fiscal or monetary policy, raising AD back to AD_0—the economy will move back to a full-employment, long-run equilibrium at a with $Y = Y_0$ (potential). Second, if the government does nothing, the unemployment at b will lead to downward pressures on the money wage rate and other resource prices (although this adjustment can be very slow). As the money wage rates decrease, the SAS curve shifts slowly rightward, eventually reaching SAS_1, with a full-employment, long-run equilibrium at d with $Y = Y_0$ (potential).

Notes:

Self-Test
True/False and Explain

Aggregate Supply

1. As the price level increases, in the long run the aggregate quantity of goods and services supplied increases.

2. Any factor that shifts the short-run aggregate supply curve rightward also shifts the long-run aggregate supply curve rightward.

3. A technological advance (other things remaining unchanged) shifts the long-run aggregate supply curve rightward, but the short-run aggregate supply curve will not shift.

4. If the wage rate decreases (other things remaining unchanged), both the long-run aggregate supply curve and the short-run aggregate supply curve shift rightward.

Aggregate Demand

5. An increase in the foreign exchange value of the dollar will increase aggregate demand in Canada.

6. An increase in the expected rate of inflation will decrease aggregate demand.

7. An increase in the quantity of money increases the quantity of real GDP demanded.

8. If the price level increases, the quantity of real GDP demanded will decrease.

Explaining Macroeconomic Trends and Fluctuations

9. A shift rightward in the aggregate demand curve increases the price level, which in turn shifts the short-run aggregate supply curve rightward in the short run.

10. If the aggregate demand curve and the short-run aggregate supply curve both shift rightward at the same time, but the aggregate demand curve shifts further rightward, the price level increases.

11. An economy is initially in short-run equilibrium and then expected future profits decrease. The new short-run equilibrium will always be a below full-employment equilibrium.

12. If the economy is in an above full-employment equilibrium, the long-run aggregate supply curve will shift rightward until the economy is at full-employment equilibrium.

13. If real GDP is higher than potential GDP, the money wage rate will rise.

Macroeconomic Schools of Thought

14. If the economy slows down, a Keynesian would argue this is the efficient response of the economy to a technological shock.

15. Under the monetarist view of the business cycle, the main cause of recessions is changes in the money supply.

Multiple-Choice

Aggregate Supply

1. A technological advance will shift
   a. both *SAS* and *AD* rightward.
   b. both *SAS* and *LAS* leftward.
   c. *SAS* rightward but leave *LAS* unchanged.
   d. *LAS* rightward but leave *SAS* unchanged.
   e. both *SAS* and *LAS* rightward.

2. An increase in the money wage rate will shift
   a. both *SAS* and *LAS* rightward.
   b. both *SAS* and *LAS* leftward.
   c. *SAS* leftward, but leave *LAS* unchanged.
   d. *LAS* rightward, but leave *SAS* unchanged.
   e. *SAS* rightward, but leave *LAS* unchanged.

3. Long-run aggregate supply will increase for all of the following reasons *except*
   a. a fall in the money wage rate.
   b. a rise in human capital.
   c. the introduction of new technology.
   d. more aggregate labour hours.
   e. more capital stock.

4. Potential GDP is the level of real GDP at which
   a. aggregate demand equals short-run aggregate supply.
   b. there is full employment.
   c. there is a recessionary gap.
   d. there is over full employment.
   e. prices are sure to increase.

5. The short-run aggregate supply curve is the relationship between the price level and the quantity of real GDP supplied, holding constant

   a. the wage rate only.
   b. the quantities of resource inputs.
   c. the level of government expenditures.
   d. the price level.
   e. the prices of resource inputs.

   a. (a)
   b. (b)
   c. (c)
   d. (d)
   e. none of the above

Aggregate Demand

6. Consider Fig. 2. Which graph illustrates what happens when resource prices decrease?

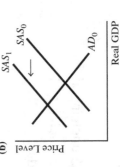

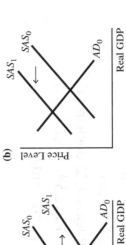

7. Consider Fig. 2. Which graph illustrates what happens when government expenditures increase?

   a. (a)
   b. (b)
   c. (c)
   d. (d)
   e. none of the above

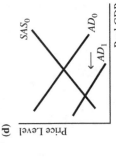

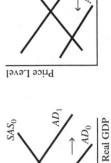

▲ FIGURE 2

8. Consider Fig. 2. Which graph illustrates what happens when the quantity of money decreases?

   a. (a)

   b. (b)

   c. (c)

   d. (d)

   e. none of the above

9. Consider Fig. 2. Which graph illustrates what happens when expected future disposable income increases?

   a. (a)

   b. (b)

   c. (c)

   d. (d)

   e. none of the above

10. Which of the following is a reason for the downward slope of the aggregate demand curve?

   a. the wealth effect

   b. the expectations effect

   c. the expected inflation effect

   d. the nominal balance effect

   e. none of the above

11. Which of the following will cause the aggregate demand curve to shift rightward?

   a. an increase in interest rates (at a given price level)

   b. an increase in expected inflation

   c. an increase in taxes

   d. a decrease in the price level

   e. an increase in the price level

Explaining Macroeconomic Trends and Fluctuations

12. Short-run macroeconomic equilibrium *always* occurs when the

   a. economy is at full employment.

   b. economy is below full employment.

   c. economy is above full employment.

   d. quantity of real GDP demanded equals the quantity of real GDP supplied.

   e. *AD* curve intersects the *LAS* curve.

13. We observe an increase in the price level and a decrease in real GDP. Which of the following is a possible explanation?

   a. The expectation of future profits has increased.

   b. The expectation of future disposable income has increased.

   c. The price of raw materials has increased.

   d. The stock of capital has increased.

   e. The money supply has increased.

14. Consider the economy represented in Table 1. In short-run macroeconomic equilibrium, the price level is _____ and the level of real GDP is _____ billion.

   a. 120; $600

   b. 120; $500

   c. 125; $550

   d. 130; $600

   e. 130; $500

TABLE 1

Price Level	Aggregate Demand (billions of 2002 $)	Short-Run Aggregate Supply (billions of 2002 $)	Long-Run Aggregate Supply (billions of 2002 $)
100	800	300	600
110	700	400	600
120	600	500	600
130	500	600	600
140	400	700	600

15. Consider the economy represented in Table 1. The economy is in a(n)

a. full-employment equilibrium and resource prices will not change.

b. above full-employment equilibrium and resource prices will increase.

c. above full-employment equilibrium and resource prices will decrease.

d. below full-employment equilibrium and resource prices will decrease.

e. below full-employment equilibrium and resource prices will increase.

16. Consider the economy represented in Table 1. There is

a. an inflationary gap equal to $100 billion.

b. an inflationary gap equal to $50 billion.

c. a recessionary gap equal to $50 billion.

d. a recessionary gap equal to $100 billion.

e. no gap; the economy is at full employment.

17. The economy cannot remain at a level of real GDP above long-run aggregate supply (LAS) because prices of productive resources will

a. decrease, shifting LAS rightward.

b. decrease, shifting SAS rightward.

c. increase, shifting LAS leftward.

d. increase, shifting SAS leftward.

e. increase, shifting SAS rightward.

18. Consider an economy starting from a position of full employment. When aggregate demand decreases, which of the following changes does not occur?

a. The price level decreases.

b. The level of real GDP decreases in the short run.

c. A recessionary gap arises.

d. Resource prices decrease in the long run, shifting the short-run aggregate supply curve rightward.

e. The long-run aggregate supply curve shifts leftward to create the new full-employment equilibrium.

19. If resource prices remain constant, an increase in aggregate demand will cause a(n)

  a. increase in the price level and an increase in real GDP.

  b. increase in the price level and a decrease in real GDP.

  c. decrease in the price level and an increase in real GDP.

  d. decrease in the price level and a decrease in real GDP.

  e. increase in the price level but no change in real GDP.

20. If real GDP is greater than potential GDP, the economy is

  a. not in short-run equilibrium.

  b. in a recessionary equilibrium.

  c. in an above full-employment equilibrium.

  d. in a below full-employment equilibrium.

  e. in full-employment equilibrium.

21. Which of the graphs in Fig. 3 illustrates a below full-employment equilibrium?

  a. (a) only

  b. (b) only

  c. (c) only

  d. (d) only

  e. both (c) and (d)

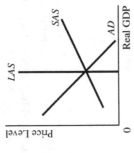
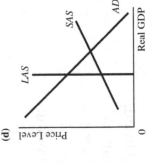
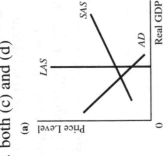
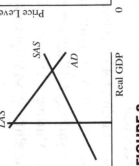

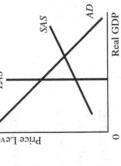

▲ **FIGURE 3**

22. Which of the graphs in Fig. 3 illustrates an above full-employment equilibrium?

    a. (a) only
    b. (b) only
    c. (c) only
    d. (d) only
    e. both (c) and (d)

23. Which one of the following newspaper quotations best describes a movement along an *SAS* curve?

    a. "The decrease in consumer spending may lead to a recession."
    b. "The increase in consumer spending is expected to lead to inflation, without any increase in real GDP."
    c. "Recent higher wage settlements are expected to cause higher inflation this year."
    d. "Growth has been unusually high the last few years due to more women entering the workforce."
    e. "The recent tornadoes destroyed many factories in Calgary and Edmonton."

Macroeconomic Schools of Thought

24. Which of the following news quotes *best* describes a *Keynesian* view of a recession?

    a. "Rapid computerization is creating obsolete workers and higher unemployment."
    b. "The unexpectedly tight fiscal policy is raising spending and lowering unemployment."
    c. "The anti-inflationary policy of the Bank of Canada is increasing spending."
    d. "The cuts in government spending have helped lower consumer spending and created unemployment."
    e. "Businesses are very worried about future sales and have lowered their purchases of capital equipment."

25. Which of the following news quotes *best* describes a *new classical* view of a recession?
   a. "Rapid computerization is creating obsolete workers and higher unemployment."
   b. "The unexpectedly tight fiscal policy is raising spending and lowering unemployment."
   c. "The anti-inflationary policy of the Bank of Canada is increasing spending."
   d. "The cuts in government spending have helped lower consumer spending and created unemployment."
   e. "Businesses are very worried about future sales and have lowered their purchases of capital equipment."

Short Answer Problems

1. The substitution effects imply that an increase in the price level will lead to a decrease in the aggregate quantity of goods and services demanded. Explain.

2. Why is the *LAS* curve vertical?

3. Why is the *SAS* curve positively sloped?

4. What are the most important factors in explaining the steady and persistent increases in the price level over time in Canada?

5. Suppose the economy is initially in full-employment equilibrium. Using the grid, graphically illustrate the short-run effects of an increase in the money wage rate. What happens to the price level and the level of real GDP?

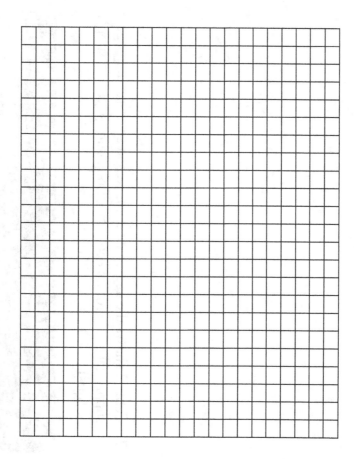

6. Consider an economy that is in above full-employment equilibrium due to an increase in *AD*. Prices of productive resources have not changed. With the help of a graph (use the grid below), discuss how the economy returns to full-employment equilibrium with no government intervention.

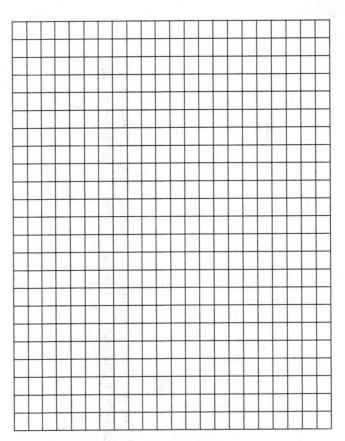

7. Table 2 shows the aggregate demand and short-run aggregate supply schedule for an economy. Long-run aggregate supply is equal to 1.1 trillion 2002 $.

TABLE 2

Price Level	Aggregate Demand (trillions of 2002 $)	Short-Run Aggregate Supply (trillions of 2002 $)
100	1.3	0.9
105	1.2	1.0
110	1.1	1.1
115	1.0	1.2
120	0.9	1.3

a. Using the grid, graph this economy's *AD*, *SAS*, and *LAS* curves, and show the original macroeconomic equilibrium. What kind of equilibrium is this—below full employment, above full employment, or full employment? If there is an inflationary or recessionary gap, identify how large it is.

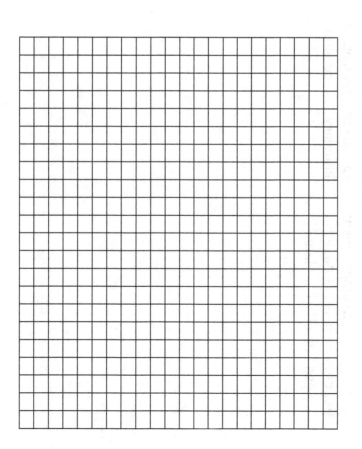

b. Next, suppose that at every price level, the quantity of real GDP demanded falls by $200 billion. Plot the new aggregate demand curve on your graph, and show the new short-run equilibrium. What kind of equilibrium is this—below full employment, above full employment, or full employment? If there is an inflationary or recessionary gap, identify how large it is.

c. Suppose that the government does not take any action and that the cause of the decrease in aggregate demand remains unchanged. What kind of adjustment occurs in the long run? Explain what happens to the price level, real GDP, AD, and AS during this adjustment, illustrating the changes on your graph.

⊛ **8.** Consider an economy for which economists have estimated that last year's real GDP was $800 billion, equal to potential GDP. The price level was 105. Suppose that this year the economists estimate that potential GDP has increased by 10 percent. However, actual real GDP has decreased by 5 percent, while the price level has also decreased by 5 percent.

Using the grid, draw an *AD–AS* graph showing last year's equilibrium, as well as last year's aggregate demand, aggregate supply (short run and long run), price level, and real GDP level. Next, given this information, show what has happened to the price level and the level of real GDP this year (show this year's equilibrium), plus what has happened to aggregate demand, short-run aggregate supply, and long-run aggregate supply since last year.

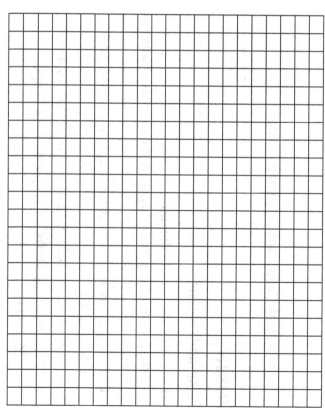

Answers

True/False and Explain

1. **F** In the long run, the money wage rates increase as well, leaving profits, real wages, and production unchanged. (624–625)

2. **F** Changes in resource prices shift only *SAS* and not *LAS*. (626–627)

3. **F** Anything that shifts *LAS* also shifts *SAS*. (626–627)

4. **F** Only the *SAS* shifts in response to a wage change. (626–627)

5. **F** Increase in the value of the dollar makes Canadian exports more expensive and imports cheaper, decreasing demand for Canadian goods. (629–632)

6. **F** If individuals expect an increased inflation rate, they will spend more today to avoid higher future prices. (629–632)

7. **T** Higher quantity of money increases spending. (629–632)

8. **T** Movement along the *AD* curve due to wealth and substitution effects. (628–629)

9. **F** Increase in *P* leads to movement along the *SAS* curve, not a shift in it. (636–637)

10. **T** Try drawing a graph. (636–637)

11. **F** Depends on where initial short-run equilibrium is relative to *LAS*, and on the size of the decrease in *AD* from the decrease in future profits—try drawing graphs. (636–637)

12. **F** *SAS* shifts, not *LAS*. (633–637)

13. **T** Unemployment is below the natural rate, which puts upward pressure on the money wage rate. (636–637)

14. **F** This is a new classical argument. (638–639)

15. **T** Monetarists believe the main source of *AD* shocks is change in money supply. (638–639)

Multiple-Choice

1. **e** Technological advances means the same inputs can produce more output, leading to an increase in quantity supplied in both the short and long run. (624–632)

2. **c** Wage rate is held constant along given *SAS*; if money wage rate increases, production is less at every price level, shifting *SAS* leftward. (626–627)

3. **a** Changes in the money wage rate change *SAS* only, not *LAS*. (626–627)

4. **b** Definition. (624)

5. **e** Short run is defined as a time period where resource prices are constant. (625)

6. **a** When resource prices decrease, firms produce more at every price level, shifting *SAS* rightward. (626–627)

7. **c** Increase in government expenditures increases aggregate spending, shifting *AD* rightward. (628–632)

8. **d** Decrease in quantity of money decreases aggregate spending, shifting *AD* leftward. (628–632)

9. **c** Increase in expected future disposable income increases household consumption, shifting *AD* rightward. (628–632)

10. **a** b and c shift AD curve, **d** doesn't exist. (628–632)

11. **b** Answers a and c cause a shift leftward; **d** and **e** are movements along the AD curve. (628–632)

12. **d** Short-run macroeconomic equilibrium always occurs where AD = SAS; equilibrium *may* occur at answers **a–c** and **e**, but doesn't *always* occur there. (636–637)

ⓣ **13.** **c** Answers **a**, **b**, and **e** increase AD, increasing real GDP, while **d** shifts LAS rightward, increasing real GDP. **c** shifts SAS leftward, increasing P and decreasing real GDP (try drawing a graph). (636–637)

14. **c** Short-run equilibrium where AD = SAS, at P = 125 and real GDP = 550—halfway between P = 120 and P = 130. (632–633)

15. **d** Real GDP = $550 billion < potential (full employment) GDP of $600 billion, so unemployed workers eventually offer to work for less. (632–637)

16. **c** Actual real GDP = $550 billion, $50 billion less than potential GDP of $600 billion. (632–633)

17. **d** Above LAS, extra demand for resources increases their prices, increasing cost of production, so SAS shifts leftward. (632–637)

18. **e** Decrease in AD creates recession, decreasing resource prices, shifting SAS rightward, pushing economy back to LAS. (636–637)

19. **a** Rightward shift in AD and movement up along the SAS curve (636–637)

20. **a** Below full-employment equilibrium occurs when AD = SAS to left of LAS. (632–633)

21. **e** Above full-employment equilibrium occurs when AD = SAS to right of LAS. (632–633)

22. **c** Equilibrium is with AD = SAS; if Y is > LAS then there is an above full-employment equilibrium. (632–633)

ⓣ **23.** **a** Decrease in consumer spending leads to shift leftward in AD, movement down SAS curve in the short run, decreasing P, and decreasing Y. (632–637)

24. **e** Expectations (animal spirits) primary cause of recession for Keynesians. (638–639)

25. **a** Fluctuations in technological advances primary cause of recession for new classicals. (638–639)

Short Answer Problems

1. There are two substitution effects. First, if the prices of domestic goods increase and foreign prices remain constant, domestic goods become relatively more expensive, so households will buy fewer domestic goods and more foreign goods. This decline in spending decreases the quantity of real GDP demanded. Thus, an increase in the price level (prices of domestic goods) decreases the aggregate quantity of (domestic) goods and services demanded.

Second, the increase in the price level increases the rate of interest, which increases saving and decreases spending. This decline in spending also decreases the quantity of real GDP demanded.

2. Long-run aggregate supply is the level of real GDP supplied when the money wage rate changes in step with the price level to achieve full employment. Since this level of real GDP equals potential GDP and is independent of the price level, the long-run aggregate supply curve is vertical. Potential GDP is the level of real GDP when resource prices freely adjust to clear resource markets.

3. The short-run aggregate supply curve is positively sloped because it holds resource prices constant. When the price level increases, firms see the prices of their output (revenues) increasing, but the prices of their input (costs) remain unchanged. With profits increasing, each firm has an incentive to increase output, and so aggregate output increases.

4. The price level increases either from an increase in aggregate demand or from a decrease in aggregate supply. Both of these forces have contributed to periods of an increasing price level. The steady and persistent increases in the price level, however, have been the result of a tendency for aggregate demand to increase faster than aggregate supply, due principally to increases in the growth rate of the quantity of money.

5. In Fig. 4, the economy is initially at point a on the SAS_0 curve. An increase in the money wage rate will shift the SAS curve leftward to SAS_1. At the new equilibrium, point b, the price level has increased and the level of real GDP has decreased.

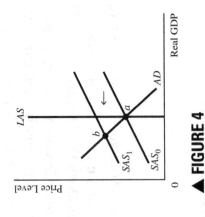

▲ **FIGURE 4**

6. In Fig. 5, the increase in AD from AD_0 to AD_1 results in above full-employment equilibrium at point b and causes the price level to increase. Since money wage rates have not changed, the real cost of labour to firms decreases, profits rise, and output is stimulated as indicated by the movement along the SAS_0 curve from point a to point b. Furthermore, the purchasing power of workers' money wage rates decreases.

   Workers eventually demand higher money wage rates and firms will be willing to pay them. Similarly, other prices of productive resources will increase. This increase in prices of productive resources shifts the SAS curve leftward, resulting in a new equilibrium. There will continue to be pressure for money wage rates and other prices of productive resources to increase until the SAS curve shifts all the way to SAS_1, where the purchasing power of the money wage rates and other prices of productive resources has been restored and the economy is again at full employment, point c.

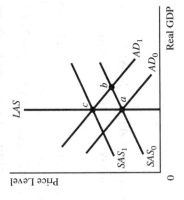

▲ **FIGURE 5**

Answers   **297**

prices, shifting the SAS curve rightward to SAS_1, raising aggregate supply, lowering prices even more, and leading to a new long-run equilibrium where SAS_1 crosses AD_1 and LAS where the price level is 100 and real GDP is back at potential GDP ($1.1 trillion).

8. Fig. 7 shows the original full-employment equilibrium, at last year's equilibrium price level of 105 and income level of 800.

For the current year, the LAS curve has shifted rightward to LAS_1, a value of 880, and the SAS curve shifts with it to SAS_1, all else equal. The new short-run equilibrium must be along the intersection of SAS_1 and an AD curve. Since prices are 5 percent lower at 100, and real GDP is 5 percent lower at 760, the new AD curve must have shifted leftward as shown.

(*Hint:* To decide where AD_1 should be, first find the intersection of $P = 100$ and $Y = 760$ on the new SAS curve, then draw in the AD curve to go through this point.)

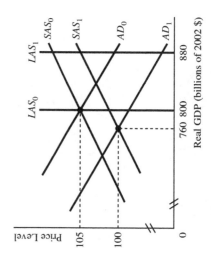

▲ **FIGURE 7**

7. a. The economy's AD_0, SAS_0, and LAS curves are graphed in Fig. 6 (ignore the AD_1 and SAS_1 curves for now). The macroeconomic equilibrium occurs where the AD and SAS curves cross, at a price level of 110 and real GDP of 1.1 trillion 2002 $. Since this level of real GDP equals potential GDP, this economy is in a full-employment equilibrium with no type of gap.

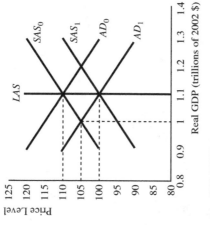

▲ **FIGURE 6**

b. This decrease in aggregate demand leads to a new short-run equilibrium where the new AD_1 crosses SAS_0, at a price level of 105 and real GDP of 1 trillion 2002 $. Since real GDP is less than potential GDP, the economy is in a below full-employment equilibrium and there is a recessionary gap (or output gap) equal to the difference between real GDP and potential GDP. The gap is $100 billion.

c. Since real GDP is below potential GDP, unemployment is above the natural rate. Eventually unemployed resources start offering to work for lower resource

11 Expenditure Multipliers: The Keynesian Model

Key Concepts

Fixed Prices and Expenditure Plans

In the very short term, price level is fixed—aggregate demand determines aggregate quantity sold.

- To understand AD, we study the aggregate expenditure model.

- **Aggregate planned expenditure** (AE) = planned consumption (C) + planned investment (I) + planned government expenditures (G) + planned exports (X) − planned imports (M) = real GDP (Y).

- C, M depend on real GDP (Y), so that increases in Y increase AE, and increases in AE increase Y.

Consumption and saving depend primarily on **disposable income** (YD) = real GDP − taxes + transfer payments.

- **Consumption function** shows the relationship between disposable income and consumption—increase in YD leads to increase in C.

- **Saving function** shows the relationship between disposable income and saving—increase in YD leads to increase in S, with $\Delta C + \Delta S = \Delta YD$.

- **Marginal propensity to consume** (MPC) = fraction of ΔYD that is consumed = $\Delta C/\Delta YD$ = slope of consumption function.

- **Marginal propensity to save** (*MPS*) = fraction of ΔYD that is saved = $\Delta S/\Delta YD$ = slope of saving function.
  - $MPC + MPS = 1$.

Influences other than ΔYD *shift* the functions.

- Increase in *expected future disposable income* or decrease in *real interest rate* or increase in *wealth* shifts S function downward, C function upward.
- Consumption and saving are a function of real GDP, since increase in real GDP increases YD.

Import function relates imports and real GDP.

- **Marginal propensity to import** is fraction of ΔY spent on imports = $\Delta M/\Delta Y$.

Real GDP with a Fixed Price Level

Components of aggregate expenditure interact to determine Y, and AE is influenced by Y.

- AE can be represented by a graph or schedule. Increase in Y leads to increase in AE.
- Aggregate planned expenditure has two parts:
  - **Autonomous expenditure** (A) = $I + G + EX$ = part of AE that does *not* vary with income.
  - **Induced expenditure** (N) = $C - I$ = part of AE that *does* vary with income.
- Actual aggregate expenditure may not equal planned expenditure if level of real GDP is not consistent with plans.
- **Equilibrium expenditure** is the level of aggregate expenditure when AE = real GDP.
  - On a graph, where AE curve crosses 45° line.
  - If real GDP is above equilibrium value, AE < real GDP. Firms cannot sell all their production, increasing unplanned inventories. Firms lower production, leading to a decrease in real GDP and convergence to equilibrium.
  - If real GDP is below equilibrium value, AE > real GDP. Firms sell all production and more, leading to unplanned decrease in inventories. Firms increase production to restore inventories, leading to increase in real GDP and convergence to equilibrium.

Notes:

The Multiplier

The **multiplier** is the amount by which change in autonomous expenditure is multiplied to determine change in equilibrium expenditure and real GDP.

- Increase in autonomous expenditure increases real GDP, leading to a further (secondary) increase in aggregate planned expenditure, leading to further increases in real GDP, etc.

- Secondary, *induced* effects means total Δ real GDP > initial Δ autonomous expenditure.

- Multiplier = (Δ real GDP)/(Δ autonomous expenditure) = 1/(1 − slope of AE function).

  - Multiplier > 1 because of induced effects.

  - Higher slope of AE function implies larger induced effects and larger multiplier.

  - Multiplier is higher if *MPC* is higher, or marginal tax rate is lower, or marginal propensity to import is lower.

- Recessions and depressions begin with expenditure fluctuations magnified by the multiplier effect.

The Multiplier and the Price Level

Aggregate demand curve shows the relationship between real GDP demanded and the price level, other things remaining the same, and can be derived from AE curve.

- Increase in price level shifts AE curve downward (due to wealth and substitution effects), lowers equilibrium real GDP, and is shown by movement up and to left on AD curve.

- Δ non-price variables (autonomous expenditures) shift both AE and AD curves.

- In the short run, an increase in AE leads to a shift rightward in the AD curve, increasing the price level, which lowers AE somewhat, offsetting the increase in Y somewhat, so multiplier is smaller.

- In the long run, vertical LAS means there is a large enough increase in the price level to cause a decrease in AE that totally offsets the initial increase, so multiplier = 0.

Helpful Hints

1. The 45° line is important for understanding the consumption function and the expenditure function. It is a *reference line* on a graph, showing the points where the two variables on the axes of the graph have the same value.

    Consider the graph of consumption and disposable income in Fig. 1. Along the 45° line, consumption equals disposable income at all points. For example, at point a, $C = YD = \$300$ billion.

    Consider point b. Consumption is still equal to $\$300$ billion, but now disposable income is only $\$200$ billion. To the left of the 45° line, variables measured on the vertical axis (here, consumption) are greater than variables measured on the horizontal axis (here, disposable income).

    Next, consider point c. Consumption is still equal to $\$300$ billion, but now disposable income is $\$400$ billion. To the right of the 45° line, variables measured on the vertical axis are less than variables measured on the horizontal axis.

    To summarize, consider the consumption function (CF) shown in Fig. 2. Using the 45° line as our reference, any point on the consumption function to the left of the 45°

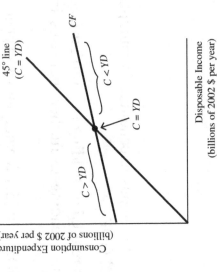

▲ **FIGURE 1**

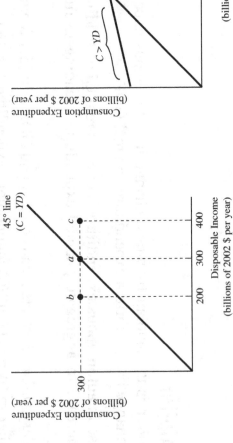

▲ **FIGURE 2**

line has consumption greater than disposable income (and therefore saving [= YD − C] is negative). Any point on the consumption function to the right of the 45° line has consumption less than disposable income (and saving is positive).

To make sure you understand, draw the graph of the aggregate expenditure function, with a 45° line, and identify the points on your graph where aggregate expenditure is greater than income, equal to income, or less than income. *Note:* For the consumption function, the 45° line is a pure reference line—it is possible in equilibrium for consumption to be greater than, less than, or equal to disposable income. However, for the aggregate expenditure function, the point on the 45° line where *AE* = *Y* is more than just a reference point; it shows the point of *equilibrium expenditure*.

2. Aggregate demand is the relationship between the price level and the quantity of goods and services demanded; in other words, it is the relationship between the price level and the level of planned aggregate expenditure. One purpose of this chapter is to help you understand planned aggregate expenditure by separating and examining its individual components. In particular, we examine consumption expenditure, investment, and net exports—the three components of private aggregate expenditure. As you put the discussion of this chapter and the next in perspective, remember that the ultimate objective is a more complete understanding of aggregate demand (and what shifts it), which combines these expenditure components with government expenditure on goods and services. This understanding of the components will help you in later chapters to understand the potential causes of past and future recessions.

Be sure you can distinguish the *AD* curve from the *AE* curve—they are based on different thought experiments. Each *AE* curve holds constant the price level, and represents only a single point on an *AD* curve. The *AD* curve allows the price level to vary. Changing the price level will shift the *AE* curve, but create a movement along the *AD* curve.

3. This chapter distinguishes between *autonomous* expenditure and *induced* expenditure. Autonomous expenditure is independent of changes in real GDP, whereas induced expenditure will vary as real GDP varies. In general, a change in autonomous expenditures creates a

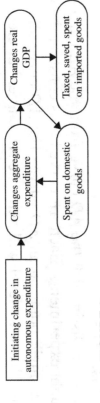

▲ **FIGURE 3**

change in real GDP, which in turn creates a change in induced expenditure. As the flow graph in Fig. 3 illustrates, these changes are at the heart of the multiplier effect.

(Even though autonomous expenditure may be independent of changes in real GDP, it will not be independent of changes in other variables—for example, the price level.)

Self-Test

True/False and Explain

Fixed Prices and Expenditure Plans

1. The sum of the marginal propensity to consume and the marginal propensity to save equals 1.

2. A change in disposable income will shift the consumption function.

3. An increase in expected future disposable income will shift both the consumption and saving functions upward.

4. Net taxes increase as real GDP increases.

Real GDP with a Fixed Price Level

5. When aggregate planned expenditure exceeds real GDP, inventories will increase more than planned.

6. Equilibrium expenditure occurs when aggregate planned expenditure equals real GDP.

7. Induced expenditure is that part of aggregate expenditure that varies as real GDP varies.

8. The aggregate expenditure schedule lists the level of aggregate planned expenditure that is generated at each level of real GDP.

The Multiplier

9. If the slope of the *AE* function is 0.75, the multiplier is equal to 3.

10. If the marginal tax rate increases, the multiplier will be higher.

11. If the marginal propensity to import decreases, the multiplier will be higher.

The Multiplier and the Price Level

12. An increase in the price level shifts the aggregate expenditure curve upward.

13. An increase in autonomous expenditure always increases equilibrium real GDP in the short run.

14. An increase in autonomous expenditure always increases equilibrium real GDP in the long run.

15. The higher the marginal propensity to consume, the higher the multiplier in the long run.

Multiple-Choice

Fixed Prices and Expenditure Plans

1. The fraction of the last dollar of disposable income saved is the

  a. marginal propensity to consume.
  b. marginal propensity to save.
  c. marginal propensity to dispose.
  d. marginal tax rate.
  e. saving function.

2. Consider Table 1. Autonomous consumption is equal to

  a. $0.
  b. $65.
  c. $100.
  d. $260.
  e. $400.

TABLE 1

Disposable Income (2002 $)	Consumption Expenditure (2002 $)
0	100
100	165
200	230
300	295
400	360

3. Consider Table 1. The marginal propensity to consume is

  a. 0.35.
  b. 0.65.
  c. 1.15.
  d. 1.65.
  e. not calculable with the information given.

4. In Table 1 on the previous page, at which of the following level(s) of *YD* is there positive saving?

a. 0

b. 100

c. 200

d. 300

e. all of the above levels

5. Which of the following events would shift the consumption function upward?

a. increase in disposable income

b. decrease in disposable income

c. decrease in the real interest rate

d. decrease in expected future disposable income

e. increase in wealth

Real GDP with a Fixed Price Level

6. The aggregate expenditure curve shows the relationship between aggregate planned expenditure and

a. disposable income.

b. real GDP.

c. the interest rate.

d. consumption expenditure.

e. the price level.

7. If there is an unplanned increase in inventories, aggregate planned expenditure is

a. greater than real GDP and firms will increase output.

b. greater than real GDP and firms will decrease output.

c. less than real GDP and firms will increase output.

d. less than real GDP and firms will decrease output.

e. less than real GDP and firms will decrease investment.

8. If $AE = 50 + 0.6Y$ and $Y = 200$, unplanned inventory

  a. increases are 75.

  b. increases are 30.

  c. decreases are 75.

  d. decreases are 30.

  e. changes are 0 and equilibrium exists.

9. Autonomous expenditure is *not* influenced by

  a. the interest rate.

  b. the foreign exchange rate.

  c. real GDP.

  d. the price level.

  e. any variable.

10. In Fig. 4, the marginal propensity to consume is

  a. 0.3.

  b. 0.6.

  c. 0.9.

  d. 1.0.

  e. none of the above.

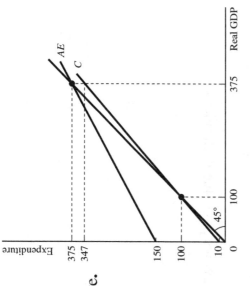

Note: There are no taxes in this economy.

▲ FIGURE 4

11. In Fig. 4, *autonomous* aggregate expenditure is

  a. 10.

  b. 100.

  c. 150.

  d. 347.

  e. 375.

12. In Fig. 4 on the previous page, *equilibrium* expenditure is

a. 10.

b. 100.

c. 150.

d. 347.

e. 375.

13. In Fig. 4 on the previous page, at the equilibrium level of real GDP, *induced* expenditure is

a. 28.

b. 150.

c. 225.

d. 347.

e. 375.

14. In Fig. 4 on the previous page, the marginal propensity to import is

a. 0.

b. 0.1.

c. 0.25.

d. 0.3.

e. 0.6.

The Multiplier

15. In Fig. 4 on the previous page, the multiplier is

a. 0.25.

b. 1.

c. 1.60.

d. 2.50.

e. 10.

16. An increase in expected future disposable income leads to a(n)

a. increase in consumption and a decrease in aggregate expenditure.

b. increase in both consumption and aggregate expenditure.

c. decrease in both consumption and aggregate expenditure.

d. decrease in consumption and an increase in aggregate expenditure.

e. increase in consumption and either an increase or a decrease in aggregate expenditure, depending on what happens to saving.

17. Which of the following quotations illustrates the idea of the multiplier?

a. "The new stadium will generate $200 million in spinoff spending."

b. "Higher expected profits are leading to higher investment spending by business and will lead to higher consumer spending."

c. "The projected cuts in government jobs will hurt the local retail industry."

d. "Taking the grain elevator out of our small town will destroy all the jobs."

e. All of the above

18. The value of the multiplier increases with a(n)

a. increase in the marginal propensity to import.

b. increase in the marginal tax rate.

c. decrease in the marginal propensity to consume.

d. decrease in the marginal propensity to save.

e. increase in the marginal propensity to save.

19. If the slope of the *AE* curve is 0.75, what is the value of the multiplier?

a. 0.25

b. 0.75

c. 1.33

d. 2.50

e. 4.0

The Multiplier and the Price Level

20. An increase in the price level will
  a. shift the *AE* curve upward and increase equilibrium expenditure.
  b. shift the *AE* curve upward and decrease equilibrium expenditure.
  c. shift the *AE* curve downward and increase equilibrium expenditure.
  d. shift the *AE* curve downward and decrease equilibrium expenditure.
  e. have no impact on the *AE* curve.

21. A decrease in the price level will
  a. increase aggregate expenditure and thus produce a movement along the aggregate demand curve.
  b. increase aggregate expenditure and thus produce a rightward shift in the aggregate demand curve.
  c. increase aggregate expenditure and thus produce a leftward shift in the aggregate demand curve.
  d. have no effect on aggregate expenditure.
  e. increase aggregate expenditure but produce no effect on the aggregate demand curve.

22. Suppose that investment increases by $10 billion. If the multiplier is 2, the *AD* curve will
  a. shift rightward by the horizontal distance of $20 billion.
  b. shift rightward by a horizontal distance greater than $20 billion.
  c. shift rightward by a horizontal distance less than $20 billion.
  d. not be affected.
  e. shift upward by a vertical distance equal to $20 billion.

23. Suppose the multiplier is 2 and the short-run aggregate supply curve is positively sloped. If investment increases by $10 billion, equilibrium real GDP will
  a. increase by $20 billion.
  b. increase by more than $20 billion.
  c. decrease by less than $20 billion.
  d. be unaffected.
  e. increase by less than $20 billion.

24. Suppose the multiplier is 2 and investment increases by $10 billion. Starting at potential GDP, in the long run equilibrium real GDP will

a. increase by $20 billion.

b. increase by more than $20 billion.

c. decrease by less than $20 billion.

d. be unaffected.

e. increase by less than $20 billion.

25. What will happen in the short run to real GDP and prices if exports increase?

a. The *AE* curve will shift rightward by an amount determined by the size of the multiplier, and the increase in real GDP will be the same size.

b. The *AE* curve will shift leftward by an amount determined by the size of the multiplier, and the decrease in real GDP will be the same size.

c. The *AE* curve will shift rightward by an amount determined by the size of the multiplier, and the increase in real GDP will be larger.

d. The *AE* curve will shift rightward by an amount determined by the size of the multiplier, and the increase in real GDP will be smaller.

e. The *AE* curve will shift rightward by an amount determined by the size of the multiplier, and the increase in real GDP will be 0.

Short Answer Problems

1. Explain how studying the circular flow in Chapters 20 and 23 helps us to understand the multiplier process of Chapter 27.

2. Suppose aggregate planned expenditure is greater than real GDP. Explain how equilibrium expenditure is achieved.

3. Define and explain autonomous expenditure, induced expenditure, and what role each plays in the multiplier process.

4. Explain (without algebraic expressions) why the multiplier is larger if the marginal propensity to consume is higher.

5. Explain how the effects of price level changes on the *AE* curve will generate an *AD* curve.

TABLE 2

Disposable Income (2002 $)	Consumption Expenditure (2002 $)	Saving (2002 $)
0	3,000	
3,000	5,250	
6,000	7,500	
9,000	9,750	
12,000	12,000	
15,000	14,250	

6. Table 2 illustrates the consumption function for a very small economy.

a. Compute the economy's saving at each level of disposable income by completing Table 2.

b. Compute the economy's *MPC* and *MPS*.

7. Consider an economy with the following components of aggregate expenditure:

- Consumption function: $C = 20 + 0.8Y$
- Investment function: $I = 30$
- Government expenditures: $G = 8$
- Export function: $X = 4$
- Import function: $M = 2 + 0.2Y$

(There are no taxes, so $YD = Y$.)

a. What is the marginal propensity to consume in this economy?

b. What is the equation of the aggregate expenditure function in this economy?

c. From the information given and computed, draw on the grid a graph for the economy's consumption function and a graph for the economy's saving function.

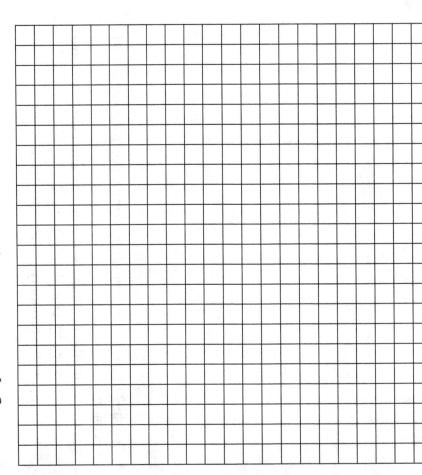

c. Find this economy's equilibrium aggregate expenditure and real GDP by completing the columns of Table 3.

TABLE 3

Y	C	I	G	X	M	AE
0						
30						
60						
90						
120						
150						
180						

8. Explain carefully what an increase in expected future disposable income will do to the consumption function, the saving function, the aggregate expenditure curve, and the aggregate demand curve.

Answers

True/False and Explain

1. **T** Last dollar of *YD* is either spent or saved. (650)

2. **F** Change in *YD* leads to movement along consumption function. (648–651)

3. **F** Shifts upward consumption function—more consumption expenditure at each level of current *YD*, but given constant current *YD*, this increase in consumption means less saving. (650–651)

4. **T** Due to induced income taxes. (651)

5. **F** *AE* > real GDP creates excess sales, leading to falling inventories. (654–655)

6. **T** Definition. (654–655)

7. **T** Definition. (653)

8. **T** Definition. (653)

9. **F** Multiplier = 1/(1 − slope of *AE* function) = 1/(1 − 0.75) = 1/0.25 = 4. (658)

ⓒ 10. **F** Higher marginal tax rate lowers slope of *AE* curve and size of multiplier. (658–659)

11. **T** Lower marginal propensity to import increases slope of *AE* curve and size of multiplier. (658–661)

12. **F** Increase in price level lowers *AE* through wealth and substitution effects. (661–663)

13. **T** Increase in *AE* shifts *AD* curve rightward, movement along *SAS* in short run with an increase in real GDP. (663–665)

14. **F** Same initial effect as for **13**, but if start at potential GDP, given vertical *LAS* curve, there is no increase in real GDP. (663–665)

15. **F** In long run, multiplier is zero due to vertical *LAS* curve. (663–665)

Multiple-Choice

1. **b** Definition. (650)

2. **c** Level of consumption when disposable income is zero. (648)

3. **b** $MPC = \Delta C/\Delta YD = (165 − 100)/(100 − 0) = 0.65$. (650)

4. **d** $YD > C$. Also true at $YD = 400$. (648–651)

5. **e** **a** and **b** are movements along curve, **c** and **d** shift it downward. (650–651)

6. **b** Definition. (653)

ⓒ 7. **d** Increase in inventories means *AE* < real GDP. Firms' sales decrease, so they decrease production in response. (654–655)

ⓒ 8. **b** $Y = 200$ implies $AE = 50 + 0.6(200) = 170$. Unplanned inventories $= Y − AE = +30$. (654–655)

9. **c** Definition. (653)

10. **c** MPC = slope of consumption function = $\Delta C/\Delta Y = 90/100 = 0.9$. (650)

11. c Intercept of *AE* function. (653)

12. e Where *AE* curve crosses 45° line. (654–655)

13. c Induced = aggregate – autonomous = 375 – 150 = 225. (654–655)

Ⓖ 14. d Marginal propensity to import = MPC – slope of AE curve = 0.9 – 0.6 = 0.3, where slope of AE curve = $\Delta AE/\Delta Y$ = 225/375 = 0.6. (653–655)

15. d Multiplier = 1/(1 – slope of AE function) = 1/(1 – 0.6) = 1/0.4 = 2.5. (658)

16. b Increase in expected future disposable income leads to more consumption spending, less saving, and an increase in autonomous expenditure. (650–657)

17. e All of the choices discuss secondary, induced effects. (656–657)

Ⓖ 18. d This change raises the MPC and multiplier. Others lower the multiplier. (657–659)

19. e Multiplier = 1/(1 – slope of AE function) = 1/(1 – 0.75) = 1/0.25 = 4.0. (658)

20. d Increase in price level decreases aggregate expenditure due to wealth and substitution effects. New equilibrium at lower real GDP = equilibrium expenditure. (661–663)

21. a Decrease in price level increases aggregate expenditure due to three effects, leading to movement along the AD curve. (661–663)

22. a Multiplier effect raises AE and Y by 2 times original Δ autonomous expenditure, which leads to a shift rightward by the same amount in the AD curve. (661–663)

23. e Multiplier effect of Question 22 is reduced by the increase in price level due to positively sloped SAS curve. (661–663)

24. d Vertical LAS curve means that there is no increase in real GDP after shift rightward in AD. (661–663)

25. d More autonomous expenditure, AD shifts rightward, but positive slope to SAS means price level increases and reduces the size of the increase in real GDP. (662–663)

Short Answer Problems

1. The circular flow shows us that firms produce goods and services, sell them to consumers, investors, governments, and the rest of the world, and use the money earned to pay factors of production, who in turn buy goods and services. The circular flow thus shows us the secondary, induced effects of the multiplier process in action. An initial increase in autonomous expenditure increases sales for firms, increasing household income, increasing consumption expenditure, etc.

2. If aggregate planned expenditure is greater than real GDP, inventories decrease more than planned, and firms increase output to replenish those depleted inventories. As a result, real GDP increases. This continues as long as real GDP is less than aggregate planned expenditure. It will stop only when equilibrium is attained—when real GDP equals aggregate planned expenditure.

3. Autonomous expenditure is the part of aggregate expenditure that does not vary with real GDP, but varies as a result of changes in other variables such as the real

interest rate. Induced expenditure is the part of aggregate expenditure that varies with real GDP. The multiplier process starts out with a change in autonomous expenditure, that changes aggregate expenditure, which in turn changes real GDP. This change in real GDP creates secondary effects by changing induced expenditure in the same direction, which in turn changes aggregate expenditure and real GDP, leading to a total effect that is a multiple of the initial change in autonomous expenditure.

4. Any initial stimulus to autonomous expenditure generates a direct increase in real GDP. The basic idea of the multiplier is that this initial increase in real GDP generates further increases in real GDP as increases in consumption expenditure are induced. At each round of the multiplier process, the increase in spending, and thus the further increase in real GDP, are partially determined by the marginal propensity to consume. A larger marginal propensity to consume means a larger increase in real GDP at each round, so the total increase in real GDP will be greater. Thus the multiplier will be larger if the marginal propensity to consume is larger.

5. The aggregate demand curve illustrates the relationship between the price level and aggregate expenditures. The aggregate expenditure diagram shows the level of equilibrium expenditure holding the price level constant. If the price level changes, the *AE* curve shifts resulting in a new level of equilibrium expenditure. Thus, for each price level, there is a different level of equilibrium expenditure. These combinations of price level and corresponding aggregate expenditure are points on the aggregate demand curve. For example, if the price level

increases, autonomous expenditure will decline and the *AE* curve shifts downward. This shift decreases equilibrium expenditure. Since an increase in the price level is associated with a reduction in equilibrium expenditure, the *AD* curve is negatively sloped.

6. **a.** The answers to **a** are shown in Table 2 Solution, where saving = *YD* − *C*.

TABLE 2 Solution

Disposable Income (2002 $)	Consumption Expenditure (2002 $)	Saving (2002 $)
0	3,000	−3,000
3,000	5,250	−2,250
6,000	7,500	−1,500
9,000	9,750	−750
12,000	12,000	0
15,000	14,250	+750

b. The *MPC* = (Δ consumption)/(Δ disposable income). Using the first two entries in Table 2 Solution, we can see that change in consumption is 2,250, and the change in disposable income is 3,000, so that the *MPC* = 0.75 = 2,250/3,000.

The *MPS* = (Δ saving)/(Δ disposable income). Using the first two entries in Table 2 Solution, we can see that Δ saving is +750, and Δ disposable income is 3,000, so that the *MPS* = 0.25 = 750/3,000. Using any other two adjacent entries in Table 2 Solution will yield the same result.

b. Substitute the various equations into:

$$AE = C + I + G + X - M,$$
$$AE = 20 + 0.8Y + 30 + 8 + 4 - 2 - 0.2Y,$$
$$AE = 60 + 0.6Y.$$

c. The answer is presented in Table 3 Solution below. The table is constructed by substituting the various values of Y into the equations. Note that equilibrium occurs when $AE = Y$ at a value of 150.

TABLE 3   Solution

Y	C	I	G	X	M	AE
0	20	30	8	4	2	60
30	44	30	8	4	8	78
60	68	30	8	4	14	96
90	92	30	8	4	20	114
120	116	30	8	4	26	132
150	140	30	8	4	32	150
180	164	30	8	4	38	168

8. An increase in expected future disposable income leads to less saving (so that the saving function shifts downward at each level of disposable income) and more consumption out of current disposable income (so that the consumption function shifts upward). This is an increase in autonomous consumption, and also an increase in aggregate expenditure, leading to a shift upward in the aggregate expenditure function. This shift creates multiplier effects and a shift rightward in the aggregate demand curve at the current price level.

c. The consumption function is shown in Fig. 5, and the saving function is illustrated in Fig. 6.

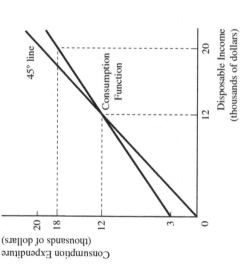

▲ FIGURE 5

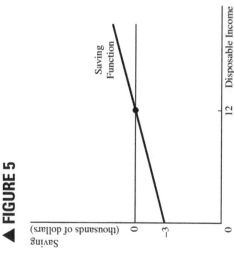

▲ FIGURE 6

7. a. From the consumption function equation we know this value is $0.8 = \Delta C/\Delta Y$.

12 Canadian Inflation, Unemployment, and Business Cycle

Key Concepts
Inflation Cycles

Inflation is caused by two sources in the short run.

Demand-pull inflation arises from increasing aggregate demand due to tax cuts or increases in quantity of money, government expenditures, exports, or investment.

- Short-run result is increased P (inflation), increased Y, and decreased unemployment to below natural rate.

- Unemployment less than the natural rate creates a labour shortage, increasing wages and costs. *SAS* shifts leftward, price level increases even more, but real GDP falls back to original level.

- If *AD* shifts rightward again, and wages increase again, a *demand-pull inflation spiral* may result.

- Persistent inflation requires persistent increases in the quantity of money.

Cost-push inflation arises from increases in costs (increases in money wage rates and money prices of raw materials).

- *SAS* shifts leftward, firms decrease production, creating **stagflation** (increased price level, decreased real GDP).

- If the government or the Bank of Canada shifts *AD* rightward in response, price level increases again, so that input owners raise input prices again, and a *cost-push inflation spiral* may result.

- If there is no government or Bank response—economy remains with high unemployment in the short run.

If inflation is expected, then money wages adjust to keep up with anticipated inflation, Δ price level only, no Δ real GDP or employment.

- Expected inflation creates actual inflation.

- To anticipate inflation, people must forecast it.

- People forecast inflation in different ways, including hiring specialists.

- Best possible forecast on basis of all available relevant information is a **rational expectation.**

Inflation and Unemployment: The Phillips Curve

The **Phillips curve** shows the relationship between inflation and unemployment.

- **Short-run Phillips curve** (*SRPC*) shows the relationship between inflation and unemployment for a given expected inflation rate and natural rate of unemployment. It is negatively sloped.

- In the short run, if actual inflation > expected, then movement up and leftward along *SRPC*.

- **Long-run Phillips curve** (*LRPC*) shows the relationship between inflation and unemployment when actual inflation = expected. It is vertical at the natural rate of unemployment.

- Decrease in expected inflation rate shifts *SRPC* downward.

- Increase in natural rate of unemployment shifts both *LRPC* and *SRPC* rightward.

Notes:

The Business Cycle

Two approaches to understanding the business cycle.

Mainstream theory states potential GDP grows steadily, but aggregate demand grows at fluctuating rate and causes cycles.

- If money wage rate is sticky and if aggregate demand grows faster than potential GDP, inflationary gap results.

- If aggregate demand grows slower than potential GDP, recessionary gap results.

Four mainstream theories with different sources of aggregate demand shocks and money wage stickiness:

- **Keynesian cycle theory**—fluctuations in business confidence create fluctuations in investment and aggregate demand; money wage assumed sticky.

- **Monetarist cycle theory**—fluctuations in investment and consumption driven by fluctuations in money growth create fluctuations in aggregate demand; money wage assumed sticky.

- **New classical cycle theory**—unexpected fluctuations in aggregate demand come from incorrect expectations; money wage sticky due to incorrect expectations.

- **New Keynesian cycle theory**—unexpected fluctuations in aggregate demand come from incorrect expectations due to the fact that money wages were negotiated over several past dates.

Real business cycle (RBC) theory regards random fluctuations in productivity (due to Δ pace of technological change) as main source of the cycle.

- RBC recession starts with technological change that makes existing capital obsolete—temporary decrease in productivity.

- Fall in productivity decreases demand for labour and capital (which decreases real rate of interest).

- Decreasing real rate of interest decreases labour supply (intertemporal substitution effect), leading to a small decrease in the real wage rate and a large decrease in employment—recession begins.

Critics of RBC theory argue that instead money wages are sticky, intertemporal substitution is weak, and technological shocks are *caused by AD* fluctuations.

- Defenders of RBC theory reply that it is consistent with facts (explains both growth *and* cycles) and microeconomic theory.

Notes:

Helpful Hints

1. An important concept introduced in this chapter is that of a *rational expectation*—the best possible forecast on the basis of all available relevant information. For example, in your textbook, when this concept is applied to the price level, the *actual* price level occurs in the short run at the intersection of the AD curve and the SAS curve, and in the long run at the intersection of the AD curve and the LAS curve. When AD is expected to increase to AD_1, the best (most likely to be correct) *forecast* of the new price level is at the intersection of AD_1 and LAS, yielding a wage demand leading to SAS_1.

   Note that the rational expectation of the price level will be at the intersection of the *expected* aggregate demand curve and the *expected short-run* aggregate supply curve in the short run, and the *expected long-run* aggregate supply curve in the long run. The *actual* equilibrium, which determines the *actual* price level, is at the intersection of the *actual* aggregate demand curve and the *actual short-run* aggregate supply curve.

2. This chapter contains competing theories for explaining real-world events. There is no dispute over the facts such as the level of prices or real GDP. The dispute centres on what changes in the economy created the facts, and what government policies might affect the economy.

   To help you remember and understand these theories, use Table 1. It highlights the similarities and differences between the theories, and how radically different real business cycle theory is.

   Theories differ based on two primary factors: the source of the cycle (AD versus AS) and the responsiveness of the labour market (sticky versus flexible wages). Be sure you can catalogue and understand these theories.

   Remember, these are theories, *not* statements of facts, and their explanations could be incorrect. Only proper empirical investigation over time will cast light on their validity.

TABLE 1 Business Cycle Theories

Labour Market Structure	Theory	Primary Source of the Cycle
Wages are sticky, U above natural rate	Keynesian	Investment (*AD* shocks)
	Monetarist	Investment, consumption, growth rate of money (*AD* shocks)
	New classical	Unexpected fluctuations in *AD*
	New Keynesian	Unexpected *and* expected fluctuations in *AD*
Wages are flexible, U = natural rate always	Real business cycle	Productivity (*AS*) shocks

Notes:

Self-Test
True/False and Explain

Inflation Cycles

1. If people expect aggregate demand to increase but it does not, the price level will increase and real GDP will decrease.

2. Increases in government expenditures alone can create persistent inflation.

3. An increase in exports cannot create demand-pull inflation.

4. Inflation resulting from expansionary monetary policy is an example of cost-push inflation.

5. Stagflation occurs when real GDP decreases and the price level increases.

6. If an increase in aggregate demand is correctly anticipated, inflation will not occur.

7. A rational expectation is a forecast that is always correct.

Inflation and Unemployment: The Phillips Curve

8. The short-run Phillips curve shows that if there is an increase in the inflation rate, unemployment will decrease.

9. The long-run Phillips curve shows a tradeoff between inflation and unemployment.

10. If there is an increase in the expected rate of inflation, the long-run Phillips curve shifts rightward.

11. If there is a decrease in the natural rate of unemployment, only the long-run Phillips curve shifts.

The Business Cycle

12. Unanticipated decreases in aggregate demand cause recessions only in new Keynesian theory, not in new classical theory.

13. A decrease in aggregate demand will cause a recession in Keynesian theory.

14. Real business cycle theorists believe that wages are flexible and adjust quickly.

15. In real business cycle theory, most fluctuations in real GDP are the best possible responses of the economy to the uneven pace of technological change.

Multiple-Choice

Inflation Cycles

1. Which one of the following is a cause of demand-pull inflation?
   a. a sharp increase in the price of oil
   b. higher wages negotiated by unions
   c. an increase in exports
   d. a decrease in the money supply
   e. a decrease in exports

2. Demand-pull inflation occurs when
   a. aggregate demand increases.
   b. aggregate supply decreases.
   c. input costs increase.
   d. people incorrectly forecast inflation.
   e. unemployment is above the natural rate.

3. Which of the following would cause the aggregate demand curve to keep shifting rightward year after year?
   a. a one-time tax cut
   b. a one-time increase in government expenditures on goods and services
   c. inflation
   d. continuous excess wage demands
   e. a positive rate of money growth

4. An increase in the price level due to an increase in the price of oil
   a. will create stagflation in the short run and *will* trigger a cost-push inflation spiral.
   b. will create stagflation in the short run and *may* trigger a cost-push inflation spiral.
   c. will raise output above potential GDP.
   d. must lead to an increase in the wage rate.
   e. must lead to a decrease in the wage rate.

5. Fig. 1 illustrates an economy initially in equilibrium at point *a*. What would cause the short-run aggregate supply curve to shift from SAS_0 to SAS_1?

a. increase in the price of oil

b. increase in the price level

c. increase in the marginal product of labour

d. increase in the demand for money

e. decrease in wages

6. If the AD curve in Fig. 1 is correctly expected to shift from AD_0 to AD_1, what will be the new equilibrium real GDP (Y) and price level (P)?

a. $Y = \$380$ billion, $P = 125$

b. $Y = \$500$ billion, $P = 150$

c. $Y = \$500$ billion, $P = 100$

d. $Y = \$620$ billion, $P = 125$

e. $Y = \$500$ billion, $P = 125$

7. If the AD curve in Fig. 1 is expected to shift from AD_0 to AD_1, but, in fact, remains at AD_0, what will be the new equilibrium real GDP (Y) and price level (P)?

a. $Y = \$380$ billion, $P = 100$

b. $Y = \$500$ billion, $P = 150$

c. $Y = \$500$ billion, $P = 100$

d. $Y = \$620$ billion, $P = 125$

e. $Y = \$380$ billion, $P = 125$

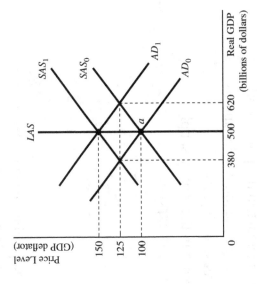

▲ **FIGURE 1**

8. If the *AD* curve in Fig. 1 is expected to remain at AD_0 but, in fact, shifts to AD_1, what will be the new equilibrium real GDP (*Y*) and price level (*P*)?

a. $Y = \$380$ billion, $P = 125$

b. $Y = \$500$ billion, $P = 150$

c. $Y = \$500$ billion, $P = 100$

d. $Y = \$620$ billion, $P = 125$

e. $Y = \$500$ billion, $P = 125$

9. Which of the following is *not* true of a rational expectation forecast?

a. It uses all available information.

b. It can be wrong.

c. It is always correct.

d. It is the best possible forecast.

e. Sometimes economic agents purchase their forecasts from specialists.

10. Stagflation results directly from a shift of the aggregate

a. demand curve leftward.

b. demand curve rightward.

c. supply curve leftward.

d. supply curve rightward.

e. demand curve rightward, followed by a shift leftward in the aggregate supply curve.

Inflation and Unemployment: The Phillips Curve

11. The short-run Phillips curve shows the relationship between

a. the price level and real GDP in the short run.

b. the price level and unemployment in the short run.

c. unemployment and real GDP in the short run.

d. inflation and unemployment, when inflation expectations can change.

e. inflation and unemployment, when inflation expectations do not change.

12. Figure 2 illustrates an economy's Phillips curves. What is the natural rate of unemployment?

a. 9 percent

b. 6 percent

c. 4 percent

d. depends on the actual inflation rate

e. cannot be determined without more information

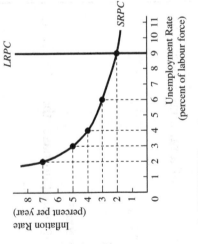

▲ FIGURE 2

13. Fig. 2 illustrates an economy's Phillips curves. What is the expected inflation rate?

a. 9 percent

b. 4 percent

c. 2 percent

d. depends on the actual inflation rate

e. cannot be determined without more information

14. Fig. 2 illustrates an economy's Phillips curves. If the current inflation rate is 4 percent, what is the current unemployment rate?

a. 9 percent

b. 6 percent

c. 4 percent

d. 3 percent

e. cannot be determined without more information

15. If the inflation rate is lower than the expected inflation rate,

a. unemployment will be above the natural rate.

b. the natural rate of unemployment will increase.

c. the expected inflation rate will increase.

d. unemployment will be below the natural rate.

e. the economy must off the *SRPC*.

16. If there is a fully anticipated increase in the inflation rate,
    a. unemployment will be below the natural rate.
    b. unemployment will be above the natural rate.
    c. the natural rate of unemployment will increase.
    d. the economy must be off the *LRPC*.
    e. the economy must be on the *LRPC*.

The Business Cycle

17. Which of the following news quotes *best* describes a *new Keynesian* view of a recession?
    a. "Rapid computerization is creating obsolete workers and higher unemployment."
    b. "The unexpectedly tight fiscal policy is raising spending and lowering unemployment."
    c. "The promised anti-inflationary policy of the Bank of Canada is increasing spending."
    d. "The promised cuts in government spending have helped lower consumer spending and created unemployment."
    e. "Businesses are very worried about future sales and have lowered their purchases of capital equipment."

18. Which of the following news quotes *best* describes a *new classical* view of a recession?
    a. "Rapid computerization is creating obsolete workers and higher unemployment."
    b. "The unexpectedly tight fiscal policy is lowering spending and creating unemployment."
    c. "The promised anti-inflationary policy of the Bank of Canada is lowering spending as promised."
    d. "The promised cuts in government spending have helped lower consumer spending and created unemployment."
    e. "Businesses are very worried about future sales and have lowered their purchases of capital equipment."

19. What is the key impulse in the Keynesian theory of the business cycle?

a. changes in expected future sales and profits

b. changes in the quantity of money

c. unanticipated changes in aggregate demand

d. anticipated changes in aggregate demand

e. changes in the pace of technological change

20. An increase in aggregate demand causes real GDP to increase by the least amount in the

a. Keynesian theory.

b. monetarist theory.

c. new Keynesian theory.

d. new classical theory.

e. real business cycle theory.

21. If the intertemporal substitution effect is weak, then RBC theory will have problems explaining

a. a large decrease in employment in a recession.

b. how a recession begins.

c. why aggregate demand decreases in a recession.

d. the automatic adjustment to full employment.

e. what creates technological change.

22. The intertemporal substitution effect states that

a. in a recession, investment is low and the capital stock increases slowly, leading to a rising marginal product of capital.

b. money wages are based on a rational expectation of the price level.

c. a decrease in productivity leads to a decrease in the demand for capital, and a decrease in the real interest rate.

d. when current real wages and real interest rates are high, people decrease their labour supply strongly.

e. when current real wages and real interest rates are high, people increase their labour supply strongly.

23. According to the real business cycle theorists, increased unemployment rate during a recession is due to an increase in the

  a. deviation of the unemployment rate from the natural rate, resulting from a real wage rate that is too high to clear the labour market.

  b. deviation of the unemployment rate from the natural rate, resulting from increased job market turnover.

  c. natural rate of unemployment resulting from a real wage that is too high to clear the labour market.

  d. natural rate of unemployment resulting from increased job market turnover.

  e. rate of new entries into the labour market.

24. Which of the following news quotes *best* describes a *real business cycle* view of a recession?

  a. "Rapid computerization is creating obsolete workers and higher unemployment."

  b. "The unexpectedly tight fiscal policy is lowering spending and creating unemployment."

  c. "The promised anti-inflationary policy of the Bank of Canada is lowering spending as promised."

  d. "The promised cuts in government spending have helped lower consumer spending and created unemployment."

  e. "Businesses are very worried about future sales and have lowered their purchases of capital equipment."

25. According to real business cycle theory, if the Bank of Canada increases the money supply when real GDP declines, real GDP

  a. will increase, but only temporarily.

  b. will increase permanently.

  c. and the price level will both be unaffected.

  d. will be unaffected, but the price level will increase.

  e. will decrease due to the inefficiencies introduced into production as a result.

Short Answer Problems

1. What happens to the price level and real GDP if the government increases expenditures on goods and services and that increase is not anticipated (the price level is not expected to change)?

2. Explain how the events in Short Answer Problem **1** might lead to a demand-pull inflation spiral.

3. List the four important features of the Canadian economy that make severe depression less likely today.

4. Explain the differences between the short-run Phillips curve and the long-run Phillips curve.

5. Sometimes politicians or other commentators say: "Unemployment is a more serious economic and social problem than inflation. Increasing inflation by a small amount in order to lower unemployment is therefore worthwhile." Briefly evaluate this statement.

6. Why does inflation start? Why does it persist?

7. Table 2 gives data for a hypothetical economy in years 1 and 2.

TABLE 2	Year 1	Year 2
Real GDP (billions of dollars)	800	750
Price level (GDP deflator)	100	105

a. If the real business cycle theory is true, what happened to aggregate demand and aggregate supply in this economy?

b. If the new Keynesian theory is true, what happened to aggregate demand and aggregate supply in this economy?

8. Consider the labour market in the economy from Short Answer Problem **7**.

a. If the real business cycle theory is true, what happened in the labour market? Is the overall unemployment natural or not?

b. If the new Keynesian theory is true, what happened in the labour market? Is the overall unemployment natural or not?

Answers

True/False and Explain

⊕ 1. **T** If expected increase in aggregate demand, it increases wage demands, leading to leftward shift in *SAS* curve, but no Δ*AD* curve, resulting in stagflation. (682)

2. **F** Persistent inflation requires persistent increases in quantity of money. (678–679)

3. **F** Increase in exports shift *AD* rightward, which can create demand-pull inflation. (678–679)

4. **F** Cost-push inflation is due to an increase in input costs. (678–679)

5. **T** Definition. (680–681)

6. **F** *AD* shifts rightward, *SAS* shifts leftward due to higher wage demands, so price level increases. (682)

7. **F** Correct on *average*. (683)

8. **T** Movement up and leftward along the *SRPC*. (684–686)

9. **F** Vertical at the natural rate of unemployment. (684–686)

10. **F** Movement upward along the *LRPC*. (684–686)

11. **F** Both *SRPC* and *LRPC* shift when the natural rate shifts. (684–686)

12. **F** In both theories, unanticipated decrease means wages are set too high, creating unemployment and recession. (687)

13. **T** Due to sticky money wages, *SAS* curve does not adjust quickly. (687)

14. **T** See text discussion. (688–691)

15. **T** See text discussion. (688–691)

Multiple-Choice

1. **c** Increase in demand. (678–679)

2. **a** Definition. (678–679)

3. **e** **a** and **b** have one-time effects, **c** caused by Δ*AD*, and **d** is supply-side effect. (678–679)

4. **b** Increase in price of oil leads to leftward shift in *SAS* curve, creating cost-push inflation (stagflation), which *may* trigger a cost-push inflation spiral if government raises aggregate demand. (680–681)

5. **a** Increase in price of crucial input leads to increase in costs of production and leftward shift of *SAS*. (680–681)

6. **b** Expected *P* at intersection of *LAS* and expected *AD* = *AD*$_1$, and actual new *SAS* is set here, and new equilibrium is where actual *AD* and new *SAS* cross. (682–683)

⊕ 7. **e** Expected *P* at intersection of expected *AD* = *AD*$_1$, and actual new *SAS* is set here, and new equilibrium is where actual *AD* and new *SAS* cross. (682–683)

⊕ 8. **d** Expected *P* at intersection of *LAS* and expected *AD* = *AD*$_1$, and actual new *SAS* is set here, and new equilibrium is where actual *AD* and new *SAS* cross. (682–683)

9. **c** Correct on *average.* (682–683)

10. **c** Definition. (680–681)

11. **e** Definition. (684)

12. **a** *LRPC* is at natural rate. (685)

13. **c** Expected inflation rate is where *SRPC* crosses *LRPC.* (685)

14. **c** Found by reading off the *SRPC.* (684–685)

15. **a** Draw a Phillips curve. (684–685)

16. **e** Economy just moves up *LRPC.* (684–685)

17. **b** One of the key impulses in new Keynesian theory is unexpected change in *AD.* (687)

18. **b** Key impulse in new classical theory is unexpected change in *AD.* (687)

19. **a** See text discussion. (687)

20. **e** Vertical *AS* curve. (687–691)

21. **a** Intertemporal substitution means Δ current real wage or real interest rate leads to big Δ labour supply. (687–691)

22. **e** Definition. (687–691)

23. **d** All unemployment is natural, and real wage rate is always correct. (687–691)

24. **a** Key impulse is Δ pace of technological change. (687–691)

25. **d** Because *LAS* is vertical. (687–691)

Short Answer Problems

1. An increase in government expenditures on goods and services shifts the aggregate demand curve rightward. If the price level is not expected to change, the short-run aggregate supply curve remains unchanged, and the increase in aggregate demand causes the price level to increase and real GDP to increase.

2. The higher price level leads to demands for higher wages, which push up the costs of production and shift the *SAS* curve leftward, leading to a further increase in the price level and a decrease in real GDP. A demand-pull inflation spiral could result *if* the government once again raises the level of their purchases or if the government continues to run a deficit (financed by printing money). *AD* will then continue to shift rightward, triggering leftward shifts in *SAS,* leading to the demand-pull inflation spiral.

3. The four important features of the Canadian economy that make severe depression less likely today are (1) bank deposits are insured; (2) the Bank of Canada is prepared to be the "lender of last resort"; (3) taxes and government spending play a stabilizing role; and (4) multi-income families are more economically secure.

4. The short-run Phillips curve assumes that the expected inflation rate is constant, and is therefore downward sloping. Therefore, an increase in the inflation rate (and therefore a decrease in real wages), will create a decrease in unemployment to a rate below the natural rate. The long-run Phillips curve is constructed assuming that the

expected inflation rate adjusts fully to reflect changes in the actual inflation rate, and is therefore vertical at the natural rate of unemployment. If there is an increase in the actual inflation rate, there is an equivalent increase in the expected inflation rate (so that the real wage rate stays constant), and the rate of unemployment stays constant at the natural rate.

5. Partially this statement is a value judgment, based on the tradeoff of a higher cost to society from the higher inflation versus the gain to society from a lower inflation rate. In this case, we would need to evaluate the costs of inflation vis-à-vis the costs of unemployment. However, there is also an objective (positive) problem with this statement. In the short run, such a tradeoff does exist, represented by the downward-sloping short-run Phillips curve. In the long run, there is no such tradeoff. As a result, a higher inflation rate leads to a lower unemployment rate in the short run, but eventually inflation expectations will increase, shifting upward the short-run Phillips curve, and unemployment returns to the natural rate. Therefore, in the long run, increasing inflation will have no impact on the unemployment rate, but will increase the costs to society that come from the higher inflation.

6. Inflation is an increase in the price level, and starts with either a shift rightward in the AD curve due to increases in the quantity of money, government spending, or exports (demand-pull inflation), or with a shift leftward in the SAS curve due to increases in wages or raw materials prices (cost-push inflation). However, the increase in the price level in either case can only persist if an inflation spiral results from the initial shock. A demand-pull or cost-push inflation spiral starts when increases in aggregate demand and shifts leftward in SAS chase each other up the long-run aggregate supply curve.

7. a. Since real GDP has decreased, the LAS curve must have shifted leftward, since the only AS curve is a vertical LAS in an RBC world. For the price level to have increased, it must be the case that either the AD curve increased, or decreased so little that in combination with the LAS curve shift the price level has increased.

b. In order to get both the price level rising and real GDP decreasing, it must be that the SAS curve shifted leftward by more than the shift rightward in the AD curve (if there was one), indicating that people anticipated an increase in AD (leading to an increase in wages and a shift leftward in the SAS), but the actual increase was less than anticipated.

8. a. A real business cycle recession starts with a temporary decrease in productivity, which leads to a decrease in the demand for investment, and a shift leftward in the AD curve. In addition, there is a decrease in the demand for labour because of the decrease in productivity, and a shift leftward in the supply of labour because of the lower real interest rate. These two shifts lead to a decrease in employment and

a shift leftward in the *LAS* curve. All unemployment is natural.

b. In the new Keynesian labour market, money wages are based on wrong expectations, so that real wages are too high since the increase in money wages is more than the increase in the price level. Labour supply is greater than labour demand, creating the unemployment. All the extra unemployment is cyclical, not natural.

13 Fiscal Policy

Key Concepts
The Federal Budget

The **federal budget** is an annual statement of revenue and outlays of the government of Canada (provincial budget is for provincial governments).

- Budgets finance government activities and achieve macroeconomic policy objectives (**fiscal policy**).

- Fiscal policy is made by government and Parliament, in consultation with bureaucrats, provincial governments, and business and consumer groups.

- Budgetary revenues—personal income taxes, corporate income taxes, indirect taxes (GST and HST), investment income.

- Budgetary outlays—transfer payments, expenditures on goods and services, debt interest payments.

- Budget balance = revenues − outlays
  - **Budget surplus** when revenues > outlays.
  - **Budget deficit** when revenues < outlays.
  - **Balanced budget** when revenues = outlays.

- **Government debt** = total borrowing by governments = sum of past deficits − sum of past surpluses.

- Persistent deficits of the 1980s increased borrowing, which increased interest payments and increased deficit, etc.

- Balanced budget of 1997 stopped this cycle—government debt is falling.

- Provincial government outlays are almost as large as federal; focused on hospitals, schools, and colleges/universities.

- Canada's current budget deficit is in the middle of the pack compared to other industrial nations.

Supply-Side Effects of Fiscal Policy

Fiscal policy may have supply-side effects on employment, potential GDP, and aggregate supply.

- Higher income taxes decrease incentives to work by creating a **tax wedge** (difference between before-tax wage rate and after-tax wage rate), decreasing labour supply and potential GDP.

- Taxes on consumption increase the wedge by increasing consumption prices, effectively lowering the real wage rate and labour supply.

- Taxes on interest income weaken incentives to save, reduce quantity of saving (quantity supplied of loanable funds), and therefore reduce investment and growth rate of real GDP.

- Since nominal interest rate is taxed, extra strong impact of tax on real *after-tax* interest rate.

- **Laffer curve** is the relationship between the tax rate and tax revenue collected. Claims high tax rate may collect less taxes than a lower tax rate due to negative incentives.

- Most economists note incentive effects of tax cuts, but believe tax cuts will reduce tax revenues and potentially increase budget deficits.

Fiscal Stimulus

Fiscal stimulus is the use of fiscal policy to increase production and employment, and can be **discretionary** (initiated by Parliament, involves changing government outlays, taxes) or **automatic** (triggered by state of economy).

- If real GDP decreases, tax revenues decrease and transfer payments increase—this *automatically* provides stimulus that shrinks a recessionary gap.
- If real GDP increases, tax revenues increase and transfer payments decrease—this *automatically* provides restraint that shrinks an inflationary gap.

Budget deficits fluctuate with business cycle due to cyclical fluctuations in net taxes, providing automatic stimulus and restraint.

- **Structural surplus or deficit** is budget balance when the economy is at full employment.
- **Cyclical surplus or deficit** = actual balance − structural balance.
- Cyclical surplus or deficit is due only to the fact that real GDP ≠ potential.
- Currently, Canada has a cyclical deficit *and* a structural deficit.

Discretionary fiscal policy works to affect *AD*, both directly and via multiplier effects.

- **Government expenditure multiplier** = quantified effect of a change in government expenditures on real GDP.
- Initial increase in *G* increases real GDP, which leads to secondary, induced effects.
- **Tax multiplier** = quantified effect of change in autonomous taxes on real GDP.
- Increase in *T* decreases *YD*, decreases *C*, and decreases real GDP, leading to secondary, induced effects.
- Increases in *G* or cuts in *T* increase government borrowing, raise interest rates, which cuts investment, partially offsetting the initial effect.

If real GDP < potential GDP, discretionary fiscal policy can be used to restore full employment.

- Increases in G, decreases in T increase aggregate expenditure and shift the AD curve rightward.
- Multiplier effect shifts the AD curve even further right, movement along the SAS curve in short run toward full-employment equilibrium.
- Reducing government expenditures or increasing taxes reduces aggregate expenditure, shifts AD leftward, reducing an inflationary gap.
- Tax cuts may work better due to reinforcing supply-side effects.

Discretionary fiscal policy is limited by

- recognition lag—recognizing fiscal policy is needed.
- law-making lag—slowness of the legislative process.
- impact lag—time it takes policy to have an impact.

Notes:

Helpful Hints

1. It is crucial to distinguish between two types of autonomous shocks. One type adds to the instability of the economy; it includes changes in autonomous consumption, investment, and exports. The other is planned to (hopefully) reduce the instability of the economy; it includes fiscal policy—changes in government expenditures and taxes. Because the two shocks work through the same multiplier process, the same process that creates instability can also help to reduce instability.

2. The size of the fiscal policy multipliers depends on the sizes of the *MPC*, the marginal tax rate, and the marginal propensity to import. Fig. 1 shows why. A crucial part of the multiplier process is the change in induced expenditure in the second round of the multiplier. These induced expenditures are reduced as income is siphoned off for saving, to pay for taxes, or to buy imported goods!

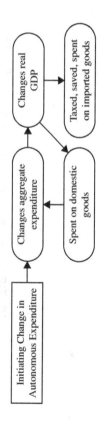

▲ **FIGURE 1**

Self-Test

True/False and Explain

The Federal Budget

1. The federal deficit is the total amount of borrowing the federal government has undertaken.

2. Only government expenditures on goods and services, not transfer payments, are crucial in analysing the federal deficit.

3. A government starts with a balanced budget. In the next year, if the percentage growth in outlays is higher than the percentage growth in revenues, the government will have a deficit.

4. Government investment income is an example of a budgetary outlay.

5. The federal government had budget deficits from 1997 to 2008.

Supply-Side Effects of Fiscal Policy

6. Cutting income taxes will shift the *AD* curve rightward, but will reduce potential GDP.

Fiscal Stimulus

10. An increase in autonomous transfer payments matched by an increase in autonomous taxes will increase real GDP by the size of the increase in transfer payments.

11. Taxes and transfer payments that vary with income automatically reduce fluctuations in real GDP.

12. If real GDP increases, so do tax revenues.

7. An increase in taxes on interest income will decrease potential GDP growth.

8. The Laffer curve claims that a cut in the tax rate always increases tax revenue.

9. If the nominal interest rate is 10 percent, the tax rate is 5 percent, and the inflation rate is 4 percent, then the real after-tax interest rate is 1 percent.

13. If an economy has a structural deficit, the budget balance at potential GDP is negative.

14. A cut in tax rates will increase equilibrium real GDP in the short run.

15. An increase in government expenditures shifts the *AD* curve rightward.

Multiple-Choice

The Federal Budget

1. Provincial government outlays

   a. are small and irrelevant to the economy.

   b. are an important source of fiscal policy.

   c. are always equal to provincial government revenues.

   d. are focused on transfer payments to individuals, such as employment insurance.

   e. tend to fluctuate with federal outlays.

2. Which of the following would *not* increase the budget deficit?

   a. an increase in interest on the government debt

   b. an increase in government expenditures on goods and services

   c. an increase in government transfer payments

   d. an increase in indirect business taxes

   e. a decrease in government investment income

3. The budget deficit grew as a percentage of GDP after 1974 because

   a. government expenditures on goods and services rose, while tax revenues remained constant.

   b. government expenditures on goods and services remained constant, while tax revenues fell.

   c. transfer payments rose, while tax revenues remained constant.

   d. debt interest payments rose, while tax revenues fell.

   e. none of the above.

4. Which of the following groups does *not* influence federal fiscal policy?

   a. government bureaucrats

   b. provincial governments

   c. Parliament

   d. business and consumer groups

   e. government unions

5. Which of the following is a budgetary outlay?

   a. personal income taxes

   b. government investment income

   c. debt interest payments

   d. indirect taxes

   e. corporate income taxes

6. The government of Ricardia's budget lists the following projected collections and spending: $25 million in personal income taxes, $15 million in corporate income taxes, $5 million in indirect taxes, $2 million in investment income, $30 million in transfer payments, $12 million in government expenditures, and $8 million in debt interest. Ricardia has a government budget

   a. surplus of $3 million.

   b. surplus of $57 million.

   c. surplus of $13 million.

   d. deficit of $13 million.

   e. deficit of $3 million.

7. The largest source of revenues for the federal government is

   a. transfer payments.

   b. expenditures on goods and services.

   c. personal income taxes.

   d. corporate income taxes.

   e. indirect taxes such as the GST.

8. Compared to the other major industrial economies, in recent years Canada

   a. is one of the heaviest borrowers.

   b. is the only one of these economies running a surplus.

   c. is the only one of these economies running a deficit.

   d. is the only economy with provincial/state governments that play a significant role.

   e. is in the middle of the pack for deficit levels.

Supply-Side Effects of Fiscal Policy

9. Which of the following quotations correctly refers to the effects of fiscal policy in the *long run?*

  a. "The increase in taxes will increase real GDP."
  b. "The increase in taxes will raise prices only."
  c. "A change in the budget has no impact on real GDP unless it changes aggregate supply."
  d. "A change in the budget has no impact on real GDP."
  e. "An increase in government expenditures on goods and services will increase real GDP."

10. Which of the following quotations correctly refers to the effects of fiscal policy in the *short run?*

  a. "The increase in taxes will increase real GDP."
  b. "The increase in taxes will raise prices only."
  c. "A change in the budget has no impact on real GDP unless it changes aggregate supply."
  d. "A change in the budget has no impact on real GDP."
  e. "The increase in government expenditures on goods and services will increase real GDP."

11. If the nominal interest rate is 11 percent, the inflation rate is 4 percent and the tax rate is 25 percent, what is the real after-tax interest rate?

  a. −1.25 percent
  b. 4.25 percent
  c. 5.25 percent
  d. 8 percent
  e. 10 percent

12. An increase in the tax rate on interest income will lead to

  a. less saving, more spending, and more economic growth.
  b. less saving, less investment, and lower economic growth.
  c. more saving, more investment, and higher economic growth.
  d. a strong intertemporal substitution effect, leading to more labour supplied.
  e. higher real after-tax interest rates.

13. Which of the following is *not* a problem created for an economy by a higher tax wedge?

   a. It lowers after-tax real interest rates.
   b. It raises before-tax wage rates and lowers employment.
   c. Potential GDP decreases.
   d. Saving decreases.
   e. The government's deficit rises.

14. Which of the following would lower potential GDP?

   a. increased tax rate on interest income
   b. increased tax rate on consumption spending
   c. increased tax rate on labour income
   d. all of the above
   e. only **a** and **c**

15. The Laffer curve has been criticized by mainstream economists because

   a. there is no theoretical possibility of higher tax rates leading to lower tax revenues.
   b. higher tax rates do not create negative incentive effects.
   c. tax cuts are just spent, not saved as predicted by the theory.
   d. savers look only at real interest rates, not nominal interest rates.
   e. empirically, tax cuts have not led to higher tax revenues.

Fiscal Stimulus

16. Suppose that the tax multiplier is −2. If taxes decrease by $4 billion and incentives to work and save are affected, in the long run real GDP will

   a. decrease by $8 billion.
   b. increase by $8 billion.
   c. be unaffected.
   d. increase, but by how much is unclear.
   e. decrease, but by how much is unclear.

17. Short-run fiscal policy is limited by the fact that

    a. the *LAS* curve is vertical.

    b. the legislative process is slow.

    c. real GDP is typically not equal to potential GDP.

    d. the policy might shift the *SAS* curve to the right.

    e. the policy might shift the *SAS* curve to the left.

18. Which of the following is an example of a fiscal policy designed to counter a recessionary gap?

    a. increasing debt interest payments

    b. increasing taxes

    c. decreasing transfer payments

    d. increasing transfer payments

    e. decreasing government expenditures on goods and services

19. During an expansion, tax revenue

    a. and government outlays decline.

    b. declines and government outlays increase.

    c. increases and government outlays decline.

    d. and government outlays increase.

    e. stays constant and government outlays increase.

20. Which of the following happens *automatically* if the economy goes into a recession?

    a. Only government outlays increase.

    b. Only net taxes increase.

    c. The deficit increases.

    d. The deficit decreases.

    e. Both government outlays and net taxes increase, and the deficit stays the same.

21. Which of the following policies will *not* shift the *AD* curve rightward?

  a. increasing government expenditures on goods and services

  b. decreasing autonomous taxes

  c. increasing autonomous transfer payments

  d. increasing government expenditures on goods and services *and* increasing autonomous taxes by the same amount

  e. decreasing government expenditures on goods and services *and* decreasing autonomous taxes by the same amount

22. Consider the economy of NoTax, where the multiplier is 2.5. If the government desires to shift the *AD* curve rightward by $5 billion, the correct increase in government expenditures is

  a. $2 billion.

  b. $2.5 billion.

  c. $3 billion.

  d. $7.5 billion.

  e. $8.33 billion.

23. If supply-side effects are strong, which of the following statements is true?

  a. The government expenditure multiplier is likely stronger than the tax multiplier.

  b. The tax multiplier is likely stronger than the government expenditure multiplier.

  c. Both the government expenditure and the tax multiplier are zero.

  d. Both the government expenditure and the tax multiplier are equally strong.

  e. Fiscal policy affects aggregate demand more than it affects aggregate supply.

24. A cyclical deficit is when

  a. government outlays are greater than revenues.

  b. government outlays are less than revenues.

  c. there is a deficit due to the fact that real GDP is greater than potential GDP.

  d. there is a deficit due to the fact that real GDP is less than potential GDP.

  e. there is a deficit even when real GDP equals potential GDP.

25. The country of Ricardia has a budget plan with constant government outlays equal to $100 billion and taxes related positively to real GDP by the equation: Taxes = $25 billion + 0.1$Y$. If the structural deficit is $10 billion, what is potential GDP in this economy?

a. $65 billion

b. $75 billion

c. $650 billion

d. $750 billion

e. $850 billion

Short Answer Problems

1. What changes in the components of the federal government budget after 1974 were the principal causes of continuing large government deficits?

2. During the summer of 1995, Saskatchewan had a provincial election. A central plank of the Saskatchewan Liberal Party's election strategy was a promise to cut taxes dramatically, stating that these cuts would create 50,000 new jobs (about 10 percent of the labour force) over the next five years. Critics claimed that this policy would have only a small effect in Saskatchewan, that most of the new jobs from the tax cuts would show up in other provinces.

a. What economic concept underlies the Liberals' promise?

b. What economic concept underlies the critics' argument?

c. The Liberals lost the election, so we did not see if the tax cuts would have had the promised effect. What do you think would have happened?

3. Suppose you are visiting the town of Elbow, Saskatchewan, which is suffering a depressed economy due to low wheat prices. You spend $100 on accommodation and another $100 golfing and dining at the excellent local golf club.

a. What factors will influence how much extra real GDP will be generated within Elbow by your $200 of expenditure? (Treat Elbow as if it were a separate economy.)

b. What does your answer imply for the argument made by the Elbow town council that the Saskatchewan government should shift a government department to the town to stimulate the town's economy?

4. Explain why the multiplier effect of a tax cut on real GDP is smaller once we consider the aggregate supply curve. Second, what happens if there are incentive effects from the tax cuts?

5. Table 1 gives some information on the real interest rates, inflation rates, and tax rates from three different countries.

TABLE 1

	Ricardia	Barroland	Lafferia
Nominal interest rate	12%	10%	10%
Inflation rate	6%	5%	6%
Tax rate	40%	50%	50%
Real, before-tax interest rate			
Real, after-tax interest rate			
Tax wedge			

a. Complete Table 1.

b. Assuming all other factors are equal, which country has the biggest negative incentive effects for lenders?

c. Assuming all other factors are equal, which country has the lowest costs for investors?

Ⓔ **6.** Some politicians and economists argue that tax cuts are beneficial for the government budget balance and are also beneficial for the economy in the short run *and* the long run. Explain their arguments and evaluate them briefly.

7. As finance minister for the government of Adanac, you have decided that to get re-elected next year, your government needs to raise real GDP by $200 billion.

a. What possible fiscal policies would work to achieve your goal?

b. Your crack team of economists has estimated the economy's government expenditure multiplier to be 4. You are confident that this estimate is correct, since you threatened to exile the economists to the North Pole should they err. If you decide to change only government expenditures, how much change is required to accomplish your goal?

c. Having carried out the increase in government expenditures, you find that the increase in real GDP is less than $200 billion, jeopardizing your chance for re-election. Before you exile the poor economists to the North Pole, is there any excuse for their mistake? (In other words, what went wrong?)

ⓒⓉ **8.** During the fall of 2008 and early 2009, Canada faced the possibility of recession as an outcome of the credit crunch. The government of Canada and the opposition parties debated what the appropriate fiscal policy might be in light of this danger. The Conservative government was worried about the potential recession, but was also worried about the long-term effects of having a deficit, and were also worried that the proposed fiscal policies might not work well to reverse a recession.

a. What are the potential dangers of having a new, larger deficit?

d. You were focused on the short run, but what other factors could have been important for long-run considerations in picking your appropriate policy?

b. Why might fiscal policy not work to prevent or reduce the effects of a recession?

c. What are the dangers of *not* carrying out an anti-recessionary fiscal policy?

d. Which danger do you think is higher—carrying out an anti-recessionary policy that doesn't work or creates deficits, or not carrying out such a policy?

Answers

True/False and Explain

1. **F** Deficit is when outlays > revenues in the current year. (704–705)

2. **F** Government expenditures on goods, transfers payments, and interest payments are all part of outlays. (704)

3. **T** If outlays grow faster than taxes, outlays > taxes next year and there is a deficit. (704–705)

4. **F** Example of revenue. (704)

5. **F** It ran surpluses. (705–709)

6. **F** An income tax cut raises *YD* and shifts *AD* rightward, and raises incentives to work and save, raising labour supply and *raising* potential GDP. (710–711)

7. **T** Due to negative incentive effects reducing investment and GDP growth. (712)

8. **F** Only if the tax rate is high enough to be past the peak of the Laffer curve. (713)

9. **T** Real after-tax rate = nominal rate × (1 − tax rate) − inflation rate = (10% × 0.5) − 4% = 1%. (712–713)

10. **F** They exactly offset each other (Δ net taxes = 0), so Δ real GDP = 0. (715–719)

11. **T** If income decreases, this decreases taxes + increases transfers, and increases disposable income, which increases aggregate expenditure, increasing income, potentially offsetting the initial decrease. (714–715)

12. **T** More is spent by households, so there is more income and indirect taxes (like GST/HST). (714–715)

13. **T** Definition. (714–715)

14. **T** Shifts *AD* rightward. (715–719)

15. **T** Increase in government expenditures = increase in quantity of goods and services demanded, so higher level of *AD*, same price level. (715–719)

Multiple-Choice

1. **e** May have a deficit, not really used for fiscal policy, almost as large as federal government outlays, *federal* government does employment insurance. (704–709)

2. **d** This is an increase in revenue. (704–705)

3. **c** See text discussion. (705–709)

4. **e** See text discussion. (704)

5. **c** Others are sources of revenue. (704–705)

6. **e** Budget balance = revenue − outlays = ($25 + $15 + $5 + $2) − ($30 + $12 + $8) = −$3 million. (704–705)

7. **c** See text discussion. (704–705)

8. **b** See text discussion. (709)

9. **c** In the long run, changes in fiscal policy have an impact only if they change potential GDP (aggregate supply). (710–713)

10. **e** A shift rightward in *AD* increases real GDP in the short run. (710–719)

11. **b** 11 × (1 − 0.25) − 4 = 4.25%. (712)

12. **b** Lower return to saving, less saving (lower quantity supplied of loanable funds), raising before-tax real interest rate, leading to lower investment and lower economic growth. (712–713)

13. **e** Deficit may or may not rise. (710–713)

14. **d** **a**, **b**, and **c** raise the tax wedge, lowering employment and saving, lowering potential GDP. (710–713)

15. **e** See text discussion. (713)

16. **d** Only the incentive effects on potential GDP matter for the long run, but size is uncertain. (710–719)

17. **b** Others are irrelevant or are not limitations. (719)

18. **d** Shifts the *AD* curve rightward. (715–719)

19. **c** Increase in real GDP increases tax revenue. Decrease in unemployment decreases transfer payments. (714–715)

20. **c** In a recession, decrease in *Y* decreases taxes and increases spending on employment insurance, etc., increasing deficit. (714–715)

21. **e** Decrease in *G* shifts *AD* leftward by government expenditure multiplier; decrease in taxes shifts *AD* rightward by tax multiplier, which has a smaller impact. (718–720)

22. **a** Invert $\Delta Y = $ multiplier $\times \Delta G$: $\Delta G = \Delta Y/$multiplier $= 5/2.5 = 2$. (718)

23. **b** Likely that the incentives effects on *AS* are strong and important, and therefore the tax multiplier is stronger. (714–719)

24. **d** Definition. (714–715)

25. **c** $10 billion $= G - T = $100 billion $- $25 billion -0.1 (potential GDP), therefore potential GDP $= (100 - 25 - 10)/0.1 = $650 billion. (714–715)

Short Answer Problems

1. The deficit increased because government outlays as a percentage of GDP increased, while taxes as a percentage of GDP fell during the late 1970s and then slowly increased. The components of spending that showed the most consistent growth were transfer payments and interest payments on government debt.

2. **a.** The Liberals were counting on the tax multiplier to boost aggregate expenditure and create new jobs.

   b. The critics argued that most of the new expenditure would be on products from outside the province—that the marginal propensity to import for a province is very high, so that the multipliers are very low.

   c. It is likely that fiscal policy multipliers are low for individual provinces due to high marginal propensities to import. For your information, imports in Saskatchewan were about 62 percent (= 15.14 billion/29.28 billion) of provincial real GDP in 1995. (*Source:* Statistics Canada, CANSIM matrices D21425 and D31874.)

3. **a.** Your $200 will trigger a multiplier process—the owners of the factors of production at the golf course will spend their extra income, for example. This spending induces second-round increases in consumption expenditure, leading to a final change in real GDP in Elbow that is a multiple of $200. The size of the multiplier effect will be determined by two things. First,

the larger the marginal propensity to consume in Elbow and the smaller the marginal propensity to import (from outside Elbow), the larger the multiplier will be. In a small town, the marginal propensity to import from outside the town is likely to be quite high, making the multiplier much smaller. Second, the effect is smaller if the aggregate supply curve is steeper—the increase in aggregate demand gets reduced by an increase in the price level.

b. Such a shift might stimulate the town's economy, since the annual increase in government expenditures will create multiplier effects. The usefulness of this shift is limited by the factors that might reduce the size of the multiplier. (This was actual government policy in Saskatchewan until the Conservatives were defeated in 1991, at least partially because of this policy.)

4. The multiplier tells us the size of the change in real GDP relative to the size of an initial change in government expenditure or taxes. Once we consider the *AS* curve, we know the price level will increase as aggregate demand increases—the increase in the price level being higher, the steeper the *AS* curve. This increase in the price level lowers aggregate expenditure, shown by the movement up the *AD* curve, leading to a smaller increase in real GDP compared to the case with no price effect.

The tax cut would reduce the tax wedge, creating incentive effects that would increase labour supply (lowering the before-tax wage rate and increasing labour demand) and the quantity supplied of loanable funds (lowering real interest rates and increasing investment). These incentive effects would increase potential GDP.

5. a. Table 1 Solution shows the answers. The real, after-tax interest rate is solved using the formula: Nominal rate × (1 − tax rate) − inflation rate. The tax wedge is the difference between the before-tax real rate (nominal rate − inflation rate) paid by borrowers and the after-tax real rate received by lenders.

TABLE 1 Solution

	Ricardia	Barroland	Lafferia
Nominal interest rate	12%	10%	10%
Inflation rate	6%	5%	6%
Tax rate	40%	50%	50%
Real, before-tax interest rate	6%	5%	4%
Real, after-tax interest rate	1.2%	0%	−1%
Tax Wedge	4.8%	5%	5%

b. Based on having the highest tax wedge, Lafferia and Barroland have the biggest negative incentive effect for lenders.

c. Lafferia has the lowest before-tax real interest rate (4 percent), and therefore would have the lowest costs for investors.

6. The Laffer curve claims a tax cut could potentially have such strong incentive effects that total tax revenues would rise, helping the government budget balance. However, when the U.S. cut its tax rates under Reagan, the result was a fall in tax revenue and a rise in the budget deficit.

With respect to the economy, a cut in taxes increases disposable income and shifts the *AD* curve rightward in the normal multiplier manner, increasing real GDP in the short run. If the *LAS* curve does not shift, in the long run the economy will return to potential GDP. However, supply-side economists argue that tax cuts will also increase the after-tax returns to work and saving, which in turn will increase labour supply and saving, increasing potential GDP and shifting the *AS* curves rightward. An evaluation is still somewhat premature. As the textbook points out, it is still a matter of political opinion whether the *AS* effects are small or large. So far, there is no hard empirical evidence one way or the other.

7. a. You would need to increase aggregate demand, which means that you would need to either increase government expenditures on goods and services, or increase transfer payments, or cut taxes.

b. If the government expenditure multiplier equals 4, to raise real GDP by $200 billion you need to increase government expenditures by $50 billion = $200/4 billion.

c. The multiplier effects we have been analysing are based on the assumption that the price level is constant. In the real world, the stimulation of aggregate demand that you have carried out would raise the price level, which lowers aggregate expenditure and partially (or completely) offsets the increase in real GDP from your policy. In addition, there was likely crowding-out effects from the higher interest rates caused by the higher deficit.

d. If you had chosen a tax cut for your policy, this might have had positive incentive effects on labour supply and saving, leading to a higher level of potential GDP in the long run.

8. a. A larger deficit increases the demand for loanable funds (see Chapter 23), and potentially increases real interest rates, crowding out private investment, and lowering long-term economic growth. In addition, a deficit increases the size of the government debt, and therefore increases the required debt payments by the government. Looking at the history of the government's deficits between 1971 and 1997, debt payments can create a vicious circle of rising debt, rising debt payments, rising deficits, rising debt, etc.

b. Fiscal policy might not work due to lags in the system. The recognition lag would not be an issue (the problem was recognized!), but the law-making lag (getting the legislation passed) is a possible problem, as is the impact lag (the time it takes the policy to have an impact). If the policy arrives after the economy has started to readjust to full employment, we may create inflationary pressures.

c. The dangers of not carrying out an anti-recessionary fiscal policy would be a longer and deeper recession, with more lost jobs and bankrupt businesses.

d. This choice depends on your personal evaluation of the pros and cons listed above, as well as your judgment on which negatives to avoid!

14 Monetary Policy

Key Concepts

Monetary Policy Objectives and Framework

Bank of Canada Act sets objectives of monetary policy.

- Bank controls quantity of money and interest rates to avoid inflation and prevent excessive swings in GDP growth and unemployment.

- Current policy is **inflation rate targeting**—explicit inflation rate target range (1 to 3 percent a year, trend of 2 percent), clear explanation of actions.

  - Inflation is measured by CPI, but Bank also focuses on *core inflation* (CPI excluding the eight most volatile prices and indirect taxes).

  - Since range was set in mid-1990s, actual inflation rate has usually been within target range.

- Benefits of a target range are clear understanding by financial markets and as anchor for inflation expectations.

  - Critics argue Bank should pay more attention to unemployment rate and real GDP growth.

- Governing Council of Bank of Canada is responsible for conduct of monetary policy, with briefings by Bank economists.

- Governor of Bank of Canada consults with Minister of Finance.

The Conduct of Monetary Policy

The Bank of Canada can control only one policy instrument: either quantity of money (monetary base) *or* exchange rate *or* short-term interest rate.

- The Bank targets the short-term interest rate, specifically the **overnight loans rate** (interest rate on overnight loans big banks make to each other).
- The Bank announces its interest rate target eight times a year.
- The tools used to achieve the chosen target are the operating band and overnight operations.
- **Operating band** is the target overnight rate plus or minus 0.25 percentage points.
  - Top of operating band = **bank rate** (overnight rate + 0.25%)—interest rate the Bank of Canada charges big banks on loans. Since a bank can always borrow at the bank rate, the overnight rate never goes higher than this.
  - Bottom of band = **settlement balances rate**—interest rate the Bank of Canada pays for reserves banks hold at the Bank of Canada. Since a bank can always earn the settlement balances rate, the overnight rate never goes lower than this.
  - The Bank of Canada can always make the overnight loans rate fall within target range.
- Open market operations move the overnight rate to the target rate.
  - If the Bank of Canada buys government bonds, this increases banking system reserves (= increased supply of overnight funds), increasing loans, lowering the overnight rate.
  - If the Bank of Canada sells government bonds, this decreases banking system reserves (= decreased supply of overnight funds), decreasing loans, raising the overnight rate.

Monetary Policy Transmission

Changing overnight rate affects aggregate demand (*AD*), real GDP growth, and inflation through several channels.

- With a lower overnight rate, other interest rates fall, quantity of money and supply of loanable funds increase, real interest rates fall.

Notes:

Key Concepts

- With lower interest rates, exchange rate falls, increasing net exports and *AD*.
- With lower real interest rates, consumption and investment increase, increasing *AD*.
- Increasing *AD* increases real GDP growth and inflation, although takes up to two years for full effects.

- Higher overnight rate has opposite effects, decreasing *AD*, real GDP growth, and inflation.
- Historical evidence shows changes in the overnight rate create different effects on long-term and short-term interest rates.
  - Because banks can easily choose between overnight loans and Treasury bills as short-term assets, they are close substitutes and the two rates move together.
  - 10-year government bond rate and long-term corporate bond rate are close substitutes (although corporate rate is slightly higher on average), so these two rates move together.
  - Short-term and long-term bond rates usually move together, but are not close substitutes, and sometimes move in different directions.

- Exchange rate responds to interest rate differential (gap between Canadian and U.S. rates), but relationship is weak since many other factors determine exchange rates.

Expenditure plans are affected by real interest rate.

- Lower real interest rate, lower opportunity cost of spending, greater consumption expenditure and investment.
- Lower real interest rate, lower Canadian dollar exchange rate, greater net exports.

Final link in transmission chain is a change in *AD* changing real GDP and price level.

- With real GDP < potential GDP, lowering the overnight rate increases the quantity of money and the supply of loanable funds. This lowers real interest rates and increases *AD*, increasing real GDP and price level, leading to faster convergence to potential GDP.
- If real GDP > potential GDP (inflationary pressure), increasing the overnight rate lowers the quantity of money and the supply of loanable funds, increasing the real interest rate and decreasing *AD*, lowering inflationary pressure.

- Monetary policy is sometimes wrong due to time lags before policy takes effect.
- When the Bank of Canada changes overnight rates, real GDP growth changes, but there is a loose link because real interest rates react to the overnight rate *and* inflation expectations, and because of time lags in the adjustment process.

Extraordinary Monetary Stimulus

The financial crisis and recession of 2008–2009 led to some extraordinary monetary policies.

- The crisis created three problems in various banks and countries:
  - Widespread falls in asset prices created solvency problems for banks if their equity became close to or below zero.
  - Some banks faced significant currency drains, creating liquidity problems.
  - For some banks, depositors lost confidence and a bank run began.
- Banks began calling in loans, and the national and global loanable funds markets dried up.
- Policymakers carried out five key policy actions:
  - Open market purchases worked to increase bank liquidity.
  - Extending deposit insurance works to reassure depositors and prevent withdrawals.
  - Governments and central banks swapped government assets for toxic bank assets, as well as buying shares in banks—both of these actions worked to reduce the solvency problem.
  - Changing accounting standards reduced problems with solvency as well.
- Despite these strong efforts, the recovery has been very slow.
- Critics argue that this slowness is due to the U.S. Fed pursuing a confusing and uncertain monetary policy, and that it should instead have a clear monetary rule such as Canada's inflation rate targeting strategy or the Taylor rule.

Notes:

Helpful Hints

1. Let's use a numerical example to review how the Bank of Canada can get the overnight rate to be in the middle of the target range. Suppose that the Bank wishes the overnight rate to be 3.5 percent, which means the operating band will be 3.25 to 3.75 percent.

    How can the Bank guarantee that the overnight rate will be within the 0.5 percent target range? Two key factors keep the rate in the range. One is that the Bank of Canada is willing to lend as much money as the banks want to borrow at the bank rate (which is set at the upper end of the target, 3.75 percent). If the overnight rate was 4 percent, no bank would borrow at this rate as they could borrow at the (lower) bank rate. Therefore, the overnight rate is less than or equal to the bank rate. The second factor is that the Bank of Canada is willing to allow the banks to hold as many deposits at the Bank of Canada as they want, and to earn the settlement balances rate of 3.25 percent. If the overnight rate was 3 percent, no bank would lend at this rate as they could earn 3.25 percent. Therefore, the overnight rate is greater than or equal to the settlements balances rate. In sum:

    Settlement balances rate ≤ overnight rate ≤ bank rate

    $3.25\% \leq$ overnight rate $\leq 3.75\%$

    As long as the Bank of Canada is willing to meet all borrowing/lending requirements implied by the rates it sets, it can force the *actual* overnight rate to be in this range. However, if the actual rate gets stuck at one end, it would be difficult for the Bank to continuously accept deposits or loan out money. In that case it must use open market operations to affect the amount of reserves and the overnight rate.

2. Open market operations affect the overnight rate via their impact on banking system reserves. One liability of the Bank of Canada is banks' deposits at the Bank of Canada (which are part of the banks' reserves). In addition, the largest class of assets of the Bank of Canada is its holdings of government securities. Finally, recall that if total

assets increase, due to the conventions of double-entry bookkeeping, total liabilities must increase by the same amount.

An open market purchase by the Bank of Canada of government securities is an increase in its assets paid for by an increase in its liabilities, principally an increase in the deposits of banks at the Bank of Canada. This increase in deposits at the Bank of Canada is an increase in banks' reserves, leaving them with excess reserves they will lend out, initially in the overnight market, pushing down the overnight rate.

Notes:

Self-Test
True/False and Explain

Monetary Policy Objectives and Framework

1. The monetary policy objective of the Bank of Canada is to avoid inflation and prevent excessive swings in the exchange rate.

2. The Bank of Canada's current inflation target is a range of 1 to 3 percent per year for core inflation.

3. The benefits of a target range include creating an anchor for inflation expectations.

The Conduct of Monetary Policy

4. Increasing the bank rate will increase the amount of lending by the banking system.

5. If the Bank of Canada sells government securities in the open market, bank reserves decrease.

6. To tighten monetary policy, the Bank of Canada raises the overnight rate target.

Monetary Policy Transmission

7. A decrease in the overnight rate shifts the *AD* curve rightward.

8. An increase in the overnight rate decreases the exchange rate.

9. A decrease in the overnight rate reduces inflationary pressures.

10. An increase in the overnight rate will increase the quantity of money and lower money demand.

11. The overnight rate and the 10-year government bond rate move very closely together.

12. A lower real interest rate creates more consumption spending.

Extraordinary Monetary Stimulus

13. A fall in the prices of the assets held by a bank creates a liquidity problem for the bank.

14. Extending deposit insurance has the goal of reducing deposit withdrawals and bank runs.

15. Inflation targeting is the sole component of the Taylor rule.

Multiple-Choice

Monetary Policy Objectives and Framework

1. Why does the Bank of Canada pay close attention to the core inflation rate in addition to the overall CPI inflation rate?

a. The core rate is more volatile and therefore a better predictor of trend inflation.

b. The core rate includes taxes, while the overall CPI rate does not.

c. The core rate has a lower average value and therefore makes the Bank look better.

d. The core rate is less volatile and a better predictor of future CPI inflation.

e. The core rate excludes eight volatile prices and is therefore more likely to stay within the target band.

2. One criticism of the Bank of Canada's focus on an inflation control target is that

a. if inflation falls below the target range a recession will result.

b. if inflation edges above the target range, the Bank decreases aggregate demand and could create a recession.

c. the Bank pays too much attention to unemployment and real GDP growth and not enough to inflation control.

d. it makes setting expectations of inflation difficult.

e. the Bank rarely achieves its target.

3. Who is responsible for setting monetary policy in Canada?

a. the government of Canada

b. the Governor of the Bank of Canada

c. the Bank of Canada's economists

d. the Governing Council of the Bank of Canada

e. the Governing Council of the Bank of Canada, after consultation with the government of Canada

The Conduct of Monetary Policy

4. The bank rate is the interest rate

  a. banks charge their very best loan customers.

  b. banks pay on term deposits.

  c. the Bank of Canada pays on reserves held by banks.

  d. the Bank of Canada charges when it lends reserves to banks.

  e. received for holding Government of Canada Treasury bills.

5. The Bank of Canada's current decision-making rule

  a. uses the overnight loans rate target to affect the current state of the economy.

  b. uses open market operations to affect the current state of the economy.

  c. uses the overnight loans rate target to hit the inflation rate target.

  d. uses open market operations to try and affect the exchange rate.

  e. uses the growth rate of the monetary base to affect lending.

6. If the Bank of Canada aims to lower the overnight rate, it will

  a. lower the bank rate and settlement balances rate, as well as buy government securities.

  b. lower the bank rate, increase the settlement balances rate, as well as buy government securities.

  c. lower the bank rate and settlement balances rate, as well as sell government securities.

  d. raise the bank rate and settlement balances rate, as well as buy government securities.

  e. raise the bank rate and settlement balances rate, as well as sell government securities.

7. Why does the Bank of Canada use open market operations together with overnight rate targeting?

  a. to ensure the overnight rate hits the target

  b. to offset the impact of the overnight rate

  c. to provide liquidity for banks

  d. to lower interest rates

  e. to raise interest rates

8. In an open market operation aimed at increasing expenditure, the Bank of Canada

a. sells government bonds, decreasing bank reserves, decreasing lending, decreasing the overnight rate.

b. sells government bonds, decreasing bank reserves, decreasing lending, increasing the overnight rate.

c. sells government bonds, decreasing bank reserves, increasing lending, increasing the overnight rate.

d. buys government bonds, increasing bank reserves, increasing lending, decreasing the overnight rate.

e. buys government bonds, increasing bank reserves, increasing lending, increasing the overnight rate.

9. The current overnight loans rate is 3 percent, with the Bank of Canada's operating band set at 2.75 to 3.25 percent. If the Bank of Canada lowers their operating band to 2.25 to 2.75 percent, which of the following is one of the reasons the overnight rate will fall to within this new range?

a. Since the banking system can now borrow from the Bank of Canada at 2.75 percent, no bank would borrow on the overnight loan market at 3 percent.

b. Since the banking system can now borrow from the Bank of Canada at 2.25 percent, no bank would borrow on the overnight loan market at 3 percent.

c. Since the banking system can now earn 2.75 percent from the Bank of Canada, no bank would lend on the overnight loan market at 3 percent.

d. Since the banking system can now earn 2.25 percent from the Bank of Canada, no bank would lend on the overnight loan market at 3 percent.

e. There is a legal requirement that the overnight rate must be within the Bank of Canada's operating band.

10. The current overnight loans rate is 3 percent, with the Bank of Canada's operating band set at 2.75 to 3.25 percent. If the Bank of Canada lowers their operating band to 2.25 to 2.75 percent, what open market operation might be used to move the overnight rate to the middle of the target?

a. buying foreign exchange in the foreign exchange market

b. buying Canadian dollars in the foreign exchange market

c. selling foreign exchange in the foreign exchange market

d. buying government securities in the open market

e. selling government securities in the open market

Monetary Policy Transmission

11. Why is the exchange rate a key monetary variable?

a. It is one of the four main policy rules.

b. It is a key policy objective.

c. It is a barometer of monetary policy.

d. It shows how much the monetary base must be multiplied to measure the resulting increase in the quantity of money.

e. It is part of the channel by which a change in the overnight rate affects aggregate demand.

12. The headline "The Bank of Canada Has Cut the Bank Rate" suggests that the Bank of Canada is trying to

a. lower inflationary pressures.

b. increase the overnight loans rate.

c. stimulate aggregate demand.

d. raise the value of the Canadian dollar.

e. help banks make profits.

13. In a situation of unemployment, a decrease in the overnight rate will lead to a(n)

a. increase in real GDP and the price level.

b. increase in real GDP, but a decrease in the price level.

c. increase in real GDP, but no change in the price level.

d. increase in the price level, but no change in real GDP.

e. decrease in the price level and real GDP.

14. A monetary policy aimed at increasing domestic expenditure will

  a. increase interest rates and decrease the exchange rate.

  b. have no impact on interest rates, but increase the exchange rate.

  c. have no impact on interest rates nor on the exchange rate.

  d. decrease interest rates and increase the exchange rate.

  e. decrease interest rates and the exchange rate.

15. Which of the following statements about historical evidence on monetary policy is *true*?

  a. The overnight interest rate moves inversely with short-term interest rates.

  b. The overnight interest rate is not related to short-term interest rates.

  c. When the Bank of Canada lowers the overnight rate, real GDP rises immediately.

  d. When the gap between Canadian and U.S. interest rates increases, the exchange rate decreases.

  e. When the gap between Canadian and U.S. interest rates increases, the exchange rate increases.

16. Consider Fig. 1. Which graph represents an anti-inflationary monetary policy?

  a. (a)

  b. (b)

  c. (c)

  d. (d)

  e. none of the above

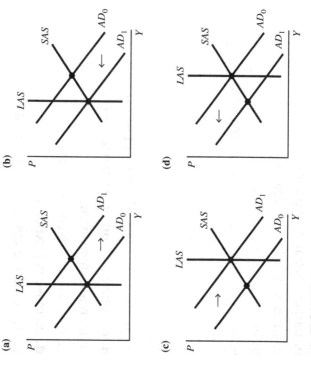

▲ **FIGURE 1**

17. Consider Fig. 1. Which graph represents an attempt to lower unemployment with monetary policy?

  a. (a)

  b. (b)

  c. (c)

  d. (d)

  e. none of the above

18. Which of the following statements *correctly* describes an anti-inflationary monetary policy?

  a. "The Bank of Canada's purchases of government securities is stimulating the housing sector."

  b. "The Bank of Canada's moves to lower interest rates are behind the decrease in the value of the Canadian dollar."

  c. "The Bank of Canada's moves to increase the overnight loans rate are leading to less lending and less consumer spending."

  d. "The Bank of Canada's sales of government securities are stimulating the housing sector."

  e. "The Bank of Canada's moves to decrease the value of the Canadian dollar are leading to more spending in the economy."

19. If the inflation rate increases by 3 percent and the nominal interest rate increases by 2 percent,

  a. the real interest rate increases.

  b. money demand increases.

  c. money demand decreases.

  d. investment decreases.

  e. consumption expenditure decreases.

20. An increase in the real interest rate will

  a. decrease consumption expenditure.

  b. increase investment.

  c. decrease the exchange rate.

  d. increase net exports.

  e. decrease the nominal interest rate.

21. An increase in the overnight interest rate will

   a. decrease the real interest rate, the inflation rate held constant.

   b. decrease nominal interest rates.

   c. decrease aggregate demand.

   d. increase aggregate demand.

   e. not change the nominal interest rate.

22. A higher Canadian interest rate will

   a. increase the demand for Canadian dollars because more people move money into Canada to take advantage of the higher interest rate.

   b. decrease the demand for Canadian dollars because more people move money out of Canada to take advantage of the higher interest rate.

   c. increase the demand for Canadian dollars because more people move money out of Canada to take advantage of the higher interest rate.

   d. decrease the demand for Canadian dollars because more people move money into Canada to take advantage of the higher interest rate.

   e. not affect the demand for Canadian dollars.

23. Changing the overnight rate affects aggregate demand through several channels. Which of the following is *not* one of those channels?

   a. Higher real interest rates lower net exports.

   b. Higher real interest rates raise consumption expenditure.

   c. Higher real interest rates lower investment spending.

   d. Lower real interest rates raise consumption expenditure.

   e. Lower real interest rates raise investment spending.

Extraordinary Monetary Stimulus

24. Which of the following policy actions increases bank reserves?

   a. an open market purchase

   b. an increase in interest rates

   c. buying toxic assets from banks

   d. buying shares in banks

   e. accounting changes that allow banks to revalue their assets

25. How does a bank run put a bank under stress?

   a. It creates a decrease in asset prices and creates liquidity problems.

   b. Deposits enter the bank creating cash surpluses.

   c. Deposits leave the bank and equity falls below zero, creating liquidity and solvency problems.

   d. Loans are paid off by borrowers and the bank cannot make profits.

   e. Loans are not repaid and the bank suffers a solvency problem.

Short Answer Problems

1. How does an open market purchase of government securities lead to a decrease in the overnight rate? What are the ripple effects of this policy on the different components of aggregate expenditure?

2. Explain what the policy action in Short Answer Problem **1** does to aggregate demand, real GDP, and the price level in the short run. How is it different in the long run?

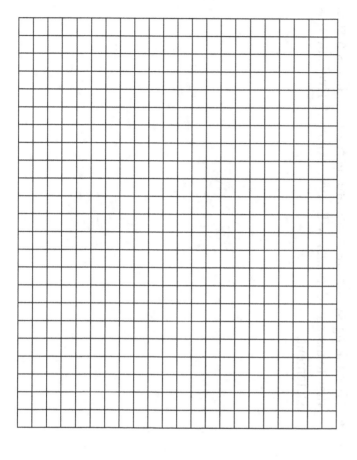

3. Suppose there is an increase in the overnight rate and therefore in other interest rates. On the grid, use a graph of the aggregate demand–aggregate supply model to show what happens to the price level and the level of real GDP in the short run and in the long run.

4. Consider the following data, from the imaginary country of Sarconia:

Current inflation rate	3% per year
Current overnight rate	4% per year
Current growth rate of real GDP	3% per year
Estimated (long-term) growth rate of potential GDP	3% per year
Current unemployment rate	5%
Estimate of natural unemployment rate	7%
Current growth rate of monetary base	12% per year

a. Is Sarconia suffering from an inflationary gap, a recessionary gap, or is it right at potential GDP? How do you know?

b. If the Bank of Sarconia has an inflationary target of 2 to 4 percent per year, what would be the appropriate policy strategy?

c. If the Bank of Sarconia follows a Taylor rule with an inflationary target of 2 to 4 percent per year, what should be its policy strategy?

5. In Short Answer Problem **4**, you should have found different policy conclusions for each of the rules in parts **b** and **c**. Explain what differences in the crucial factors underlying each rule lead to the different policy conclusions.

6. "If banking system reserves are increasing, this is a sign that loans and deposits will soon expand." Evaluate this statement.

7. Consider the following "quotation" from the *Regional Post*:

Interest Rates Crash after Bank of Canada Action

by J. S. Smith

The Bank of Canada cut interest rates dramatically yesterday. … [T]he bank cut its target for overnight rates to 3.25% from 4.00%. The major banks quickly followed suit, cutting the cost of borrowing for their best customers (the prime rate) to 5.50% from 6.25%. This change was followed by reductions in other rates, including mortgage rates.

Explain the link from the overnight rate target to the prime rate that the major banks charge their best customers.

8. If the Bank of Canada wishes to reduce inflationary pressure, explain briefly what steps it will have to carry out in the overnight loans market.

Answers

True/False and Explain

1. **F** Avoid inflation and prevent excessive swings in real GDP growth and unemployment. (728)

2. **F** 1 to 3 percent for overall inflation. (728–729)

3. **T** See text discussion. (729)

4. **F** Higher bank rate increases cost of borrowing reserves, so banks wish to hold more reserves, and *decrease* loans. (730–732)

5. **T** People buy securities with deposits that are transferred to the Bank of Canada, decreasing reserves. (731–732)

6. **T** They must raise the bank rate and the settlement balances rate, and potentially carry out an open market operation. (731)

7. **T** A lower overnight rate pushes down short-term and long-term interest rates, which increases consumption, investment, and net exports, shifting *AD* curve rightward. (735)

8. **F** A higher overnight rate pushes up interest rates, raising Canadian interest rate differential, raising demand for Canadian dollar, and therefore the exchange rate. (735)

9. **F** A lower overnight rate pushes down short-term and long-term interest rates, increasing consumption, investment, and net exports, shifting the *AD* curve rightward, pushing up price level. (733–740)

10. **F** A higher overnight rate leads to lower bank reserves,

money. Lower quantity of money raises interest rate and lowers money demand. (735)

11. **F** They move together, but not that closely. (733–734)

12. **T** A lower real rate leads to less saving and more consumption. (741)

13. **F** Creates solvency problem. (741)

14. **T** Depositors have less incentive to withdraw. (742)

15. **F** It looks at both inflation and the output gap. (747)

Multiple-Choice

1. **d** See text discussion. (728)

2. **b** Anti-inflationary policy leads to decreased *AD*, which can lead to recession and unemployment. (728)

3. **e** See text discussion. (730)

4. **d** Definition. (731)

5. **c** Overnight loan rate is a policy instrument aimed at policy objective of inflation rate. (731–732)

6. **a** Lowering two rates will force the overnight rate down in between these two rates (see Helpful Hint **1**), and buying securities increases banking system reserves, leading to more overnight loans, pushing rate down. (731–732)

7. **a** The target range will guarantee the overnight rate is within the range, but not at the desired level unless open market operations support the target range.

8. **d** Buying bonds increases reserves to pay for them, which creates excess reserves, leading to an increase in funds available for lending in the overnight loans market, pushing down the overnight rate. (732)

9. **a** Upper end of band is the bank rate—the rate the Bank of Canada charges for borrowing from it. No profit-seeking bank will pay more than this rate to borrow, forcing down the actual overnight rate to less than or equal to this rate. (731–732)

10. **d** They need to buy securities to raise banking system reserves to increase funds for lending in the overnight market to push down the overnight rate. (731–732)

11. **e** Δ overnight rate leads to Δr, which Δ demand for Canadian dollar and exchange rate, which ΔX, ΔM, and AD. (735)

12. **c** Lowering the bank rate lowers costs of borrowing to replenish reserves, so banking system will maintain lower reserves, lend out more money, lowering interest rates and stimulating consumption, investment, net exports, and AD. (733–740)

13. **a** Decrease in the overnight rate shifts AD rightward, increasing real GDP and the price level if initial equilibrium is left of full employment (draw a graph). (736–740)

14. **e** Decrease in overnight rate decreases interest rates, decreasing demand for the Canadian dollar and therefore exchange rate. (733–735)

15. **e** See text discussion. (733–740)

16. **b** Output is above natural rate (inflationary gap). Policy is attempting to reduce AD to reduce the gap. (736–740)

17. **c** Output is below natural rate (recessionary gap). Policy is attempting to increase AD to reduce the gap. (736–740)

18. **c** All other changes lead to lower interest rates and higher aggregate expenditure, shifting AD rightward. (733–740)

19. **c** Nominal interest rate increases, money demand decreases. Real interest rate decreases since increase in inflation rate > increase in nominal interest rate, so investment and consumption expenditure increase. (735)

20. **a** Higher cost of borrowing decreases borrowing and spending. (735)

21. **c** Higher overnight rate increases other interest rates and decreases consumption, investment, and net exports. (735)

22. **a** People trying to earn more on their money buy Canadian assets and must buy Canadian dollars to buy Canadian assets. (735)

23. **b** Higher real interest rates lower borrowing and spending. (733–740)

24. **a** Bank of Canada buys government securities from banks (crediting their reserves held at the Bank). (742)

25. **c** Withdrawals create cash shortages and the bank has to use up reserves and its equity to match withdrawals. (741)

Short Answer Problems

1. An open market purchase of government securities by the Bank of Canada increases the reserves of the banking system by increasing one of its components—banks' deposits at the Bank of Canada. When the securities are purchased from banks, the Bank of Canada pays for the securities by crediting the bank's deposit at the Bank of Canada, which directly increases their reserves. The banks now have more reserves, and will try to lend more on the overnight market (and will need to borrow less), putting downward pressure on overnight rates.

   The lower overnight rates create substitution effects, pushing down other interest rates, increasing consumption expenditure and investment spending. The lower interest rates also lower demand for the Canadian dollar, which lowers the value of the exchange rate and increases net exports.

2. The impact of the extra consumption, investment, and net exports is that the aggregate demand curve shifts rightward. In the short run, this increases real GDP and the price level. In the long run, if the economy started out in recession, it will converge towards potential GDP without other effects. However, if it started out at potential GDP, the increase in aggregate demand will create inflationary pressures, which in turn will create wage increases. Short-run aggregate supply shifts leftward, creating further increases in the price level and decreases in real GDP as the economy moves back towards potential GDP.

3. Fig. 2 illustrates the consequences of an increase in the overnight rates. The economy is initially in long-run

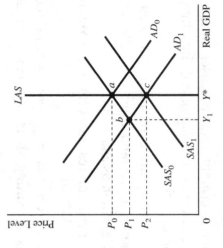

▲ **FIGURE 2**

equilibrium at point *a*, the intersection of AD_0 and SAS_0 (and *LAS*). The price level is P_0 and GDP is at potential, Y^*. An increase in the overnight rate lowers consumption, investment, and net exports and shifts the *AD* curve leftward, from AD_0 to AD_1. The new short-run equilibrium is at point *b*. The price level decreases to P_1 and real GDP decreases to Y_1. In the long run, however, input prices also decrease, which shifts *SAS* rightward, from SAS_0 to SAS_1. A new long-run equilibrium occurs at point *c*. In the long run, the price level decreases further to P_2, while real GDP returns to potential, Y^*.

4. **a.** Since unemployment is below the natural rate, real GDP is above potential GDP and there is an inflationary gap.

   b. Since inflation is exactly in the middle of the inflationary target range, the appropriate policy would be to do nothing different.

   c. A Taylor rule follows the following formula:

R is the overnight rate, INF is the inflation rate, and GAP is an estimate of the output gap. Substituting in the information from the question, we see:

$$R = 2 + 3 + 0.5\,(3 - 2) + 0.5\ GAP, \text{ or}$$

$$R = 5.5 + 0.5\ GAP$$

We do not know what GAP is, but if there is an inflationary gap, $GAP > 0$. Therefore, the overnight rate should be higher than 5.5 percent. Since it is currently 4 percent, it needs to be raised.

5. The simple inflationary rule of part **b** only focuses on the inflation target, which was currently being met, and not on any future problems. The Taylor rule (which also looks at the output gap as a source of future inflationary pressures) tries to forecast future pressures and offset them before they occur.

6. Banking system reserves might be increasing for two reasons, which will have opposite future effects on loans and deposits. It might be as a result of an open market operation, where the Bank of Canada is buying securities and pumping up the reserves of the banking system.

This creates *excess* reserves, which will be lent out, creating deposits expansion.

A second reason might be because the Bank of Canada has raised the overnight loan rate, making it more expensive for banks to be short of reserves. Then, banks will raise their *desired* reserves in order to avoid being short. In this case, they will be shrinking their loans (and therefore deposits) to increase their desired reserves.

7. The overnight rate is the rate banks in the banking system charge each other when there are shortages in reserves at the end of the day. If this rate climbs dramatically, banks will want to hold more reserves. To do this, they will call in loans to their other customers and raise loan rates, since these are substitutes for overnight loans.

8. To reduce inflationary pressure, the Bank of Canada needs to reduce aggregate demand. To do this, the Bank must raise nominal and real interest rates. To raise the overnight rate, the Bank would raise its target range for the overnight rate. In addition, they would probably carry out an open market sale of government securities. If they sell securities to the banking system, these securities will be paid for out of reserves, reducing the amount of reserves.

15 International Trade Policy

Key Concepts

How Global Markets Work

Imports are goods and services we buy from other countries; **exports** are what we sell to other countries.

- Canada's major exports (imports) are crude petroleum and motor vehicles/parts (machinery and consumer goods); our major trading partner is the United States.

  - Trade includes trade in services, such as tourism.

National comparative advantage drives international trade—a country exports goods/services that it can produce at a lower opportunity cost than any other nation, and imports goods/services that other nations can produce at a lower opportunity cost.

- For import goods, world price < pre-trade domestic price.

  - Quantity demanded (= quantity bought) increases with international trade.

  - Quantity supplied decreases with international trade and is lower than quantity demanded.

  - Imports = quantity demanded − supplied > 0.

- For export goods, world price > pre-trade domestic price.

  - Quantity supplied increases with international trade.

- Quantity demanded decreases with international trade and is lower than quantity supplied.
- Exports = quantity supplied − demanded > 0.

Different parts of economy gain or lose from international trade.

- *Lower* price for imported goods leads to *more* consumption by consumers—consumers of imported goods *gain* from international trade.
- *Lower* price for imported goods leads to *less* production by producers—producers of import-competing goods *lose* from international trade.
- Consumers' gain = producers' loss + gain from more consumption—society gains from imported goods.

For export goods, we also see overall gain to society.

- *Higher* price for exported goods leads to *less* consumption by consumers—consumers of exported goods *lose* from international trade.
- *Higher* price for exported goods leads to *more* production by producers—producers of exported goods *gain* from international trade.
- Producers' gain = consumers' loss + gain from more production—society gains from exporting.

International Trade Restrictions

Governments use four different tools to influence international trade and protect domestic industries: tariffs, import quotas, other import barriers, and export subsidies.

Tariffs are taxes on imported goods, providing revenue for government and helping the self-interest of import-competing industries.

- Higher domestic price = world price + tariff.
- Higher price means lower domestic quantity bought *and* higher domestic quantity produced—quantity imported shrinks.

Notes:

- Government *gains* tariff revenue = tariff rate × quantity imported.
- Domestic producers *gain* from higher price and higher production.
- Consumers *lose* from higher price and lower consumption.
- Society loses: Producers' gains + tariff revenue < consumers' losses.
- Tariffs have been decreasing due to **General Agreement on Tariffs and Trade** (international treaty to limit trade restriction) and other free trade agreements.
- Recent attempts by the **World Trade Organization (WTO)** to lower barriers to trade via the **Doha Round** of trade talks has failed due to disputes between rich and developing nations.

Import quotas restrict import quantities, with quota licences distributed to importers.

- New supply curve = domestic supply curve + quota amount.
- Domestic price higher than world price—quantity demanded and bought falls, quantity supplied rises.
- Consumers lose due to higher price.
- Domestic producers gain due to higher price.
- Importers gain profits from buying at the world price and selling at a higher domestic price.
- Society loses in a similar manner to effects of tariffs.

Other import barriers restrict supply of imports, which increases domestic price and domestic production.

- Examples include health, safety, and regulation barriers, and voluntary export restraints (similar to a quota allocated to foreign exporters).

Export subsidies are payments from government to producers of exported goods.

- Export subsidies are illegal under international trade agreements, but agricultural subsidies to farmers have the effect of increasing domestic production, leading to overproduction.

The Case Against Protection

Trade restrictions are used despite losses of gains from trade for two somewhat credible reasons—to protect **infant industries** as they mature and to prevent foreign companies from **dumping** their products on world markets at prices less than cost.

A country may restrict trade for the following less credible reasons:

- to save jobs lost from free trade
- to compete with cheap foreign labour
- to penalize lax environmental standards
- to prevent rich countries from exploiting developing countries

One new worry is **offshoring** (hiring foreign labour or buying goods/services from abroad), especially **offshore outsourcing** (hiring foreign labour to produce in other countries).

- Lower transportation and communications costs have increased offshoring in recent years.
- Benefits, costs, winners, and losers from offshoring are similar to those for free trade, with losers concentrated in the domestic services industry.

The biggest problem with protection is that it invites retaliation from other countries (trade wars).

- There are still trade restrictions because
- Tariff revenue is an attractive tax base for governments in developing countries.
- **Rent-seeking** (lobbying) by groups/industries that suffer disproportionately under freer trade.

- In Canada, employment insurance and interprovincial transfers provide some compensation for losses due to free trade, but in general losers are not compensated.

Helpful Hints

1. The crucial result of this chapter is the demonstration that a country gains from trading internationally, both from exporting and from importing.

   A country gains from exporting because the world price is higher than the domestic price. Producers gain from selling internationally at this higher price. Even though consumers lose some (due to the higher price), the producers' gain more than outweighs this loss, so that the country gains overall.

   Similarly, a country gains from importing because the world price is lower than the domestic price. Consumers gain from buying at this lower price. Even though producers lose some (due to the lower price), the consumers' gain more than outweighs this loss, and the country gains overall.

   Note that this latter effect means that an importing country even gains from buying a good that is dumped at below-cost on the world market by another country. In essence, the dumping country is giving the importing country a subsidy!

2. Given the considerable gains from free trade, why then do countries have such a strong tendency to impose trade restrictions? The key is that while free trade creates benefits to the economy as a whole, there are both winners and losers. The winners gain more in total than the losers lose, but the losers tend to be concentrated in a few industries.

   Given this concentration, free trade will be resisted by some acting on the basis of rational self-interest. Even though only a small minority benefit while the overwhelming majority will be hurt, it is not surprising to see trade restrictions implemented. The cost of a given trade restriction to *each* of the majority will be individually quite small, while the benefit to *each* of the few will be individually large. Thus the minority will have a significant incentive to see that restriction takes place, while the majority will have little incentive to expend time and energy in resisting trade restriction.

3. To understand the source of pressures for trade restrictions, let us summarize those who win and lose from trade restrictions.

Under the three forms of restrictions (tariffs, quotas, and voluntary export restraints) *consumers* lose, because the price of the imported good increases. *Domestic producers* of the imported good and their factors of production gain from all three, because the price of the imported good increases. *Foreign producers* and their factors of production lose under all three schemes, because their export sales decrease. Under quotas and voluntary export restraints, the *holders of import licences* gain from buying low and selling high (they may be foreign or domestic). *Government* gains tariff revenue under tariffs and, potentially, votes under other schemes.

Given this list, it is hardly surprising that the main supporters of trade restrictions are domestic producers and their factors of production.

Self-Test
True/False and Explain

How Global Markets Work

1. When a Canadian citizen stays in a hotel in France, Canada is exporting a service.

2. Countries will export goods and services which they can produce at a lower opportunity cost than other nations.

3. In order to export a good, the world price must be lower than the domestic price.

4. If Canada starts importing widgets, the price of widgets in Canada will fall and the quantity bought will increase.

5. All parts of society gain from being able to export goods at a higher price than the domestic price.

6. Domestic producers gain from the introduction of imports.

7. Domestic consumers gain from the introduction of imports.

International Trade Restrictions

8. When governments impose import quotas, they increase their country's gains from trade.

9. A tariff on a good will raise its price and reduce the quantity traded.

10. An import quota will cause the price of the imported good to decrease.

11. The government revenue plus the gain to producers offsets the losses to consumers from a tariff.

The Case Against Protection

12. Japan is dumping steel if it sells steel in Japan at a lower price than it sells it in Canada.

13. Since Mexican labour is paid so much less than Canadian labour, entering into a free trade agreement with Mexico guarantees Canada will lose jobs to Mexico.

14. Elected governments are slow to reduce trade restrictions because there would be more losers than gainers.

15. Entering a trade agreement that increases both imports and exports will decrease jobs domestically.

Multiple-Choice

How Global Markets Work

1. Which of the following is a Canadian service export?
   a. A Canadian buys dinner while travelling in Switzerland.
   b. A Swiss buys dinner while travelling in Canada.
   c. A Canadian buys a clock made in Switzerland.
   d. A Swiss buys a computer made in Canada.
   e. A Canadian buys a Canadian computer in Switzerland.

2. If Canada imports widgets, it must be the case that
   a. Canada has a comparative advantage in widget production.
   b. widgets are cheaper in Canada than the rest of the world.
   c. the Canadian supply of widgets is greater than the Canadian demand for widgets at the world price.
   d. the Canadian supply of widgets is less than the Canadian demand for widgets at the world price
   e. there is no tariff on widgets.

3. If Canada starts exporting gadgets, then the domestic price of gadgets
   a. decreases, leading to a decline in production and imports fill the gap.
   b. decreases, leading to a decline in demand and the different is exported.
   c. stays the same, but Canada increases production in response to the world demand.
   d. increases, demand declines and production increases and the difference is exported.
   e. increases, demand increases too and imports fill the gap.

4. Table 1 shows Glazeland's doughnut market before international trade. Glazeland opens up to international trade. If the world price is $0.60, then Glazeland will produce _____ doughnuts and will _____ doughnuts.

   a. 2 million; import 3 million
   b. 4 million; import 1 million
   c. 4 million; export 1 million
   d. 5 million; import 3 million
   e. 5 million; export 3 million

TABLE 1 Glazeland's Doughnut Market

Price (dollars per doughnut)	Glazeland's Supply (millions)	Glazeland's Demand (millions)
0.20	1	10
0.30	2	8
0.40	3	6
0.50	4	4
0.60	5	2
0.70	6	0

5. Table 1 shows Glazeland's doughnut market before international trade. Glazeland opens up to international trade. If the world price is $0.40, then Glazeland will produce _____ doughnuts and will _____ doughnuts.

   a. 3 million; import 3 million
   b. 3 million; export 3 million
   c. 4 million; import 1 million
   d. 4 million; export 1 million
   e. 6 million; export 3 million

6. If the widget market enters the world market, and the world price is higher than the domestic price, then the

   a. higher price will make consumers better off.
   b. higher price will make producers worse off.
   c. increased production will make consumers better off.
   d. decreased production will make producers worse off.
   e. amount of exports will be positive.

7. Fig. 1 shows an export market. At the world price, domestic production is _____ units and domestic consumption is _____ units.

a. 100; 175
b. 100; 125
c. 125; 175
d. 175; 125
e. 175; 100

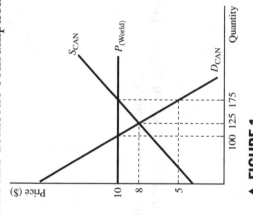

▲ **FIGURE 1**

8. Fig. 1 shows an export market. At the world price, producers have gained _____ per unit sold, and exports are _____ units.

a. $2; 25
b. $2; 50
c. $2; 75
d. $5; 50
e. $5; 75

9. Fig. 2 shows an import market. At the world price, domestic production is _____ units and domestic consumption is _____ units.

a. 4,000; 14,000
b. 7,000; 12,000
c. 7,000; 10,000
d. 10,000; 14,000
e. 14,000; 4,000

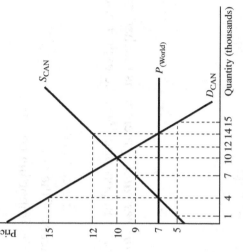

▲ **FIGURE 2**

10. Fig. 2 shows an import market. At the world price, consumers have gained _____ per unit sold, and imports are _____ units.

a. $2; 10,000
b. $2; 5,000
c. $2; 4,000
d. $3; 10,000
e. $3; 4,000

International Trade Restrictions

11. Fig. 2 shows an import market. A tariff of $2 would lead to domestic production of _____ units and imports of _____ units.

   a. 12,000; 5,000

   b. 12,000; 2,000

   c. 7,000; 5,000

   d. 10,000; 2,000

   e. 15,000; 14,000

12. Fig. 2 shows an import market. Under an import quota of 5,000 units, what is the new domestic price?

   a. $5

   b. $7

   c. $9

   d. $10

   e. $12

13. When an *import quota* is imposed, the gap between the domestic price and the export price is captured by

   a. consumers in the importing country.

   b. the domestic producers of the good.

   c. the government of the importing country.

   d. foreign exporters.

   e. the importers of the good.

14. When a *voluntary export restraint* agreement is reached, the gap between the domestic import price and the export price is captured by

   a. consumers in the importing country.

   b. the domestic producers of the good.

   c. the government of the importing country.

   d. foreign exporters.

   e. the domestic importers of the good.

15. When a *tariff* is imposed, the gap between the domestic price and the export price is captured by

a. consumers in the importing country.
b. the domestic producers of the good.
c. the government of the importing country.
d. foreign exporters.
e. the domestic importers of the good.

16. A tariff on watches that are imported by Atlantis will cause the domestic price of watches to

a. decrease and imports to increase.
b. increase and watch production in Atlantis to increase.
c. increase and watch production in Atlantis to decrease.
d. decrease and watch production in Atlantis to increase.
e. decrease and watch production in Atlantis to decrease.

17. Table 2 on the next page shows the Canadian supply of and demand for widgets. Widgets are available on the world market for $7. If the Canadian government imposes a tariff of $1, the selling price will be _____ and quantity bought will be _____.

a. $6; 48 million
b. $7; 44 million
c. $8; 16 million
d. $8; 24 million
e. $8; 40 million

TABLE 2 Canada's Market for Widgets		
Price (dollars per widgets)	Canadian Supply (millions)	Canadian Demand (millions)
5	12	52
6	16	48
7	20	44
8	24	40
9	28	36
10	32	32
12	36	28

18. Table 2 shows the Canadian supply of and demand for widgets. Widgets are available on the world market for $7. If the Canadian government imposes a tariff of $1, how much will be imported by Canada?

    a. 32 million
    b. 24 million
    c. 16 million
    d. 24 million
    e. 40 million

19. Table 2 shows the Canadian supply of and demand for widgets. Widgets are available on the world market for $7. Canadian widget producers convince their government that there is a need to protect the domestic industry from cheap imports. In response, the Canadian government sets an import quota of 8 million widgets. The resulting price of a widget in Canada will be _____, and domestic production will be _____.

    a. $6; 40 million
    b. $7; 36 million
    c. $8; 32 million
    d. $9; 28 million
    e. $10; 32 million

20. The introduction of a tariff will

    a. make consumers better off, make producers better off, and make society better off overall.
    b. make consumers better off, make producers worse off, and make society better off overall.
    c. make consumers worse off, make producers better off, and make society better off overall.
    d. make consumers better off, make producers worse off, and make society worse off overall.
    e. make consumers worse off, make producers better off, and make society worse off overall.

The Case Against Protection

21. Which of the following is *not* an argument for protectionism?

    a. to prevent dumping
    b. to save jobs in import-competing industries
    c. to gain a comparative advantage
    d. to allow infant industries to grow
    e. to prevent rich nations from exploiting poor nations

22. The biggest problem with protection is that
  a. it invites retaliation from trading partners.
  b. losers are not compensated.
  c. it worsens environmental standards.
  d. it can worsen national security.
  e. it lowers wages.

23. Why is international trade restricted?
  a. because government revenue is costly to collect via tariffs
  b. in order to get higher consumption possibilities
  c. to realize the gains from trade
  d. due to rent-seeking
  e. because free trade creates economic losses on average

24. The effects of offshoring from opening up call centres in India are similar to the effects from
  a. free trade.
  b. tariffs.
  c. import quotas.
  d. voluntary export restraints.
  e. export subsidies.

25. In Canada, when international trade hurts producers and reduces jobs in import-competing industries, the government response is
  a. to introduce tariffs.
  b. to do absolutely nothing.
  c. to fully compensate all losers.
  d. to guarantee every job loser retraining.
  e. to allow employment insurance to help job losers with temporary relief.

Short Answer Problems

1. It is often argued by union leaders that tariffs are needed to protect domestic jobs. In light of the explanation in the textbook, evaluate this argument.

   b. Dumping duties are put in place to protect the U.S. economy from the "unfair" low price of the dumped imports. Did the dumping duties on bras make the U.S. economy better off?

2. In a recent case, the U.S. government investigated Chinese bra manufacturers for suspected "dumping" of bras in the United States. The U.S. Department of Trade determined that the cost of making a bra in China was equivalent to $12 per bra, although they were being sold in the United States for $11 each. They then imposed dumping duties (tariffs) on Chinese bras of $1 per bra.

   a. Define dumping, and explain whether this is a case of dumping.

3. Consider a simple world in which there are two countries, Atlantis and Beltran, each producing and consuming gadgets. The Atlantean gadget market is shown in Table 3, and the Beltranian market is given in Table 4. Both countries use the dollar as their currency.

TABLE 3 Atlantis's Market for Gadgets

Price (dollars per gadgets)	Atlantean Supply (millions)	Atlantean Demand (millions)
0	0	240
10	50	210
20	100	180
30	150	150
40	180	120
50	210	90
60	240	60
70	270	30
80	300	0

b. If they do trade, who will be the exporter and who will be the importer?

c. Using the information in the tables, find the trading price of gadgets, and indicate how much will be exported from one country to another, and how much will be imported.

TABLE 4 Beltran's Market for Gadgets

Price (dollars per gadgets)	Beltranian Supply (millions)	Beltranian Demand (millions)
0	0	200
10	25	190
20	50	180
30	75	170
40	100	160
50	120	150
60	140	140
70	160	130
80	180	120

a. Do the conditions exist for the two countries to trade in gadgets? Explain briefly.

4. Suppose that Atlantis and Beltran engage in trade. (You should have been able to show in Short Answer Problem **3** that Atlantis will export gadgets to Beltran.) On the grid below, graph the Atlantis market for gadgets, indicating the pre-trade equilibrium and the free trade equilibrium. Indicate the winners and losers in Atlantis from free trade.

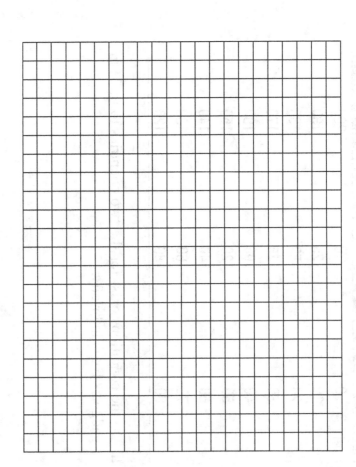

5. Suppose that Atlantis and Beltran engage in trade. (You should have been able to show in Short Answer Problem **3** that Atlantis will export gadgets to Beltran.) On the grid below, graph the Beltran market for gadgets, indicating the pre-trade equilibrium and the free trade equilibrium. Identify the winners and losers in Beltran from free trade.

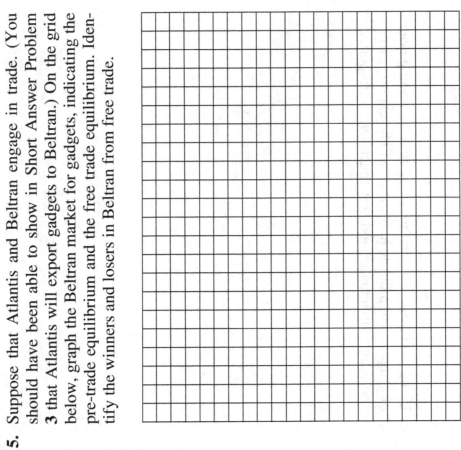

6. Continue the analysis of Atlantis and Beltran trading gadgets. Suppose that the importing country (Beltran) introduces a tariff of $10. Show on your graph from Short Answer Problem **5** what this will do to the quantity demanded in Beltran, quantity produced, and amount imported. Indicate in the space provided who will gain and who will lose from the tariff in Beltran. How much is the tariff revenue for Beltran?

7. Continue the analysis of Atlantis and Beltran trading gadgets. What will be the impact of the tariff introduced by Beltran be on the quantity exported from Atlantis, and what will be the impact on the domestic price of gadgets, quantity produced, and quantity demanded in Atlantis? Indicate in words in the space provided who will gain and who will lose from the tariff in Atlantis. (It is likely easier to work with Table 3 instead of doing this graphically.)

8. Rich countries are often worried about the impact of off-shoring of services (such as call centres for computers or software) to developing countries such as India. Suppose that Canada was to ban the use of off-shoring for call centres. Explain in words who would gain and who would lose from this ban in Canada, and in India.

Answers

True/False and Explain

1. **F** Canada is importing (using) a service. (752)
2. **T** Definition of national comparative advantage. (752)
3. **F** Consumers lose from higher price. (755)
4. **F** Must be higher to generate needed profits. (754)
5. **T** (753)
6. **F** Introducing imports lowers prices for import-competing goods, hurting producers. (755)
7. **T** Introducing imports lowers prices for import-competing goods, benefiting consumers. (755)
8. **F** Trade restrictions reduce gains from trade. (756–758)
9. **T** Tariff raises price paid inside the country, which decreases quantity traded. (756–758)
10. **F** Quota decreases supply, which increases price. (758)
11. **F** Loss to consumers more than offsets gains to producers + tariff revenue because of higher cost domestic production. (758)
12. **F** Dumping would be selling in Canada at lower price than in Japan. (761)
13. **F** We must also examine the productivity of workers in each country, and Canadian workers are more productive. (762)
14. **F** They will be slow because losers' losses are individually much greater than winners' gains. (764)
15. **F** More imports will likely decrease jobs, but more exports will increase them—net outcome is not clear. (762)

Multiple-Choice

1. **b** **a** and **c** are imports, **d** and **e** are exports of a *good*. (752)
2. **d** If we import, world price is lower and our supply is therefore too low compared to demand. Could still have a tariff. (753)
3. **e** Price = $0.60 implies supply of 5 million, but demand is only 2 million, so 3 million are exported. (753–754)
4. **a** Price = $0.40 implies supply of 3 million, but demand is 6 million, so 3 million are imported. (753–754)
5. **d** (754)
6. **e** Higher price and higher production benefits producers and hurts consumers. (755)
7. **e** Read off demand and supply curves at world price. (754)
8. **c** Difference between domestic price (where *D* and *S* cross) and world price; quantity supplied − quantity demanded. (754–755)
9. **a** Read off demand and supply curves at world price. (753)
10. **d** Difference between domestic price (where *D* and *S* cross) and world price; quantity supplied − quantity demanded. (753–754)
11. **c** New price = $9 (world price + tariff)—quantity produced is read off supply curve, quantity demanded off demand curve, imports = difference. (756–758)

12. **c** Add 5,000 units to the supply curve and see where it crosses demand curve. (758–760)
13. **e** Under quota, domestic government allocates the licence to import. (758)
14. **d** Because they have the right to export. (760)
15. **c** They collect tariff revenue = import price – world price. (756–758)
16. **b** Tariff increases domestic price = export price + tariff, and domestic production increases in response. (756–758)
17. **e** New price is $1 + $7 = $8, so quantity bought is 40 million off demand curve. (756–758)
18. **c** Difference between quantity demanded and supplied at $8. (758–760)
19. **d** Equilibrium is price where quota of 8 million = import demand = quantity demanded – quantity supplied. (758–760)
20. **e** See text discussion. (758)
21. **c** See text discussion. (761–765)
22. **a** See text discussion. (761–765)
23. **d** See text discussion. (761–765)
24. **a** Similar effect on domestic price of good, domestic production, imports, and winners and losers. (763)
25. **e** See text discussion. (764–765)

Short Answer Problems

1. This argument has some truth to it. As the textbook shows on pages 756–757, the tariff will lead an increase in domestic production of the protected good, which will lead to an increase in jobs in that industry. However, the same tariff could trigger a trade war, which would reduce foreign purchases of goods, reducing exports and export production, and reducing jobs in the export industry. The net effect on jobs is unclear.

2. a. Dumping occurs when a foreign firm sells its exports at a lower price than the cost of production. Since the cost of production is higher than the export price, this is indeed a case of dumping.

   b. The dumping duties are exactly like a tariff, and the effect of a tariff is to increase the domestic price of bras, reduce domestic bra consumption (and hurt consumers) and increase domestic bra production (and help producers), and hurt the U.S. economy overall.

3. a. The pre-trade price of gadgets in Atlantis would be $30, while the pre-trade price in Beltran would be $60. If a trading price between $30 and $60 could come about, both sides would gain. Therefore, the appropriate conditions exist for trade.

   b. The exporter would be Atlantis, with the lower price, and Beltran would be the importer with the higher price.

   c. We can find the trading price ($40) in a variety of manners. We could combine the two supply schedules into a "world" supply schedule, and combine the two demand schedules into a "world" demand schedule, and find the equilibrium world price. Such a schedule is shown below in Table 5, and world equilibrium occurs with a quantity of 280 million and price of $40.

TABLE 5 "World" Market for Gadgets

Price (dollars per gadgets)	World Supply (millions)	World Demand (millions)
0	0	440
10	75	400
20	150	360
30	225	320
40	280	280
50	330	240
60	380	200
70	430	160
80	480	120

We can also find the trading price ($40) by looking at Tables 3 and 4, and noting that at a price of $40, supply in Atlantis exceeds demand by 60 million, while supply in Beltran is short of demand by 60 million, indicating that sending 60 million from Atlantis to Beltran would create equilibrium. In summary, Atlantis exports 60 million gadgets and Beltran imports 60 million.

4. Fig. 3 shows the Atlantean market. The initial pre-trade equilibrium occurs at a price of $30 and a quantity traded of 150 million. We have established the world price will be $40. At this price, Atlantis will demand only 120 million gadgets (read off the demand curve), and will produce 180 million gadgets (read off the supply curve), and will export the surplus of 60 million gadgets.

Producers will gain from the higher price and the higher production. Consumers will lose from the higher

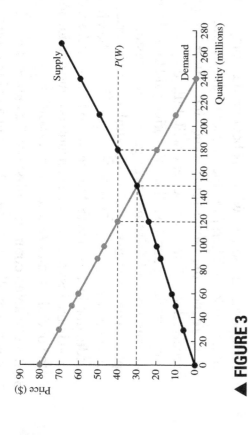

▲ FIGURE 3

price and the lower consumption. Since producers gain what the consumers lose *and* gain from exporting, there is an overall gain to Atlantis.

5. Fig. 4 shows the Beltran market.

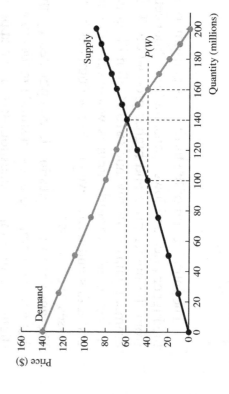

▲ FIGURE 4

The introduction of the tariff hurts consumers, due to the higher price and lower consumption. Producers gain from the higher price and higher production. The government gains tariff revenue ($10 × 30 million gadgets imports), but overall Beltran is worse off—the producers' gains and tariff revenue do not compensate for the losses to consumers.

The initial pre-trade equilibrium occurs at a price of $60 and a quantity traded of 140 million. At this price, Beltran will demand 160 million gadgets (read off the demand curve), and will produce only 100 million gadgets (read off the supply curve), and will import the shortage of 60 million gadgets.

Producers will lose from the lower price and the lower production. Consumers will gain from the lower price and the higher consumption. Since consumers gain what the producers lose *and* gain from importing, there is an overall gain to Beltran.

6. Fig. 5 shows the impact of the tariff on Beltran's market. The tariff adds $10 to the world price, leading to a domestic price of $50. At this price, demand is only 150 million gadgets, and supply increases to 120 million gadgets, leading to a decreased amount of imports at 30 million units.

7. The answer to this question is complicated by the fact that we are attempting to use a simple model to answer a slightly more complex question, so only an approximate answer is possible. Beltran is now importing only 30 million gadgets from Atlantis, instead of the previous 60 million units. Therefore, Atlantis will export only 30 million units. Looking at Table 31.3, we can see that this will occur at some price between $30 and $40 (we cannot exactly tell where without a mathematical model incorporating the tax, which is beyond the complexities of this model). Therefore, the impact of the Beltran tariff is to reduce the world price somewhat. Since the price received by Atlantean sellers will fall, they will lose some producer surplus. Since the price paid by Atlantean consumers will fall, they will gain some consumer surplus. The overall impact of the fall in world price for Atlantis will be a reduction in exports, and therefore a reduction in the gains to Atlantean producers (and a reduction in the loss to Atlantean consumers), and a reduction in the overall gain to Atlantis from exporting.

8. If a Canadian company "offshores" a call centre to India, it is essentially the same as the company importing a service from India. All the gains and losses to individuals and the overall economy are identical to the normal case

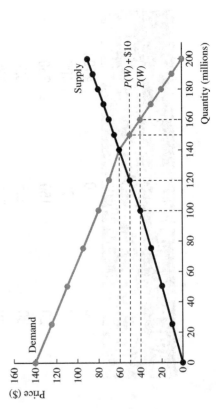

▲ FIGURE 5

of an import. The company as an importer gains the less expensive service, which means lower costs and presumably more profits for the Canadian company (and potentially lower prices for its buyers). The losers are the potential sellers in Canada (people who operate or work in call centres), who lose from a lower price in Canada for what they sell. Overall, Canada gains from being to import the cheaper product.

Similarly, for India, this is an export of a service, and we can see that the Indian suppliers of the call centre services gain from being able to sell more at a higher price, Indian consumers lose from the higher Indian price, and overall India gains from being able to export this service.

If the use of offshore call centres is banned, then all these gains and losses are reversed. The Canadian buyers of call centre services lose (they face higher costs). The Canadian import-competing call centres gain back from the now-higher Canadian prices, but overall Canada is worse off from the ban (just like a tariff makes Canada worse off). For India, the Indian suppliers lose the higher prices, the Indian consumers gain from the lower prices, and overall India is worse off.